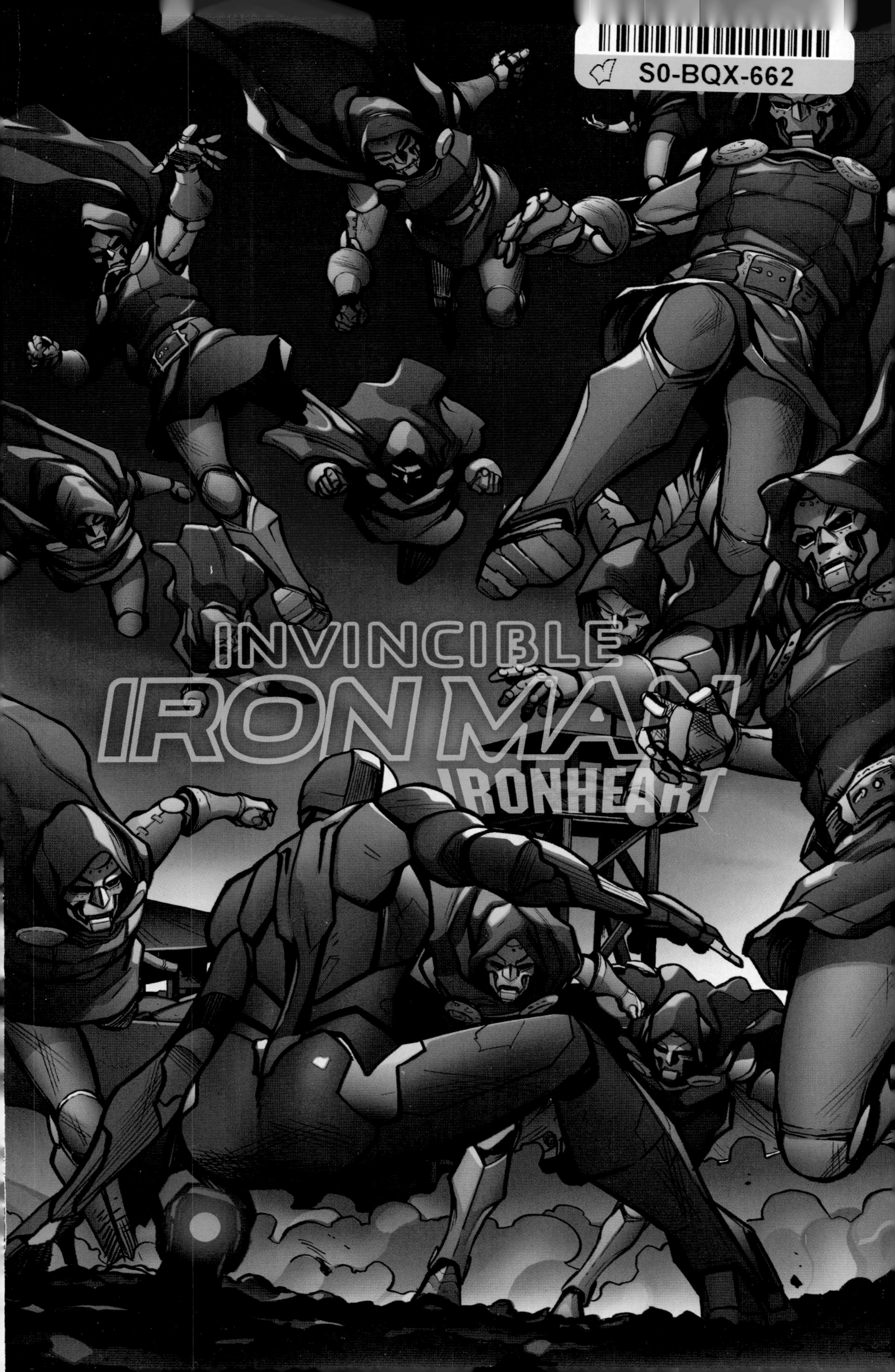
INVINCIBLE
IRON MAN
IRONHEART

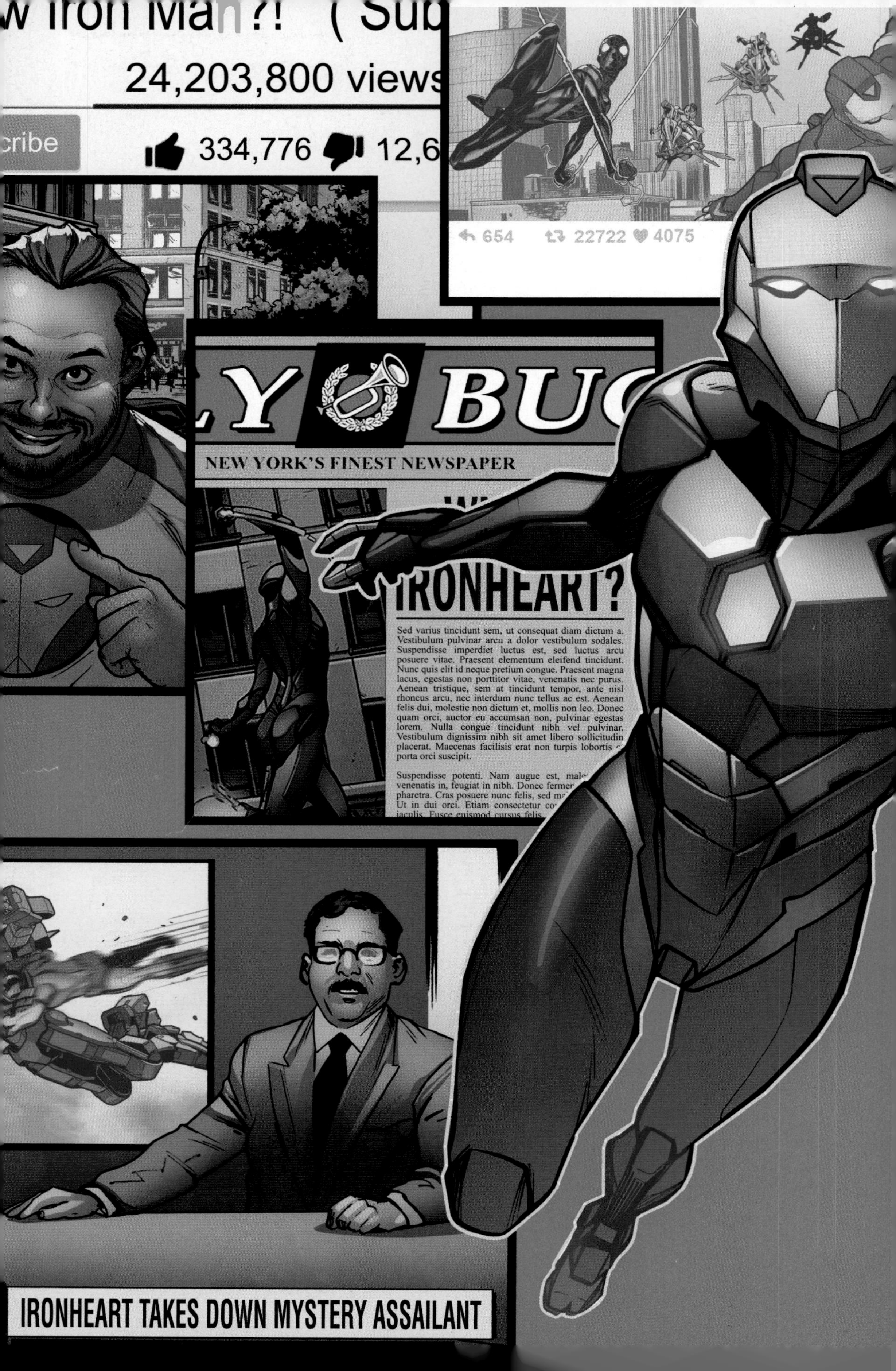
w Iron Ma ?! (Sub
24,203,800 views
cribe
334,776
12,6
654
22722
4075
LY BUG
NEW YORK'S FINEST NEWSPAPER
IRONHEART?
Sed varius tincidunt sem, ut consequat diam dictum a. Vestibulum pulvinar arcu a dolor vestibulum sodales. Suspendisse imperdiet luctus est, sed luctus arcu posuere vitae. Praesent elementum eleifend tincidunt. Nunc quis elit id neque pretium congue. Praesent magna lacus, egestas non porttitor vitae, venenatis nec purus. Aenean tristique, sem at tincidunt tempor, ante nisl rhoncus arcu, nec interdum nunc tellus ac est. Aenean felis dui, molestie non dictum et, mollis non leo. Donec quam orci, auctor eu accumsan non, pulvinar egestas lorem. Nulla congue tincidunt nibh vel pulvinar. Vestibulum dignissim nibh sit amet libero sollicitudin placerat. Maecenas facilisis erat non turpis lobortis
porta orci suscipit.
Suspendisse potenti. Nam augue est, male
venenatis in, feugiat in nibh. Donec fermer
pharetra. Cras posuere nunc felis, sed m
Ut in dui orci. Etiam consectetur co
iaculis. Fusce euismod cursus felis.
IRONHEART TAKES DOWN MYSTERY ASSAILANT

INVINCIBLE IRON MAN
IRONHEART

CHOICES

BRIAN MICHAEL BENDIS
WRITER

STEFANO CASELLI WITH
KATE NIEMCZYK (#11), TAKI SOMA (#11) & KIICHI MIZUSHIMA (#11)
ARTISTS

MARTE GRACIA WITH ISRAEL SILVA (#9-10)
COLOR ARTISTS

VC's CLAYTON COWLES
LETTERER

STEFANO CASELLI & MARTE GRACIA (#6-8, #10), DANIEL ACUÑA (#9) AND JESÚS SAIZ (#11)
COVER ART

ALANNA SMITH
ASSISTANT EDITOR

TOM BREVOORT
EDITOR

INVINCIBLE IRON MAN: IRONHEART VOL. 2 — CHOICES. Contains material originally published in magazine form as INVINCIBLE IRON MAN #6-11. First printing 2018. ISBN 978-1-302-90674-0. Published by MARVEL WORLDWIDE, INC., a subsidiary of MARVEL ENTERTAINMENT, LLC. OFFICE OF PUBLICATION: 135 West 50th Street, New York, NY 10020. Copyright © 2018 MARVEL No similarity between any of the names, characters, persons, and/or institutions in this magazine with those of any living or dead person or institution is intended, and any such similarity which may exist is purely coincidental. **Printed in the U.S.A.** DAN BUCKLEY, President, Marvel Entertainment; JOHN NEE, Publisher; JOE QUESADA, Chief Creative Officer; TOM BREVOORT, SVP of Publishing; DAVID BOGART, SVP of Business Affairs & Operations, Publishing & Partnership; DAVID GABRIEL, SVP of Sales & Marketing, Publishing; JEFF YOUNGQUIST, VP of Production & Special Projects; DAN CARR, Executive Director of Publishing Technology; ALEX MORALES, Director of Publishing Operations; DAN EDINGTON, Managing Editor; SUSAN CRESPI, Production Manager; STAN LEE, Chairman Emeritus. For information regarding advertising in Marvel Comics or on Marvel.com, please contact Vit DeBellis, Custom Solutions & Integrated Advertising Manager, at vdebellis@marvel.com. For Marvel subscription inquiries, please call 888-511-5480. **Manufactured between 4/20/2018 and 5/22/2018** by LSC COMMUNICATIONS INC., KENDALLVILLE, IN, USA.

10 9 8 7 6 5 4 3 2 1

IRON MAN CREATED BY
STAN LEE, LARRY LIEBER,
DON HECK & JACK KIRBY

COLLECTION EDITOR: **JENNIFER GRÜNWALD**
ASSISTANT EDITOR: **CAITLIN O'CONNELL**
ASSOCIATE MANAGING EDITOR: **KATERI WOODY**
EDITOR, SPECIAL PROJECTS: **MARK D. BEAZLEY**
VP PRODUCTION & SPECIAL PROJECTS: **JEFF YOUNGQUIST**
SVP PRINT, SALES & MARKETING: **DAVID GABRIEL**
BOOK DESIGNER: **ADAM DEL RE**

EDITOR IN CHIEF: **C.B. CEBULSKI**
CHIEF CREATIVE OFFICER: **JOE QUESADA**
PRESIDENT: **DAN BUCKLEY**
EXECUTIVE PRODUCER: **ALAN FINE**

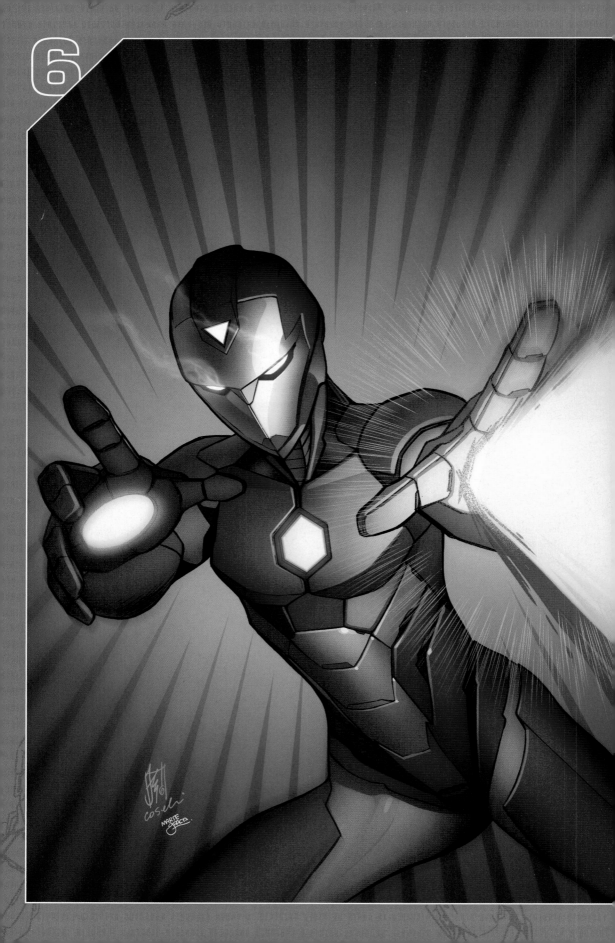

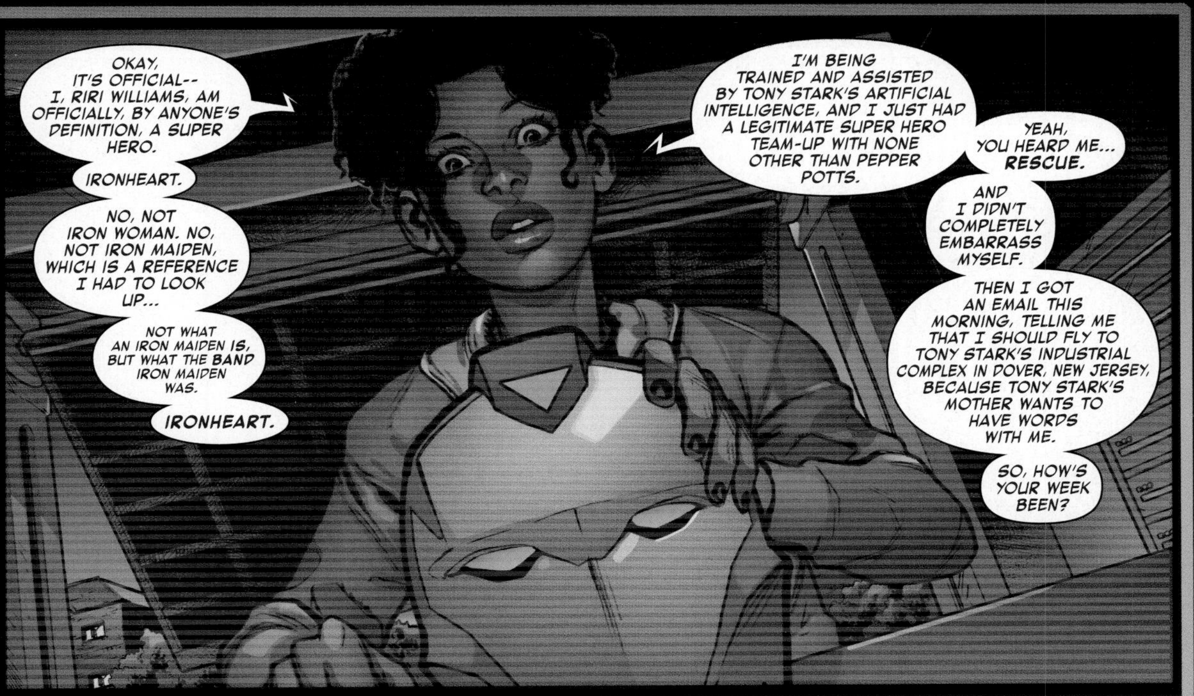
OKAY, IT'S OFFICIAL-- I, RIRI WILLIAMS, AM OFFICIALLY, BY ANYONE'S DEFINITION, A SUPER HERO.
IRONHEART.
NO, NOT IRON WOMAN. NO, NOT IRON MAIDEN, WHICH IS A REFERENCE I HAD TO LOOK UP...
NOT WHAT AN IRON MAIDEN IS, BUT WHAT THE BAND IRON MAIDEN WAS.
IRONHEART.
I'M BEING TRAINED AND ASSISTED BY TONY STARK'S ARTIFICIAL INTELLIGENCE, AND I JUST HAD A LEGITIMATE SUPER HERO TEAM-UP WITH NONE OTHER THAN PEPPER POTTS.
YEAH, YOU HEARD ME... RESCUE.
AND I DIDN'T COMPLETELY EMBARRASS MYSELF.
THEN I GOT AN EMAIL THIS MORNING, TELLING ME THAT I SHOULD FLY TO TONY STARK'S INDUSTRIAL COMPLEX IN DOVER, NEW JERSEY, BECAUSE TONY STARK'S MOTHER WANTS TO HAVE WORDS WITH ME.
SO, HOW'S YOUR WEEK BEEN?

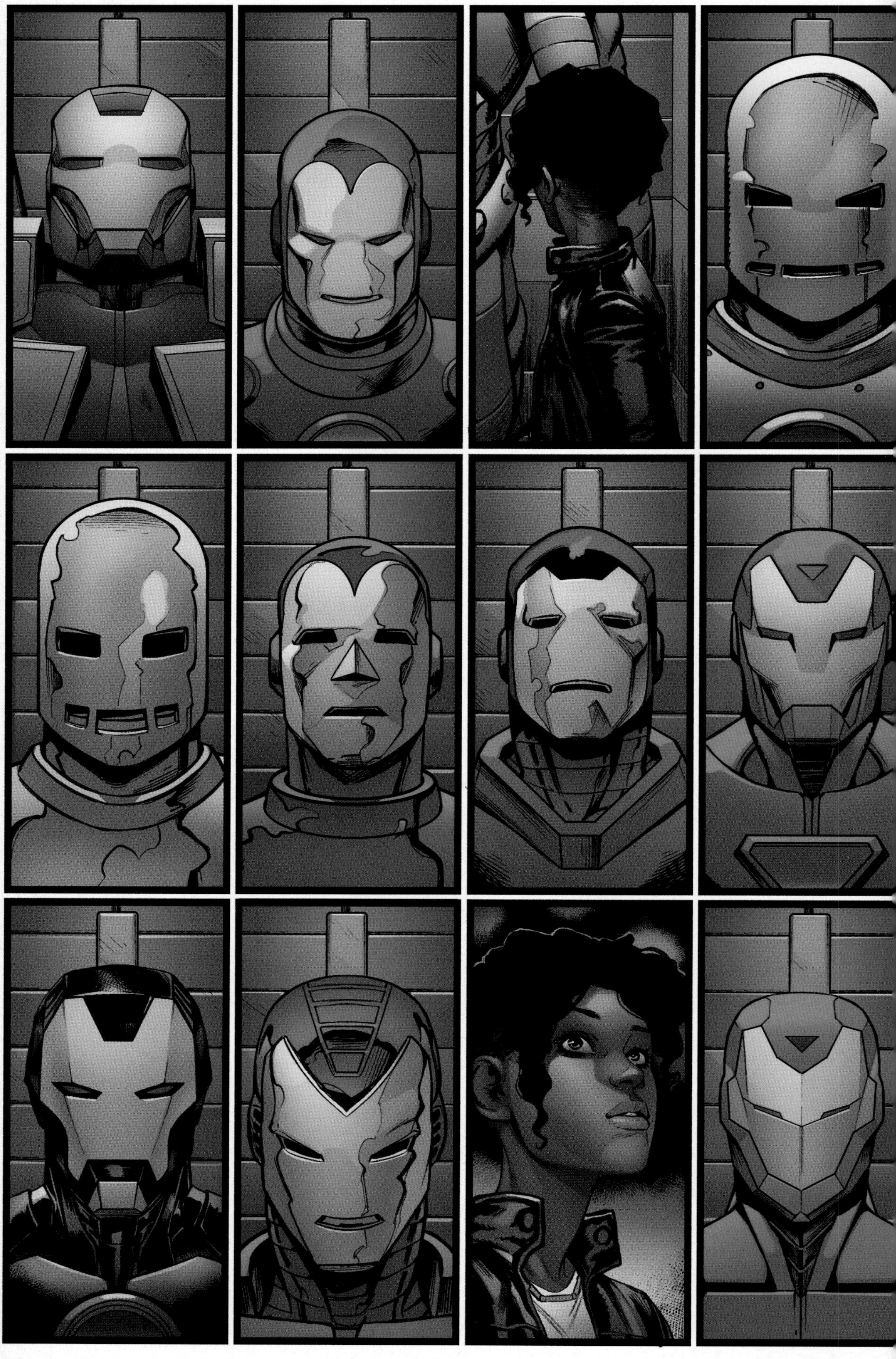

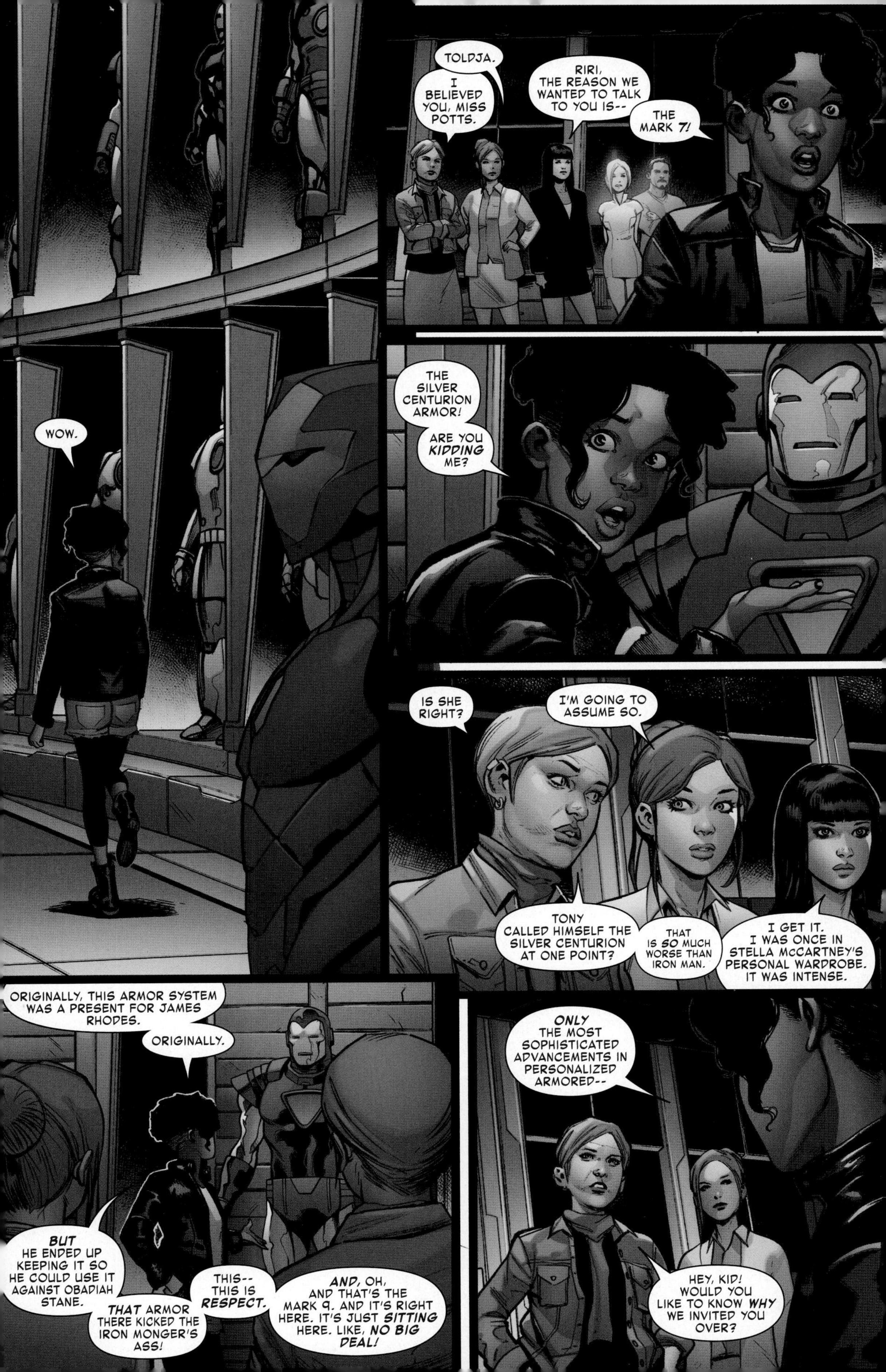
TOLDJA.
I BELIEVED YOU, MISS POTTS.
RIRI, THE REASON WE WANTED TO TALK TO YOU IS--
THE MARK 7!
WOW.
THE SILVER CENTURION ARMOR!
ARE YOU KIDDING ME?
IS SHE RIGHT?
I'M GOING TO ASSUME SO.
TONY CALLED HIMSELF THE SILVER CENTURION AT ONE POINT?
THAT IS SO MUCH WORSE THAN IRON MAN.
I GET IT. I WAS ONCE IN STELLA McCARTNEY'S PERSONAL WARDROBE. IT WAS INTENSE.
ORIGINALLY, THIS ARMOR SYSTEM WAS A PRESENT FOR JAMES RHODES.
ORIGINALLY.
BUT HE ENDED UP KEEPING IT SO HE COULD USE IT AGAINST OBADIAH STANE.
THAT ARMOR THERE KICKED THE IRON MONGER'S ASS!
THIS-- THIS IS RESPECT.
AND, OH, AND THAT'S THE MARK 9. AND IT'S RIGHT HERE. IT'S JUST SITTING HERE. LIKE, NO BIG DEAL!
ONLY THE MOST SOPHISTICATED ADVANCEMENTS IN PERSONALIZED ARMORED--
HEY, KID! WOULD YOU LIKE TO KNOW WHY WE INVITED YOU OVER?

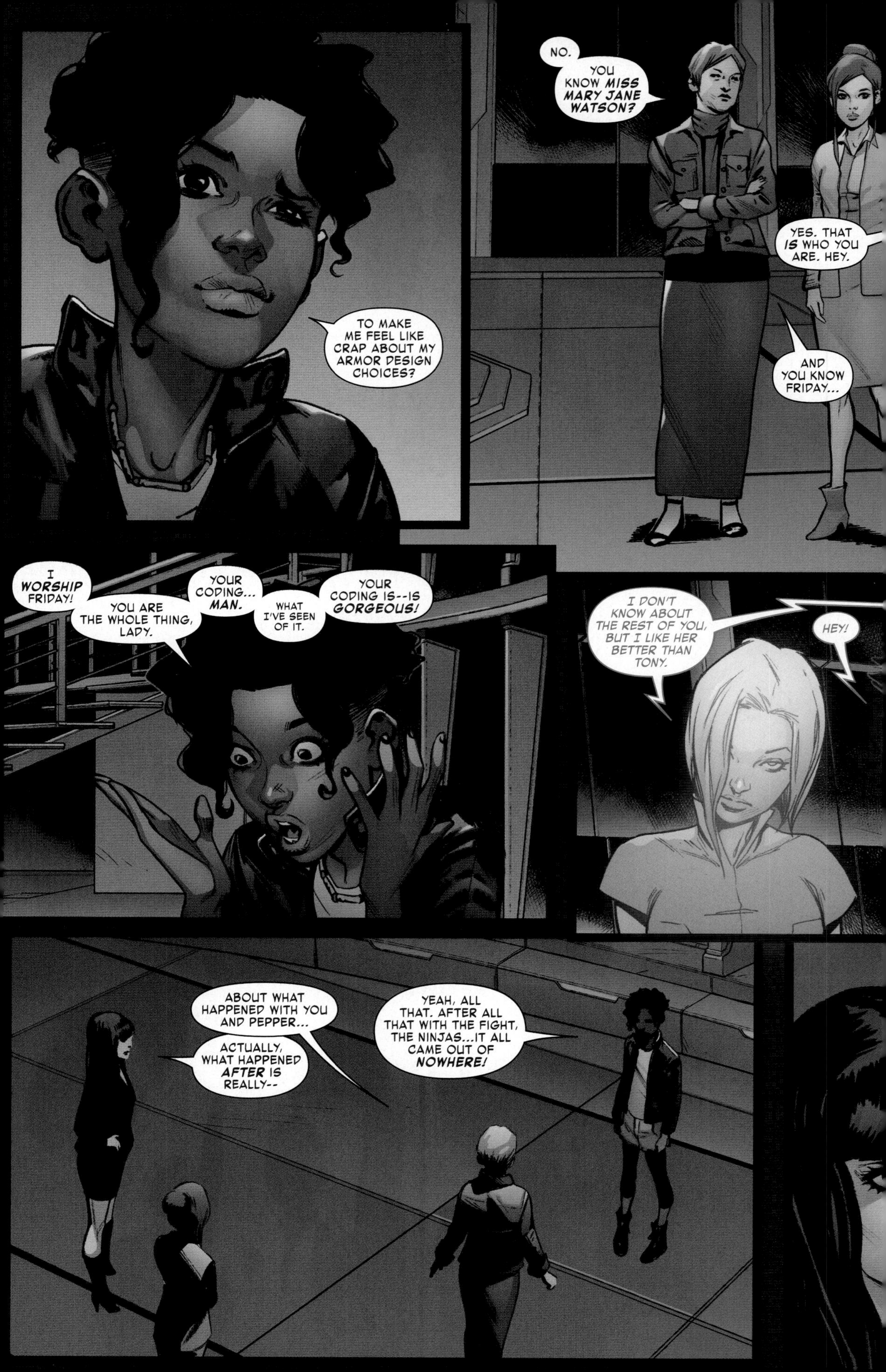
TO MAKE ME FEEL LIKE CRAP ABOUT MY ARMOR DESIGN CHOICES?
NO.
YOU KNOW MISS MARY JANE WATSON?
YES. THAT IS WHO YOU ARE. HEY.
AND YOU KNOW FRIDAY...
I WORSHIP FRIDAY!
YOU ARE THE WHOLE THING, LADY.
YOUR CODING... MAN.
WHAT I'VE SEEN OF IT.
YOUR CODING IS--IS GORGEOUS!
I DON'T KNOW ABOUT THE REST OF YOU, BUT I LIKE HER BETTER THAN TONY.
HEY!
ABOUT WHAT HAPPENED WITH YOU AND PEPPER...
ACTUALLY, WHAT HAPPENED AFTER IS REALLY--
YEAH, ALL THAT. AFTER ALL THAT WITH THE FIGHT, THE NINJAS...IT ALL CAME OUT OF NOWHERE!

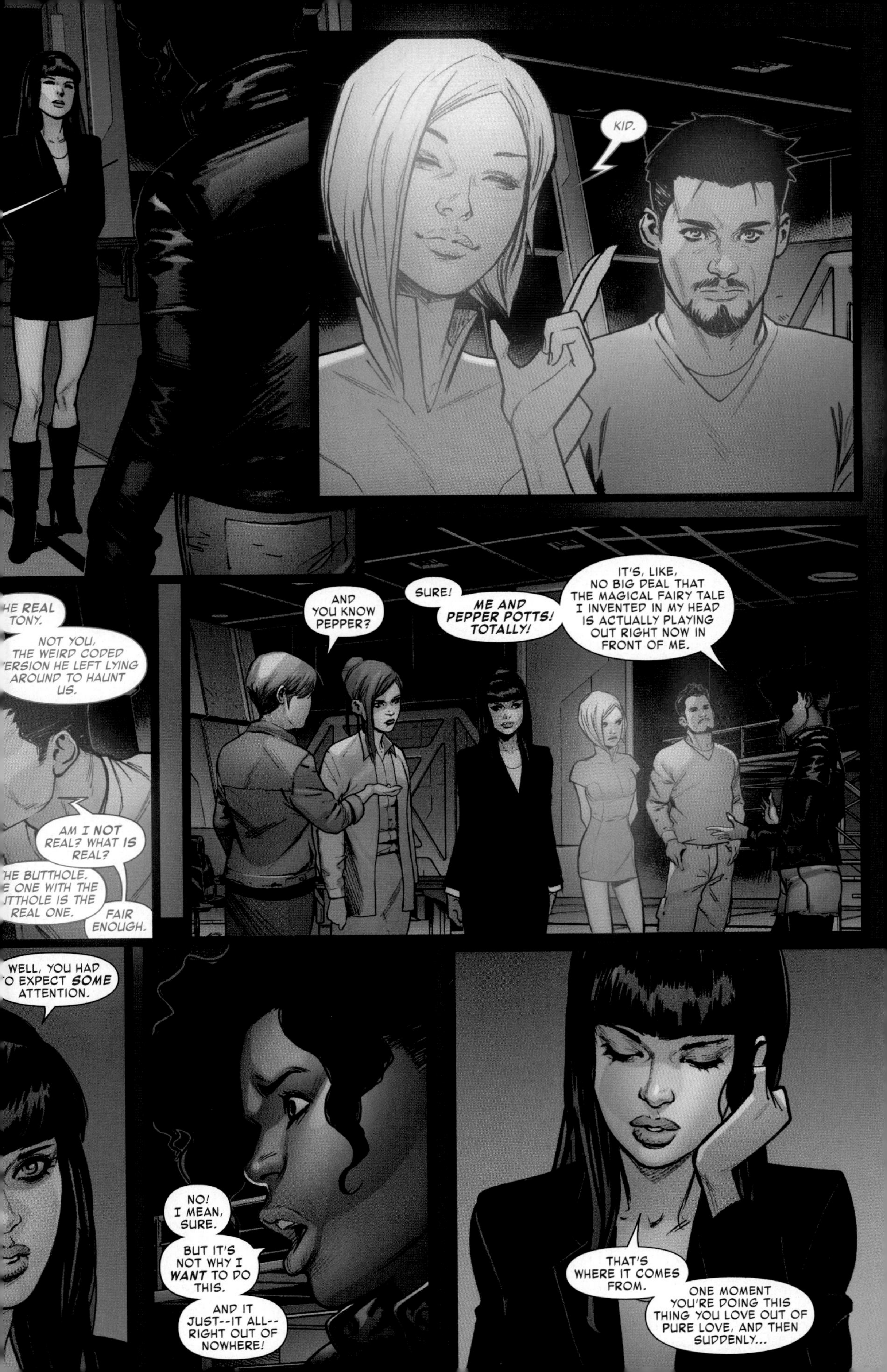
KID.
HE REAL TONY.
NOT YOU, THE WEIRD CODED VERSION HE LEFT LYING AROUND TO HAUNT US.
AM I NOT REAL? WHAT IS REAL?
THE BUTTHOLE. THE ONE WITH THE BUTTHOLE IS THE REAL ONE.
FAIR ENOUGH.
AND YOU KNOW PEPPER?
SURE!
ME AND PEPPER POTTS! TOTALLY!
IT'S, LIKE, NO BIG DEAL THAT THE MAGICAL FAIRY TALE I INVENTED IN MY HEAD IS ACTUALLY PLAYING OUT RIGHT NOW IN FRONT OF ME.
WELL, YOU HAD TO EXPECT SOME ATTENTION.
NO! I MEAN, SURE.
BUT IT'S NOT WHY I WANT TO DO THIS.
AND IT JUST--IT ALL--RIGHT OUT OF NOWHERE!
THAT'S WHERE IT COMES FROM.
ONE MOMENT YOU'RE DOING THIS THING YOU LOVE OUT OF PURE LOVE, AND THEN SUDDENLY...

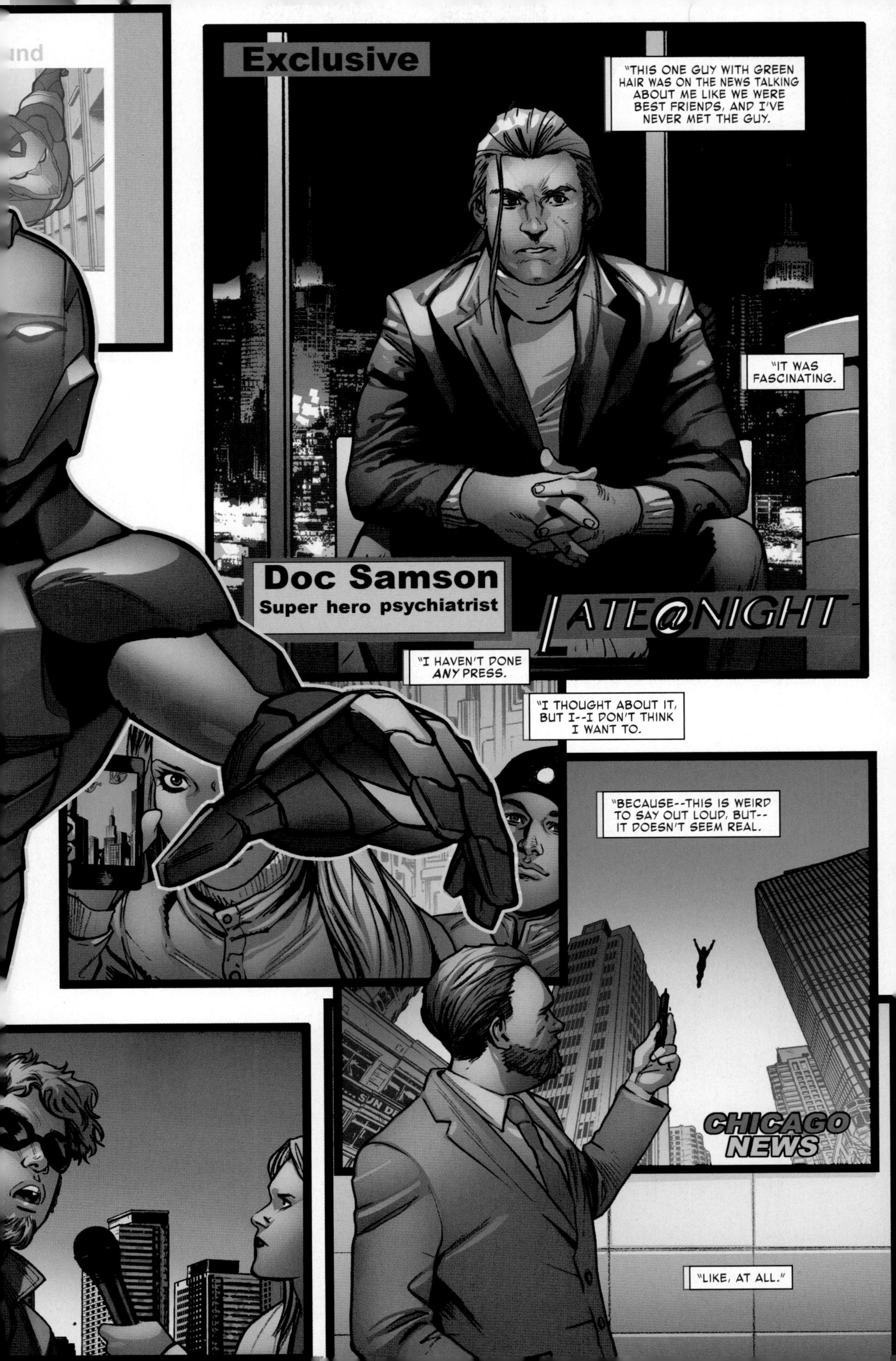

und
Exclusive
"THIS ONE GUY WITH GREEN HAIR WAS ON THE NEWS TALKING ABOUT ME LIKE WE WERE BEST FRIENDS, AND I'VE NEVER MET THE GUY.
"IT WAS FASCINATING.
Doc Samson
Super hero psychiatrist
LATE@NIGHT
"I HAVEN'T DONE ANY PRESS.
"I THOUGHT ABOUT IT, BUT I--I DON'T THINK I WANT TO.
"BECAUSE--THIS IS WEIRD TO SAY OUT LOUD, BUT--IT DOESN'T SEEM REAL.
CHICAGO NEWS
"LIKE, AT ALL."

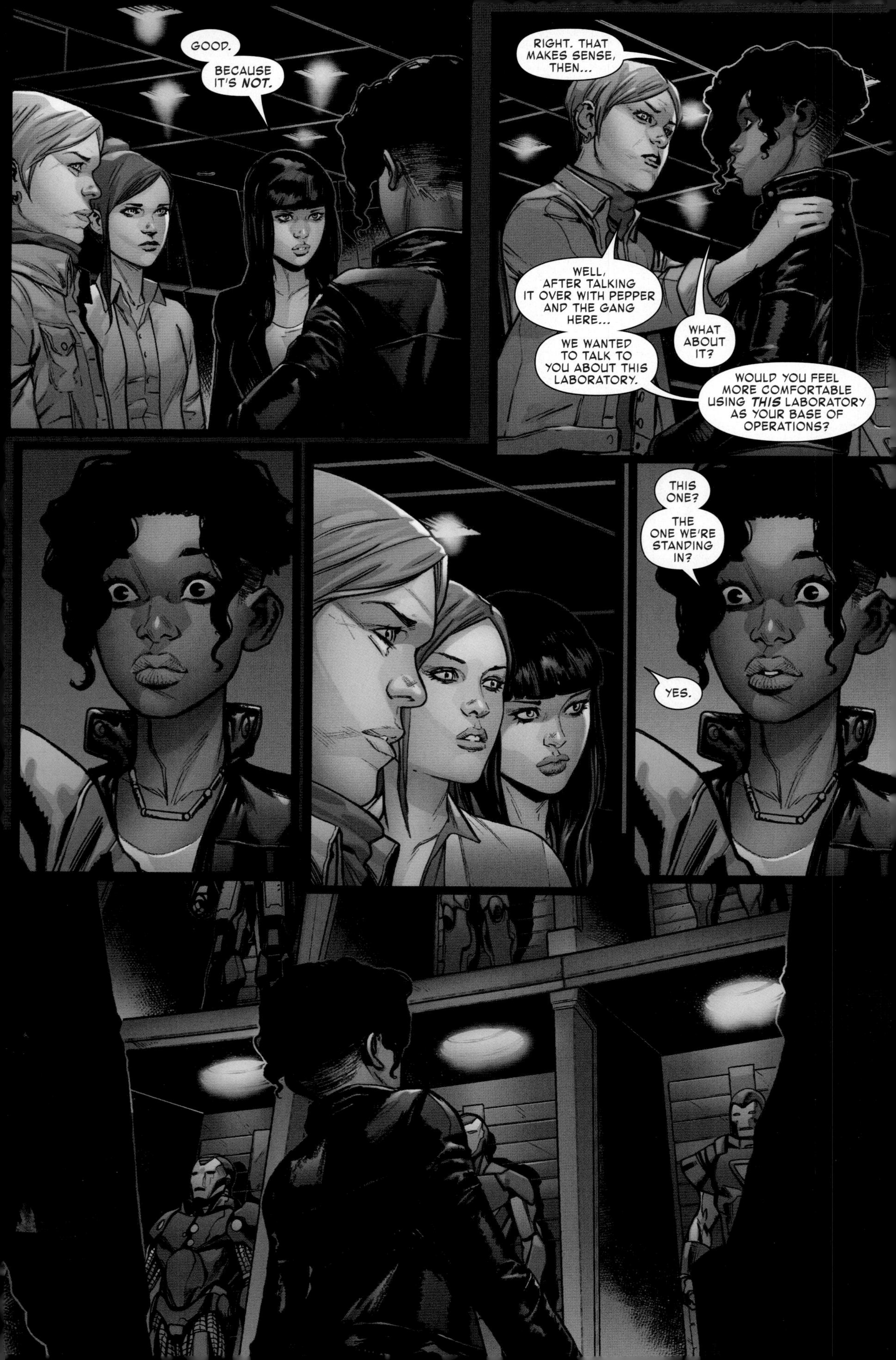
GOOD.
BECAUSE IT'S NOT.
RIGHT. THAT MAKES SENSE, THEN...
WELL, AFTER TALKING IT OVER WITH PEPPER AND THE GANG HERE...
WE WANTED TO TALK TO YOU ABOUT THIS LABORATORY.
WHAT ABOUT IT?
WOULD YOU FEEL MORE COMFORTABLE USING THIS LABORATORY AS YOUR BASE OF OPERATIONS?
THIS ONE?
THE ONE WE'RE STANDING IN?
YES.

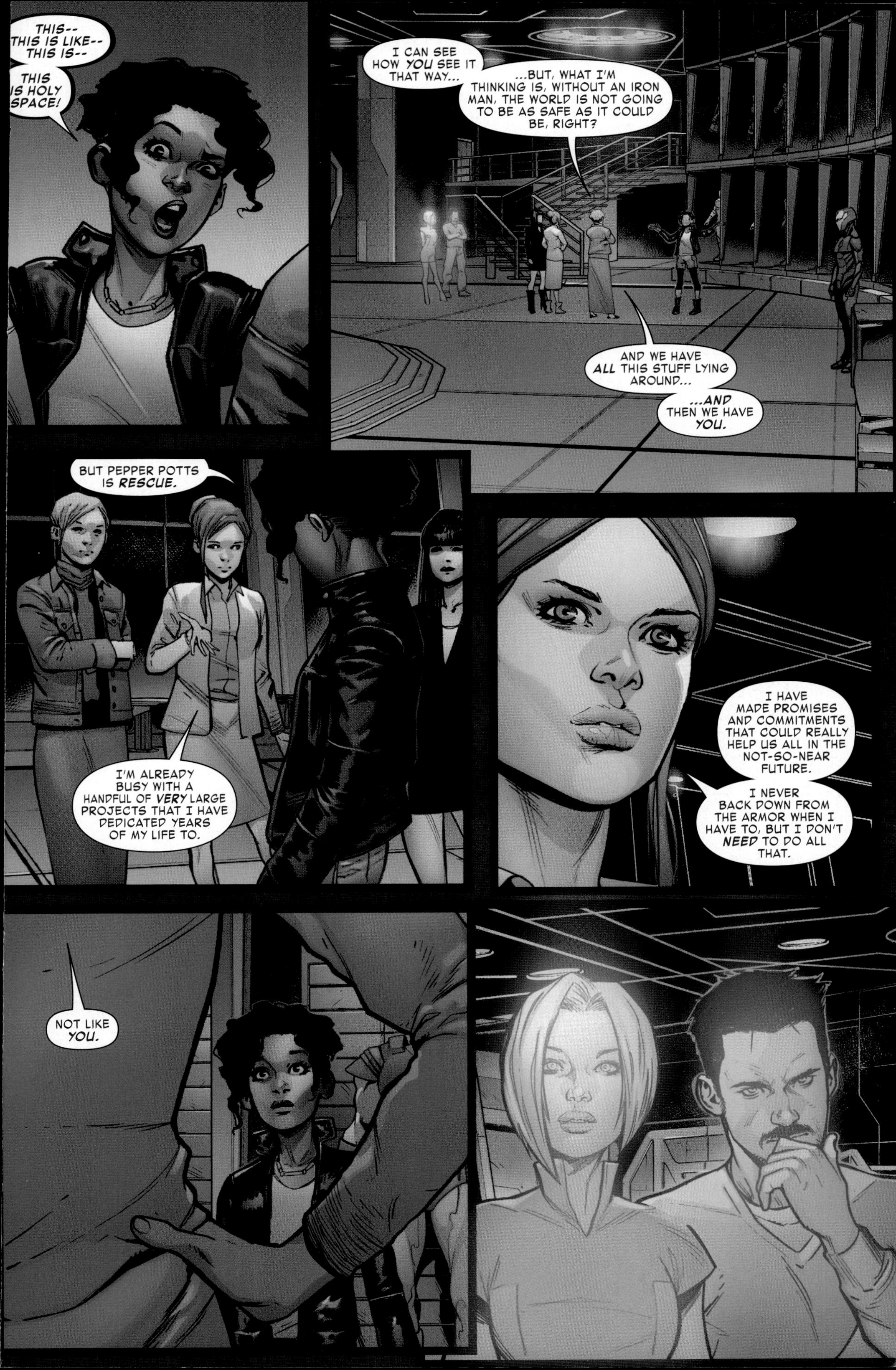
THIS-- THIS IS LIKE-- THIS IS--
THIS IS HOLY SPACE!
I CAN SEE HOW YOU SEE IT THAT WAY...
...BUT, WHAT I'M THINKING IS, WITHOUT AN IRON MAN, THE WORLD IS NOT GOING TO BE AS SAFE AS IT COULD BE, RIGHT?
AND WE HAVE ALL THIS STUFF LYING AROUND...
...AND THEN WE HAVE YOU.
BUT PEPPER POTTS IS RESCUE.
I'M ALREADY BUSY WITH A HANDFUL OF VERY LARGE PROJECTS THAT I HAVE DEDICATED YEARS OF MY LIFE TO.
I HAVE MADE PROMISES AND COMMITMENTS THAT COULD REALLY HELP US ALL IN THE NOT-SO-NEAR FUTURE.
I NEVER BACK DOWN FROM THE ARMOR WHEN I HAVE TO, BUT I DON'T NEED TO DO ALL THAT.
NOT LIKE YOU.

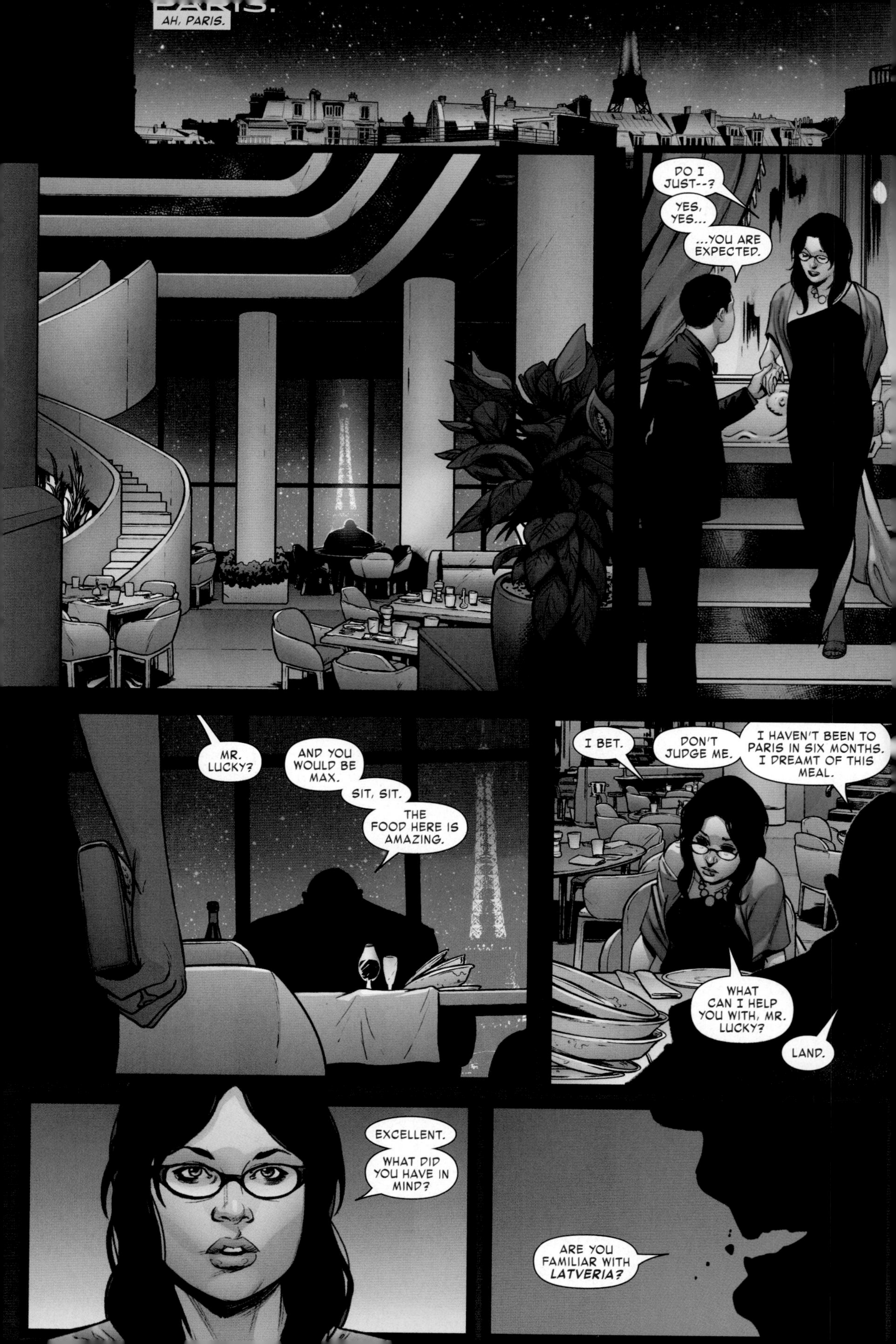
AH, PARIS.
DO I JUST--?
YES, YES...
...YOU ARE EXPECTED.
MR. LUCKY?
AND YOU WOULD BE MAX.
SIT, SIT.
THE FOOD HERE IS AMAZING.
I BET.
DON'T JUDGE ME.
I HAVEN'T BEEN TO PARIS IN SIX MONTHS. I DREAMT OF THIS MEAL.
WHAT CAN I HELP YOU WITH, MR. LUCKY?
LAND.
EXCELLENT.
WHAT DID YOU HAVE IN MIND?
ARE YOU FAMILIAR WITH *LATVERIA?*

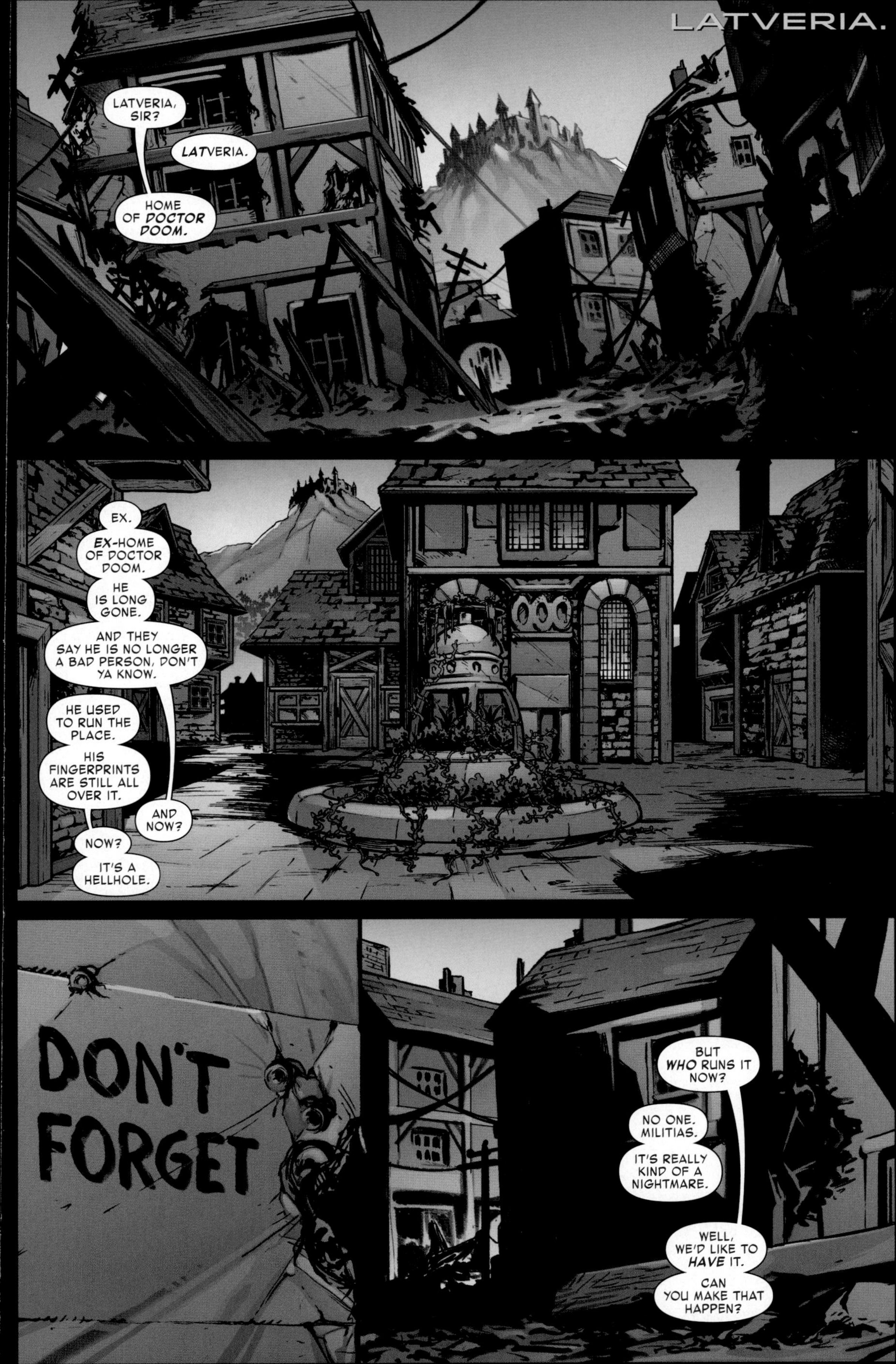
LATVERIA.
LATVERIA, SIR?
LATVERIA.
HOME OF DOCTOR DOOM.
EX.
EX-HOME OF DOCTOR DOOM.
HE IS LONG GONE.
AND THEY SAY HE IS NO LONGER A BAD PERSON, DON'T YA KNOW.
HE USED TO RUN THE PLACE.
HIS FINGERPRINTS ARE STILL ALL OVER IT.
AND NOW?
NOW?
IT'S A HELLHOLE.
DON'T FORGET
BUT WHO RUNS IT NOW?
NO ONE. MILITIAS.
IT'S REALLY KIND OF A NIGHTMARE.
WELL, WE'D LIKE TO HAVE IT.
CAN YOU MAKE THAT HAPPEN?

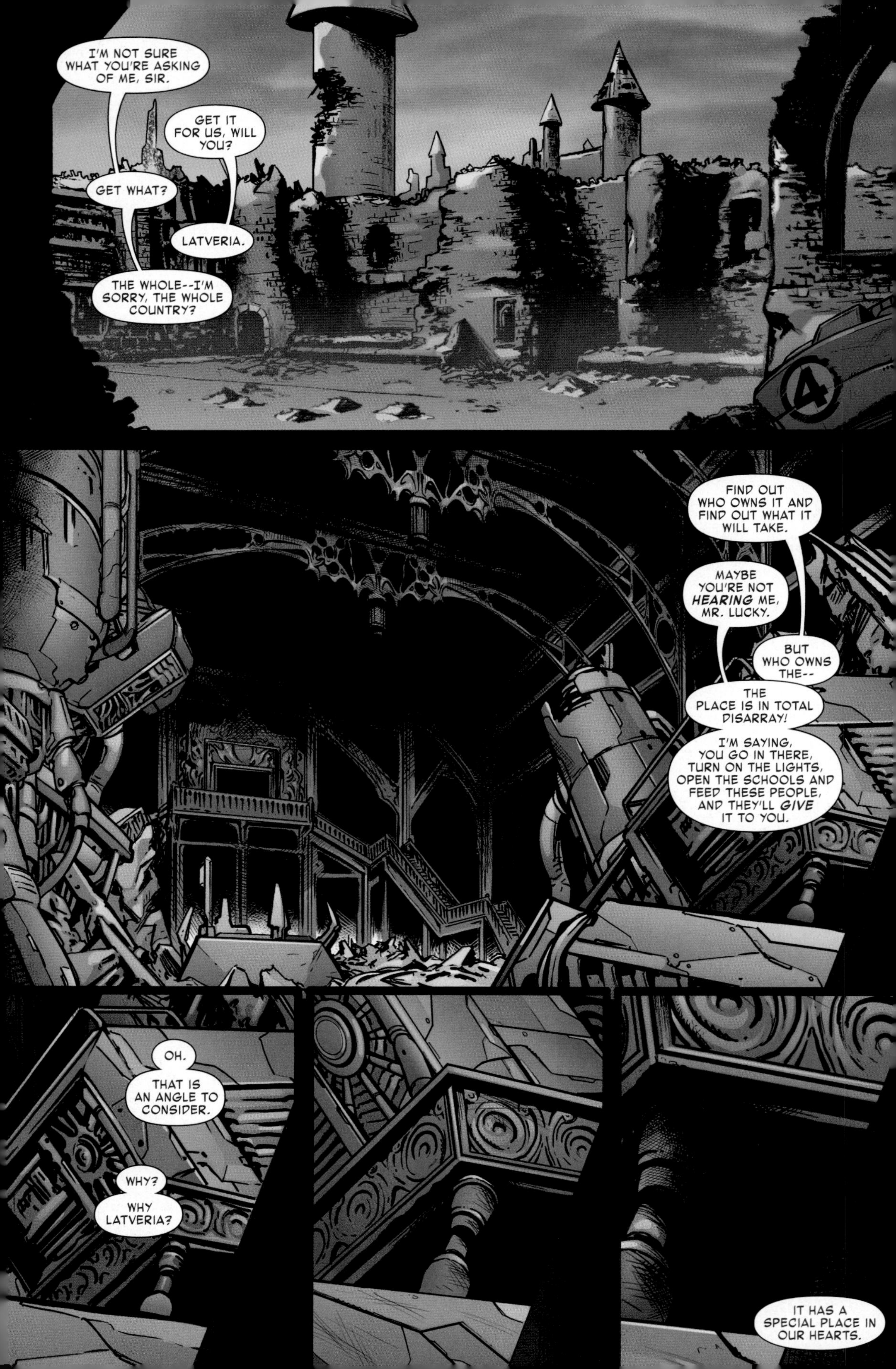
I'M NOT SURE WHAT YOU'RE ASKING OF ME, SIR.
GET IT FOR US, WILL YOU?
GET WHAT?
LATVERIA.
THE WHOLE--I'M SORRY, THE WHOLE COUNTRY?
FIND OUT WHO OWNS IT AND FIND OUT WHAT IT WILL TAKE.
MAYBE YOU'RE NOT *HEARING* ME, MR. LUCKY.
BUT WHO OWNS THE--
THE PLACE IS IN TOTAL DISARRAY!
I'M SAYING, YOU GO IN THERE, TURN ON THE LIGHTS, OPEN THE SCHOOLS AND FEED THESE PEOPLE, AND THEY'LL *GIVE* IT TO YOU.
OH.
THAT IS AN ANGLE TO CONSIDER.
WHY?
WHY LATVERIA?
IT HAS A SPECIAL PLACE IN OUR HEARTS.

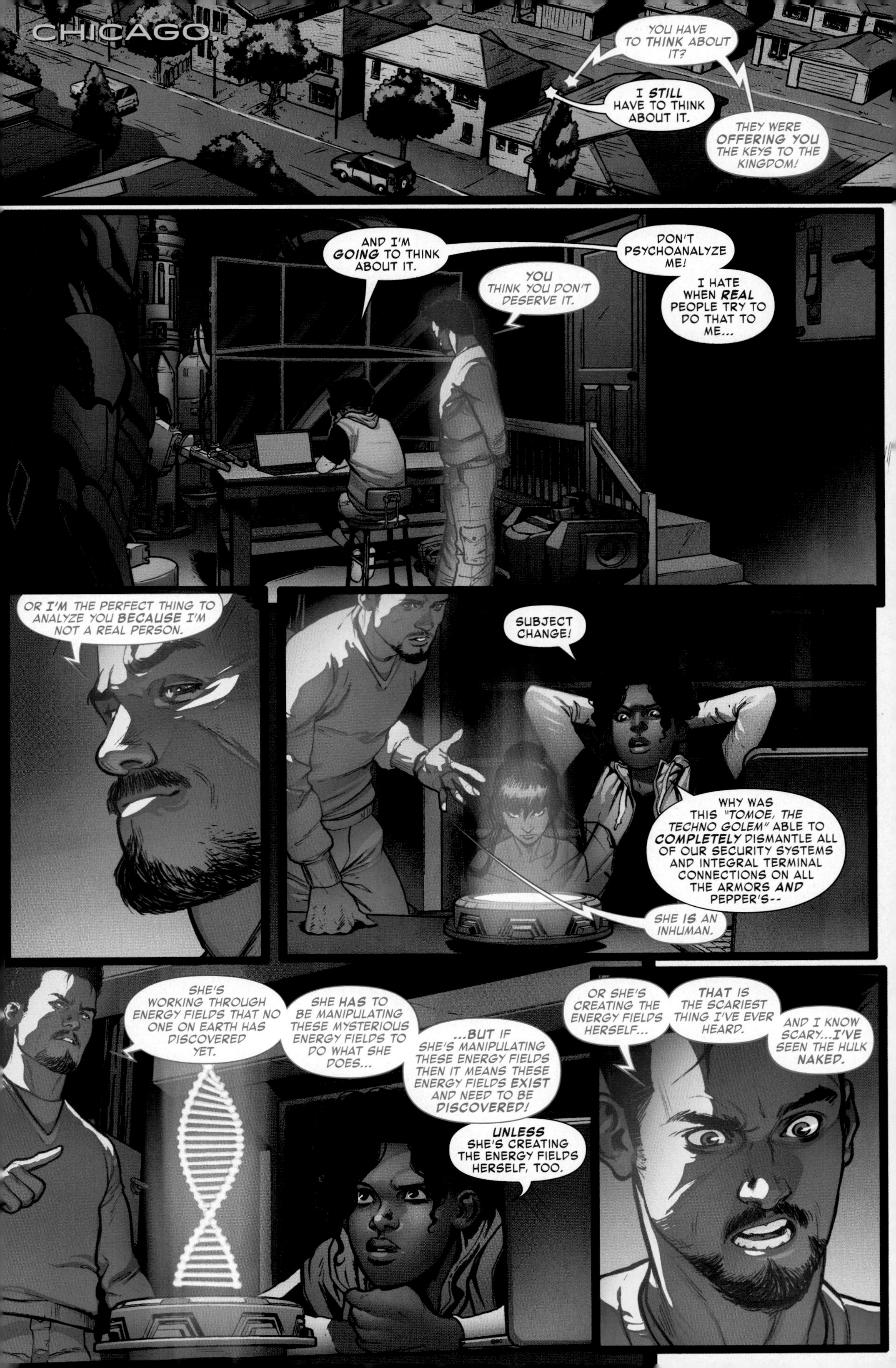
CHICAGO.
YOU HAVE TO THINK ABOUT IT?
I STILL HAVE TO THINK ABOUT IT.
THEY WERE OFFERING YOU THE KEYS TO THE KINGDOM!
AND I'M GOING TO THINK ABOUT IT.
YOU THINK YOU DON'T DESERVE IT.
DON'T PSYCHOANALYZE ME!
I HATE WHEN REAL PEOPLE TRY TO DO THAT TO ME...
OR I'M THE PERFECT THING TO ANALYZE YOU BECAUSE I'M NOT A REAL PERSON.
SUBJECT CHANGE!
WHY WAS THIS "TOMOE, THE TECHNO GOLEM" ABLE TO COMPLETELY DISMANTLE ALL OF OUR SECURITY SYSTEMS AND INTEGRAL TERMINAL CONNECTIONS ON ALL THE ARMORS AND PEPPER'S--
SHE IS AN INHUMAN.
SHE'S WORKING THROUGH ENERGY FIELDS THAT NO ONE ON EARTH HAS DISCOVERED YET.
SHE HAS TO BE MANIPULATING THESE MYSTERIOUS ENERGY FIELDS TO DO WHAT SHE DOES...
...BUT IF SHE'S MANIPULATING THESE ENERGY FIELDS THEN IT MEANS THESE ENERGY FIELDS EXIST AND NEED TO BE DISCOVERED!
UNLESS SHE'S CREATING THE ENERGY FIELDS HERSELF, TOO.
OR SHE'S CREATING THE ENERGY FIELDS HERSELF...
THAT IS THE SCARIEST THING I'VE EVER HEARD.
AND I KNOW SCARY...I'VE SEEN THE HULK NAKED.

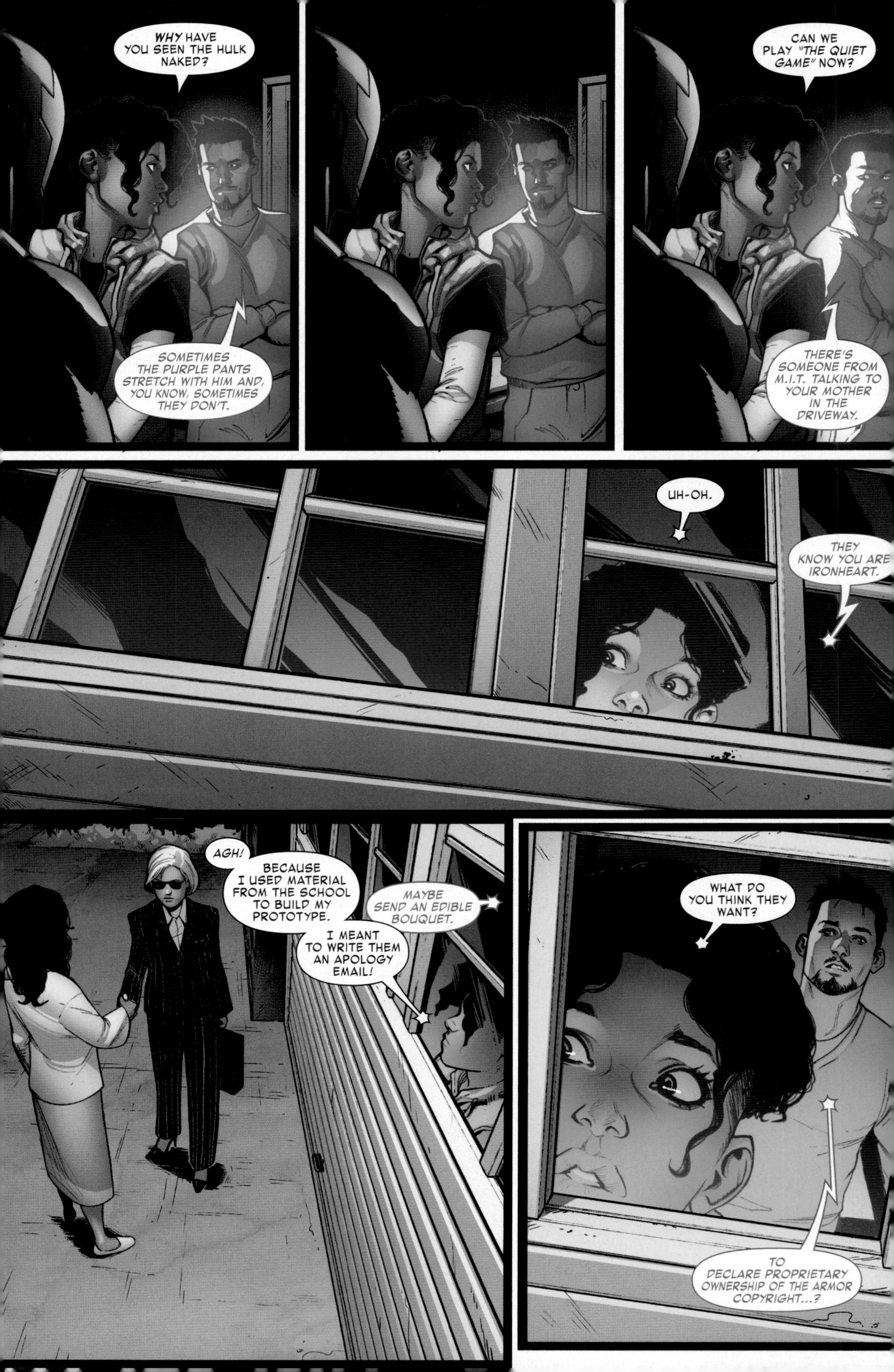
WHY HAVE YOU SEEN THE HULK NAKED?
SOMETIMES THE PURPLE PANTS STRETCH WITH HIM AND, YOU KNOW, SOMETIMES THEY DON'T.
CAN WE PLAY "THE QUIET GAME" NOW?
THERE'S SOMEONE FROM M.I.T. TALKING TO YOUR MOTHER IN THE DRIVEWAY.
UH-OH.
THEY KNOW YOU ARE IRONHEART.
AGH!
BECAUSE I USED MATERIAL FROM THE SCHOOL TO BUILD MY PROTOTYPE.
MAYBE SEND AN EDIBLE BOUQUET.
I MEANT TO WRITE THEM AN APOLOGY EMAIL!
WHAT DO YOU THINK THEY WANT?
TO DECLARE PROPRIETARY OWNERSHIP OF THE ARMOR COPYRIGHT...?

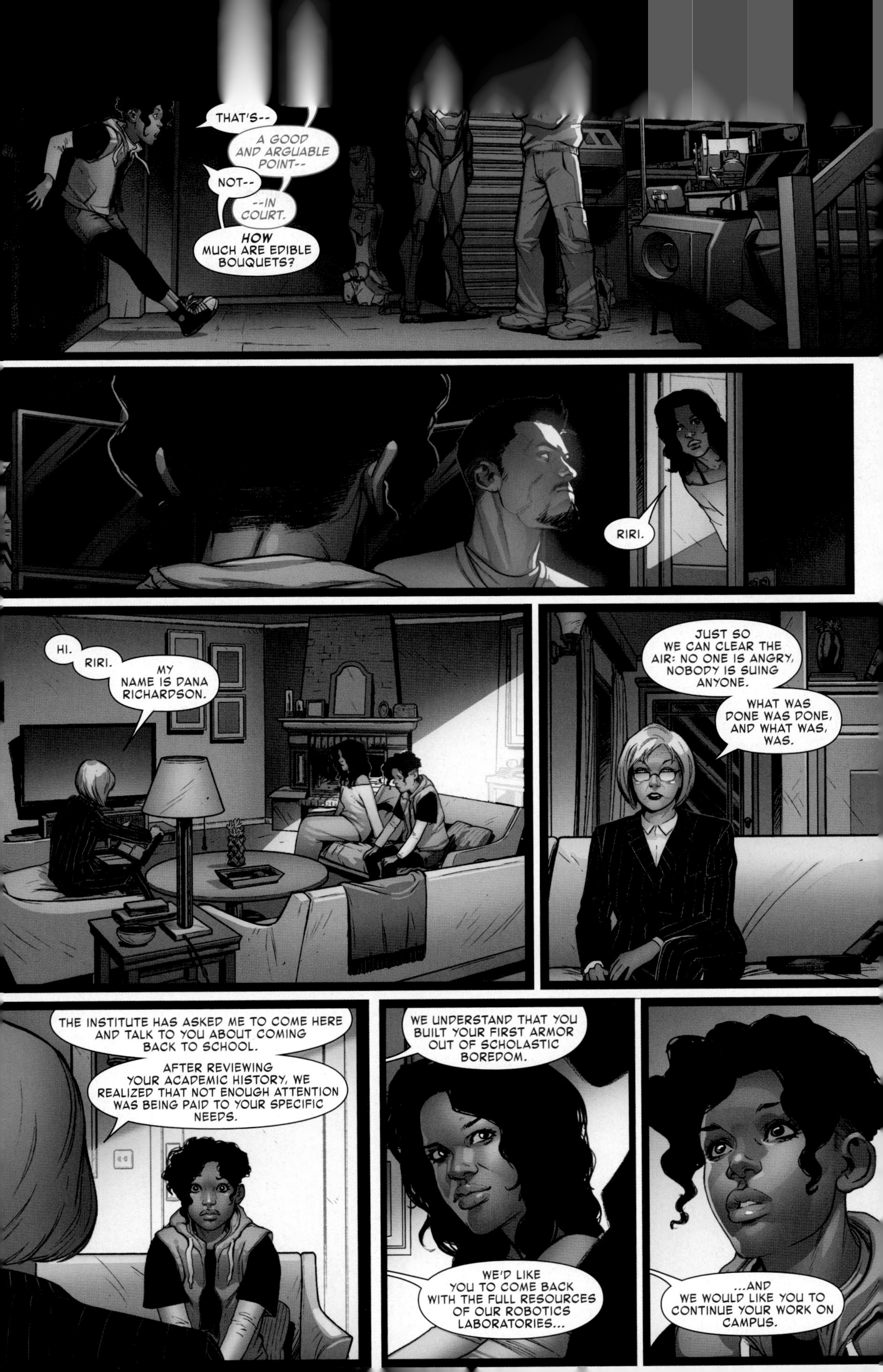
THAT'S--
A GOOD AND ARGUABLE POINT--
NOT--
--IN COURT.
HOW MUCH ARE EDIBLE BOUQUETS?
RIRI.
HI.
RIRI.
MY NAME IS DANA RICHARDSON.
JUST SO WE CAN CLEAR THE AIR: NO ONE IS ANGRY, NOBODY IS SUING ANYONE.
WHAT WAS DONE WAS DONE, AND WHAT WAS, WAS.
THE INSTITUTE HAS ASKED ME TO COME HERE AND TALK TO YOU ABOUT COMING BACK TO SCHOOL.
AFTER REVIEWING YOUR ACADEMIC HISTORY, WE REALIZED THAT NOT ENOUGH ATTENTION WAS BEING PAID TO YOUR SPECIFIC NEEDS.
WE UNDERSTAND THAT YOU BUILT YOUR FIRST ARMOR OUT OF SCHOLASTIC BOREDOM.
WE'D LIKE YOU TO COME BACK WITH THE FULL RESOURCES OF OUR ROBOTICS LABORATORIES...
...AND WE WOULD LIKE YOU TO CONTINUE YOUR WORK ON CAMPUS.

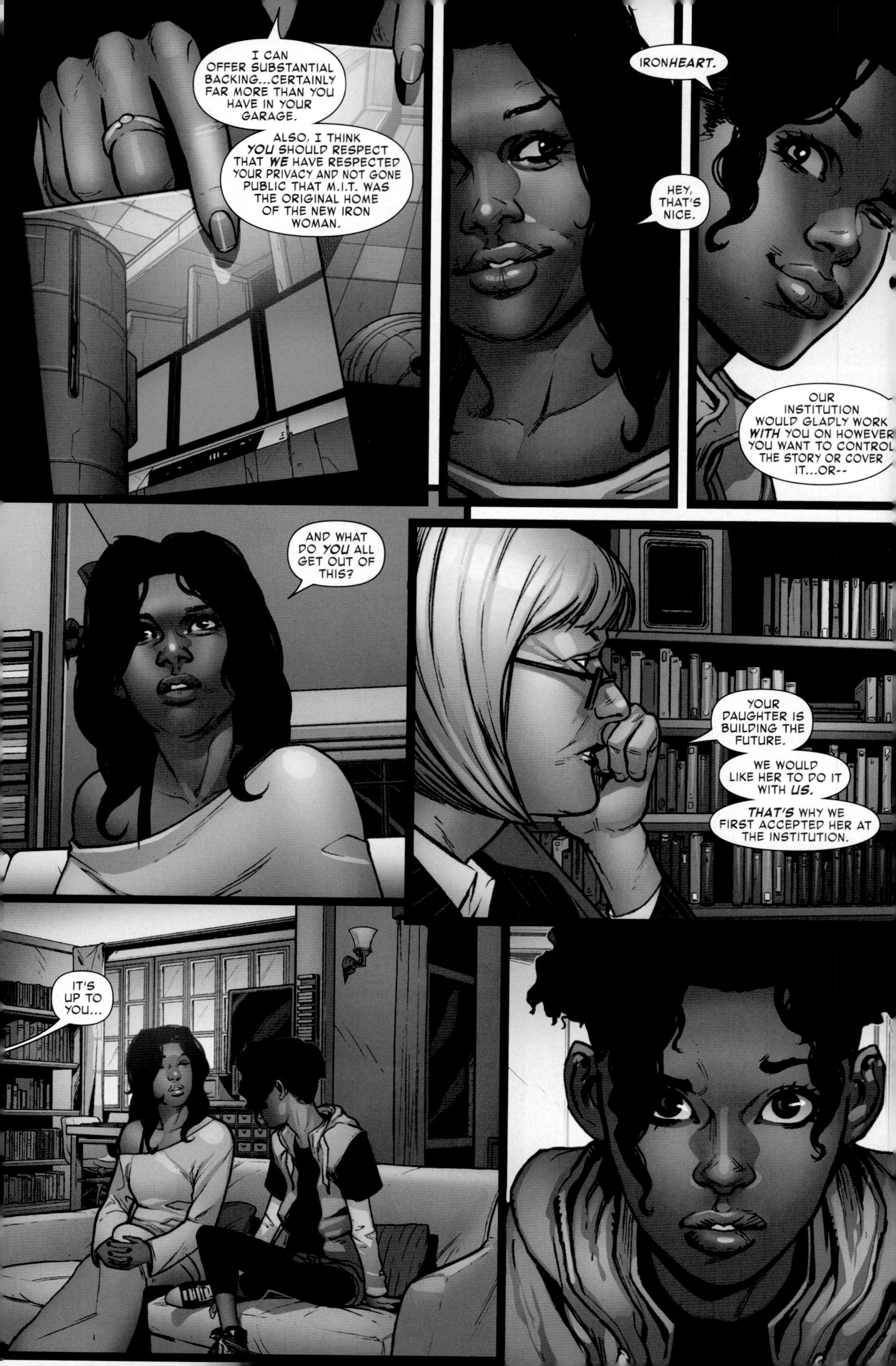
I CAN OFFER SUBSTANTIAL BACKING...CERTAINLY FAR MORE THAN YOU HAVE IN YOUR GARAGE.
ALSO, I THINK *YOU* SHOULD RESPECT THAT *WE* HAVE RESPECTED YOUR PRIVACY AND NOT GONE PUBLIC THAT M.I.T. WAS THE ORIGINAL HOME OF THE NEW IRON WOMAN.
IRON*HEART.*
HEY, THAT'S NICE.
OUR INSTITUTION WOULD GLADLY WORK *WITH* YOU ON HOWEVER YOU WANT TO CONTROL THE STORY OR COVER IT...OR--
AND WHAT DO *YOU* ALL GET OUT OF THIS?
YOUR DAUGHTER IS BUILDING THE FUTURE.
WE WOULD LIKE HER TO DO IT WITH *US.*
THAT'S WHY WE FIRST ACCEPTED HER AT THE INSTITUTION.
IT'S UP TO YOU...

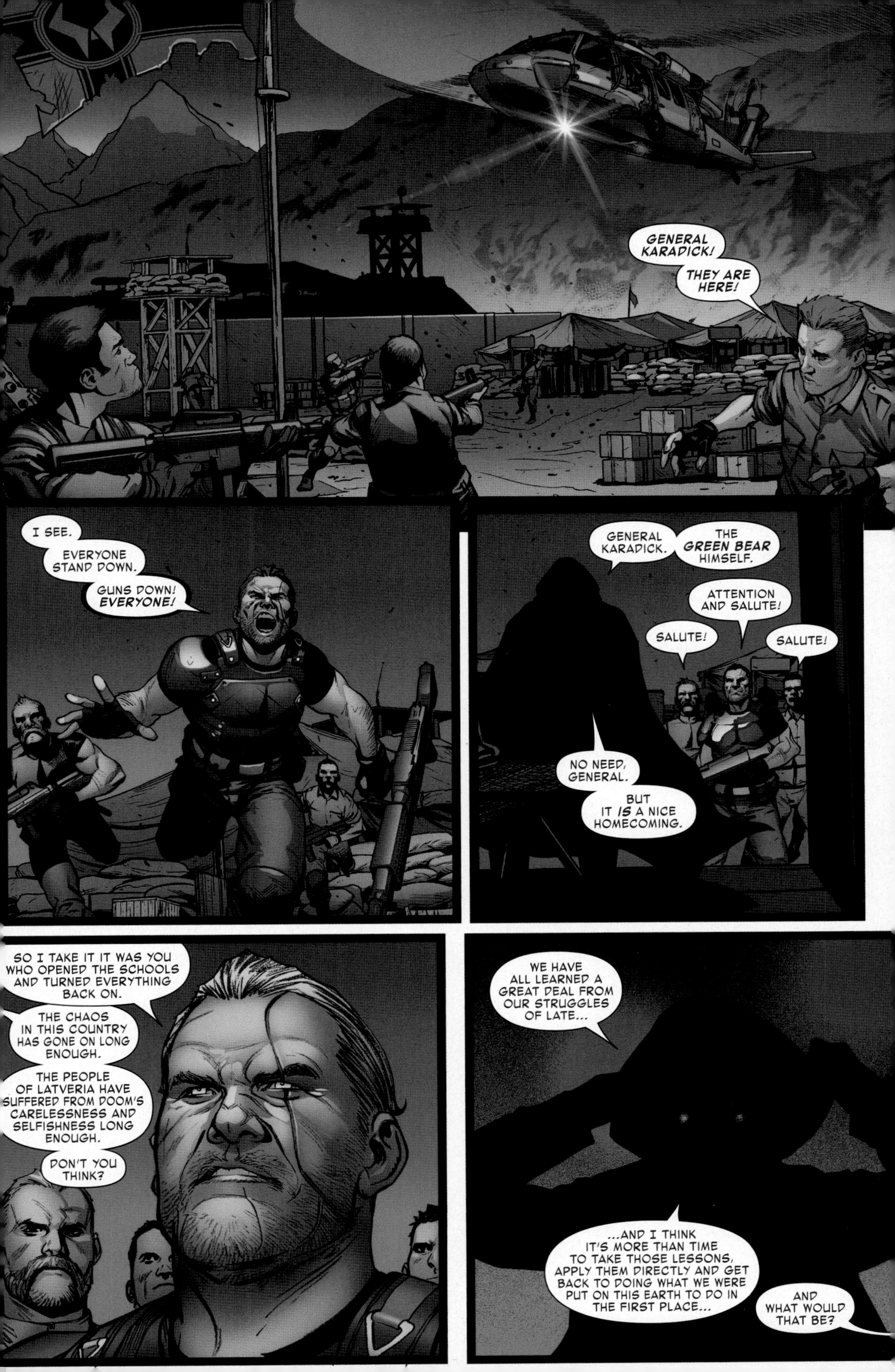
GENERAL KARADICK!
THEY ARE HERE!
I SEE.
EVERYONE STAND DOWN.
GUNS DOWN! EVERYONE!
GENERAL KARADICK.
THE GREEN BEAR HIMSELF.
ATTENTION AND SALUTE!
SALUTE!
SALUTE!
NO NEED, GENERAL.
BUT IT IS A NICE HOMECOMING.
SO I TAKE IT IT WAS YOU WHO OPENED THE SCHOOLS AND TURNED EVERYTHING BACK ON.
THE CHAOS IN THIS COUNTRY HAS GONE ON LONG ENOUGH.
THE PEOPLE OF LATVERIA HAVE SUFFERED FROM DOOM'S CARELESSNESS AND SELFISHNESS LONG ENOUGH.
DON'T YOU THINK?
WE HAVE ALL LEARNED A GREAT DEAL FROM OUR STRUGGLES OF LATE...
...AND I THINK IT'S MORE THAN TIME TO TAKE THOSE LESSONS, APPLY THEM DIRECTLY AND GET BACK TO DOING WHAT WE WERE PUT ON THIS EARTH TO DO IN THE FIRST PLACE...
AND WHAT WOULD THAT BE?

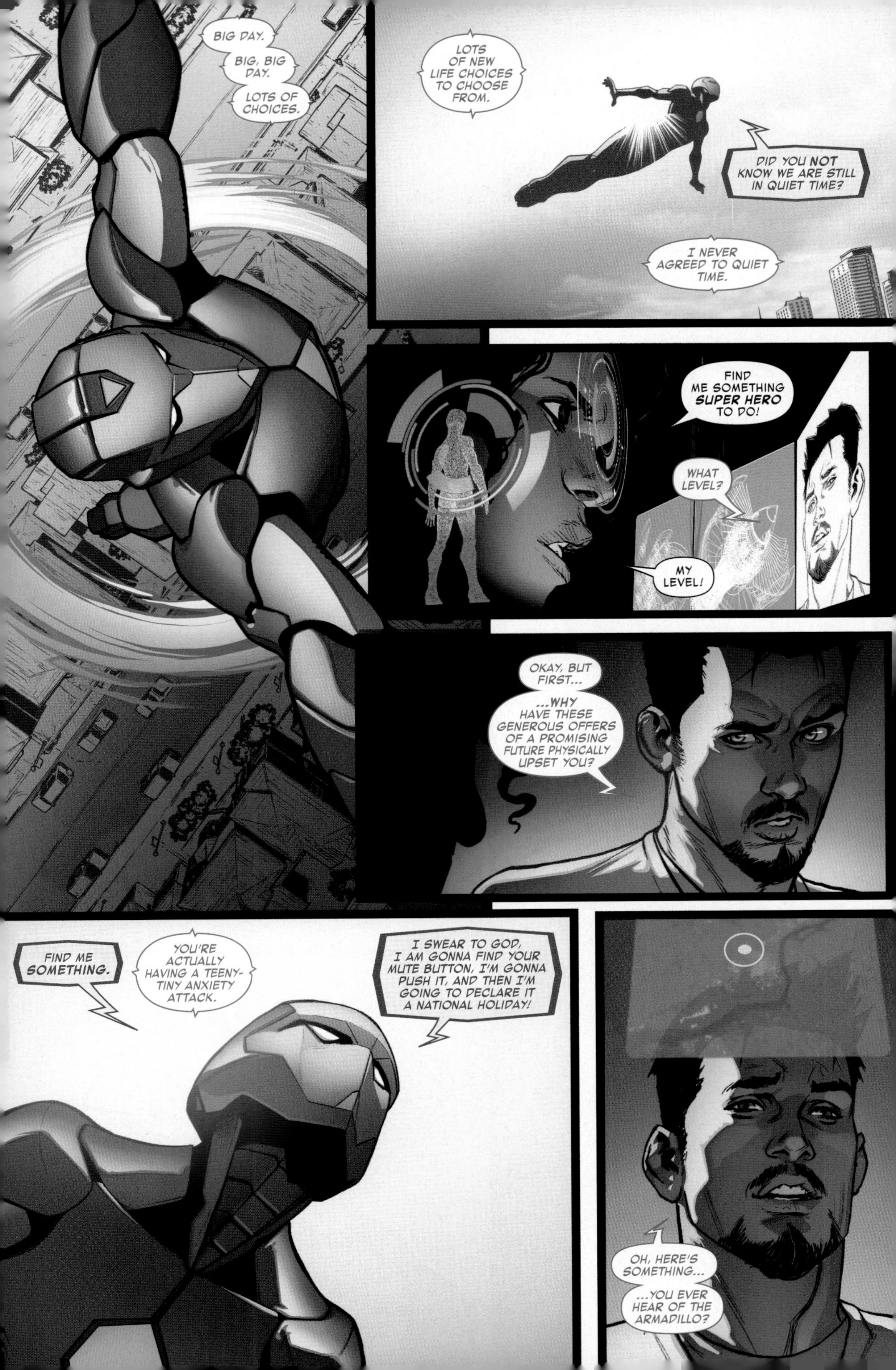
BIG DAY.
BIG, BIG DAY.
LOTS OF CHOICES.
LOTS OF NEW LIFE CHOICES TO CHOOSE FROM.
DID YOU NOT KNOW WE ARE STILL IN QUIET TIME?
I NEVER AGREED TO QUIET TIME.
FIND ME SOMETHING SUPER HERO TO DO!
WHAT LEVEL?
MY LEVEL!
OKAY, BUT FIRST...
...WHY HAVE THESE GENEROUS OFFERS OF A PROMISING FUTURE PHYSICALLY UPSET YOU?
FIND ME SOMETHING.
YOU'RE ACTUALLY HAVING A TEENY-TINY ANXIETY ATTACK.
I SWEAR TO GOD, I AM GONNA FIND YOUR MUTE BUTTON, I'M GONNA PUSH IT, AND THEN I'M GOING TO DECLARE IT A NATIONAL HOLIDAY!
OH, HERE'S SOMETHING...
...YOU EVER HEAR OF THE ARMADILLO?

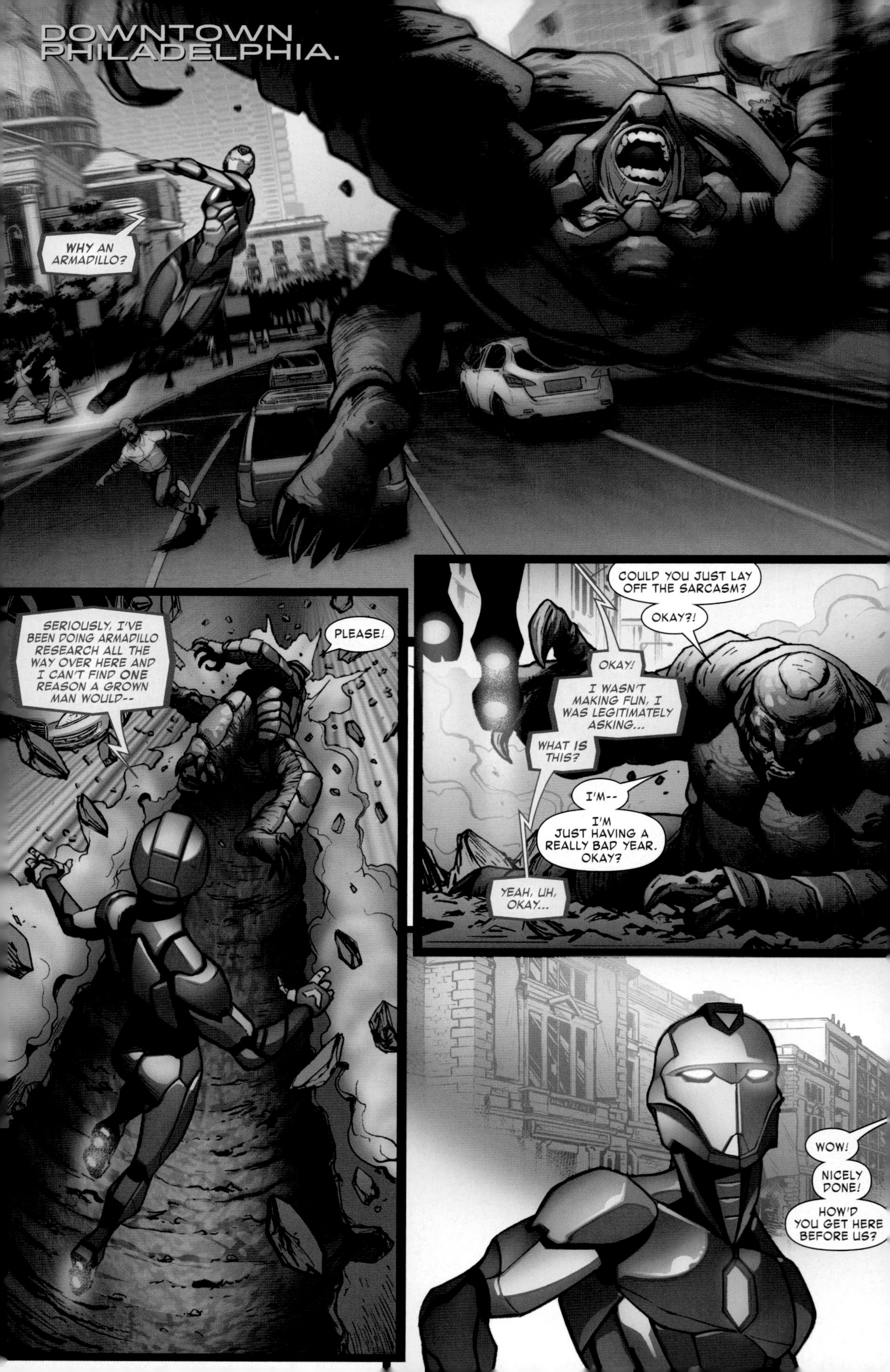
DOWNTOWN PHILADELPHIA.
WHY AN ARMADILLO?
SERIOUSLY, I'VE BEEN DOING ARMADILLO RESEARCH ALL THE WAY OVER HERE AND I CAN'T FIND ONE REASON A GROWN MAN WOULD--
PLEASE!
COULD YOU JUST LAY OFF THE SARCASM?
OKAY?!
OKAY!
I WASN'T MAKING FUN, I WAS LEGITIMATELY ASKING...
WHAT IS THIS?
I'M--
I'M JUST HAVING A REALLY BAD YEAR. OKAY?
YEAH, UH, OKAY...
WOW!
NICELY DONE!
HOW'D YOU GET HERE BEFORE US?

7

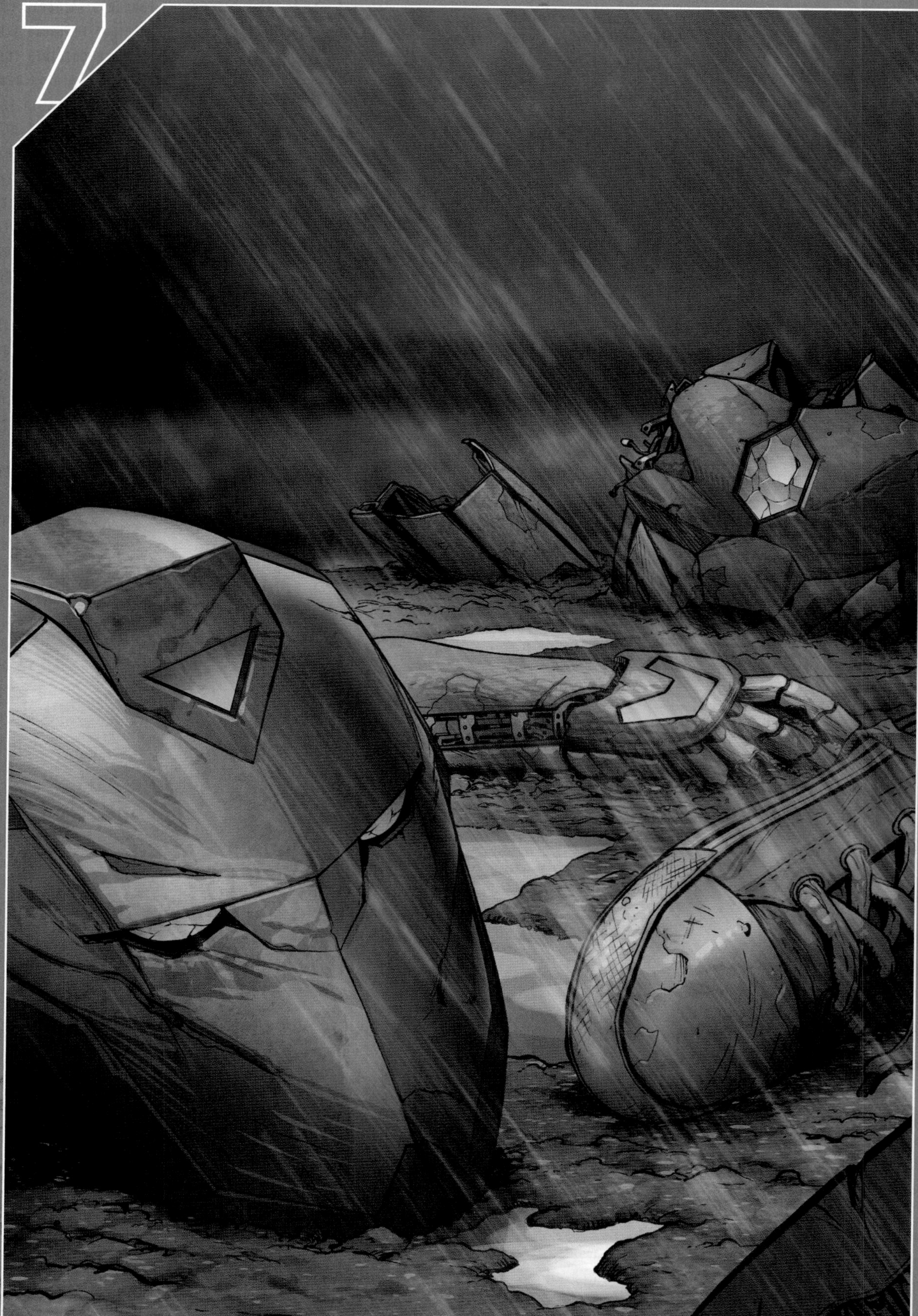

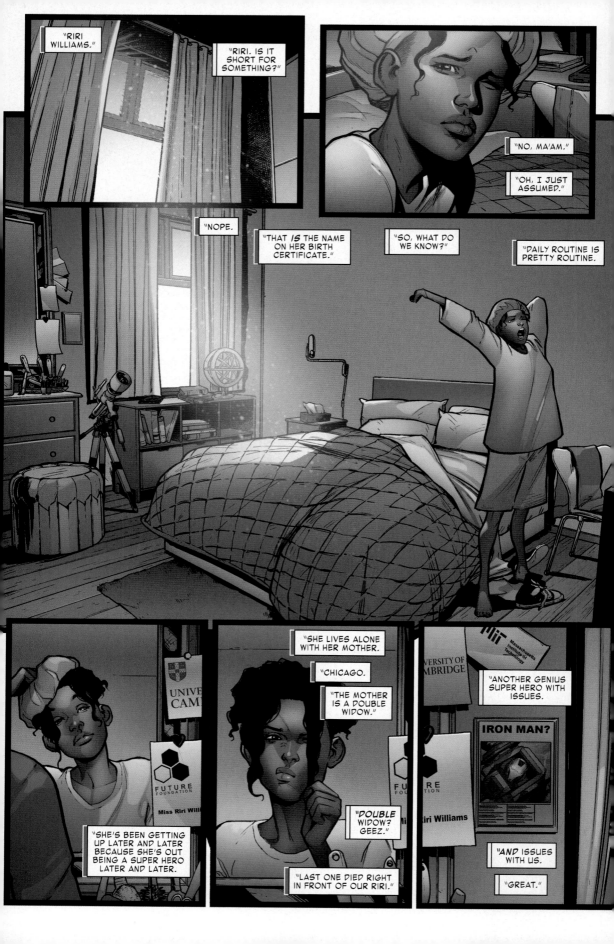

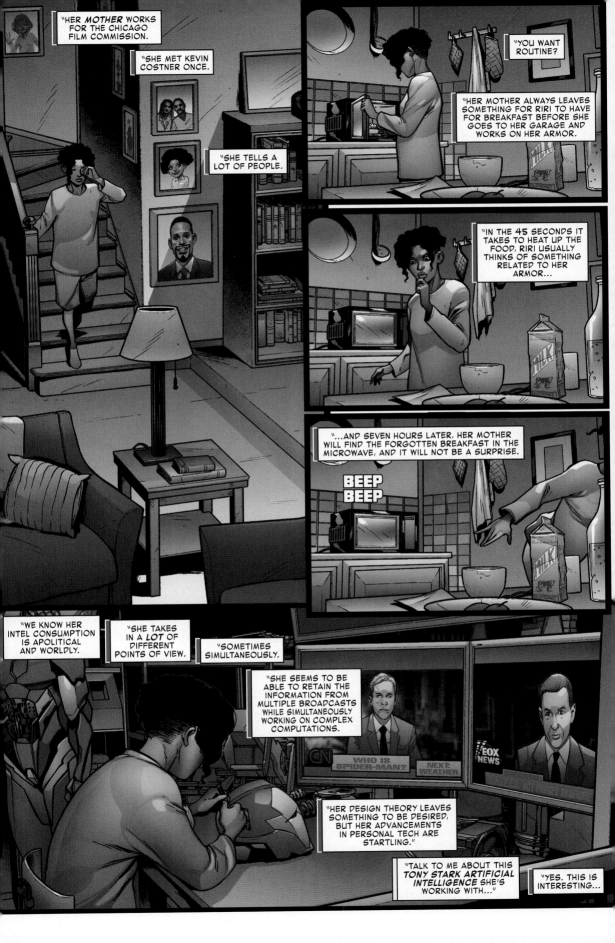

"HER *MOTHER* WORKS FOR THE CHICAGO FILM COMMISSION.

"SHE MET KEVIN COSTNER ONCE.

"SHE TELLS A LOT OF PEOPLE.

"YOU WANT ROUTINE?

"HER MOTHER ALWAYS LEAVES SOMETHING FOR RIRI TO HAVE FOR BREAKFAST BEFORE SHE GOES TO HER GARAGE AND WORKS ON HER ARMOR.

"IN THE 45 SECONDS IT TAKES TO HEAT UP THE FOOD, RIRI USUALLY THINKS OF SOMETHING RELATED TO HER ARMOR...

"...AND SEVEN HOURS LATER, HER MOTHER WILL FIND THE FORGOTTEN BREAKFAST IN THE MICROWAVE, AND IT WILL NOT BE A SURPRISE.

BEEP BEEP

"WE KNOW HER INTEL CONSUMPTION IS APOLITICAL AND WORLDLY.

"SHE TAKES IN A *LOT* OF DIFFERENT POINTS OF VIEW.

"SOMETIMES SIMULTANEOUSLY.

"SHE SEEMS TO BE ABLE TO RETAIN THE INFORMATION FROM MULTIPLE BROADCASTS WHILE SIMULTANEOUSLY WORKING ON COMPLEX COMPUTATIONS.

WHO IS SPIDER-MAN?

NEXT WEATHER

FOX NEWS

"HER DESIGN THEORY LEAVES SOMETHING TO BE DESIRED, BUT HER ADVANCEMENTS IN PERSONAL TECH ARE STARTLING."

"TALK TO ME ABOUT THIS *TONY STARK ARTIFICIAL INTELLIGENCE* SHE'S WORKING WITH..."

"YES. THIS IS INTERESTING...

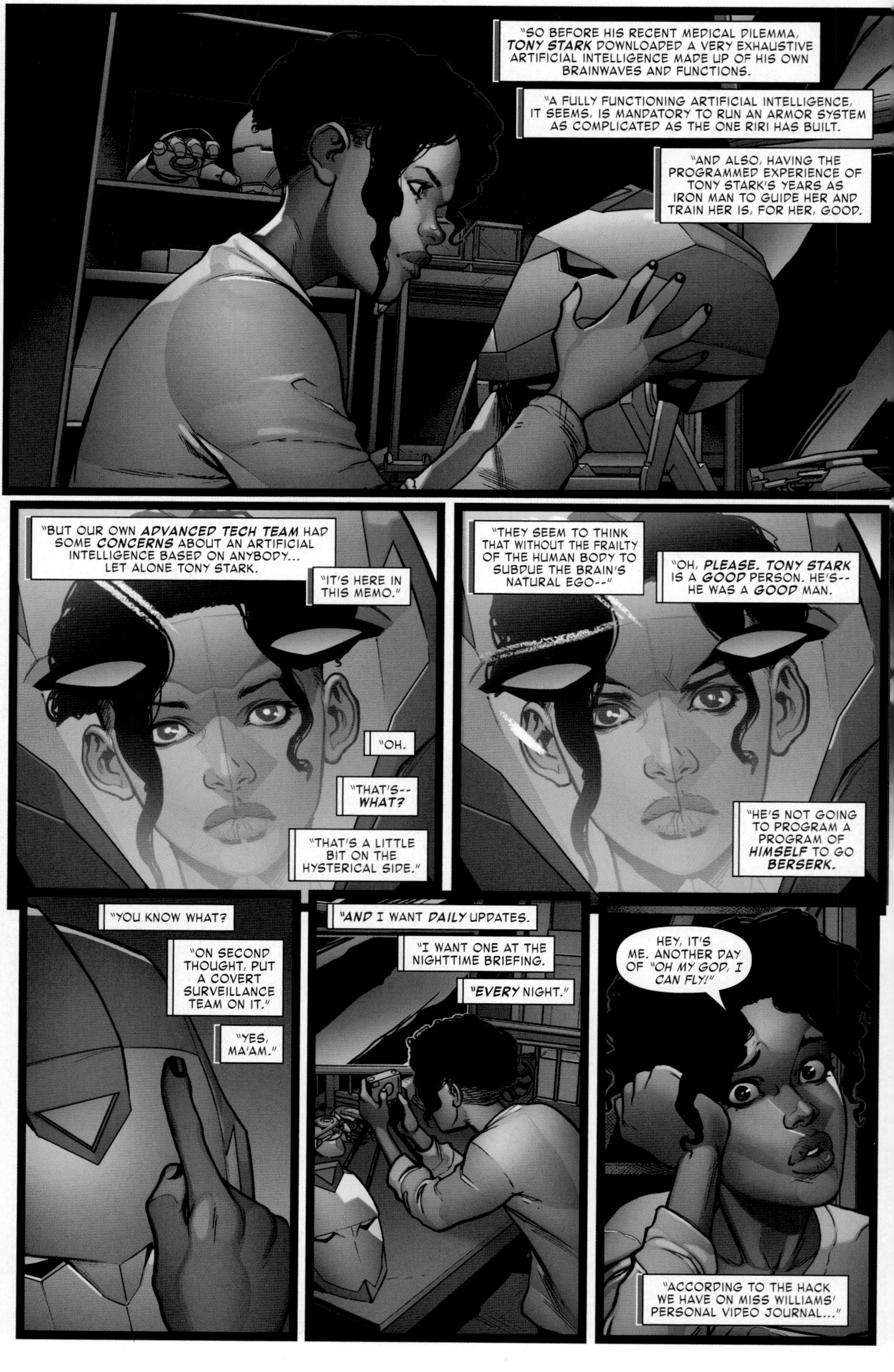
"SO BEFORE HIS RECENT MEDICAL DILEMMA, TONY STARK DOWNLOADED A VERY EXHAUSTIVE ARTIFICIAL INTELLIGENCE MADE UP OF HIS OWN BRAINWAVES AND FUNCTIONS.
"A FULLY FUNCTIONING ARTIFICIAL INTELLIGENCE, IT SEEMS, IS MANDATORY TO RUN AN ARMOR SYSTEM AS COMPLICATED AS THE ONE RIRI HAS BUILT.
"AND ALSO, HAVING THE PROGRAMMED EXPERIENCE OF TONY STARK'S YEARS AS IRON MAN TO GUIDE HER AND TRAIN HER IS, FOR HER, GOOD.
"BUT OUR OWN ADVANCED TECH TEAM HAD SOME CONCERNS ABOUT AN ARTIFICIAL INTELLIGENCE BASED ON ANYBODY... LET ALONE TONY STARK.
"IT'S HERE IN THIS MEMO."
"OH.
"THAT'S-- WHAT?
"THAT'S A LITTLE BIT ON THE HYSTERICAL SIDE."
"THEY SEEM TO THINK THAT WITHOUT THE FRAILTY OF THE HUMAN BODY TO SUBDUE THE BRAIN'S NATURAL EGO--"
"OH, PLEASE. TONY STARK IS A GOOD PERSON. HE'S-- HE WAS A GOOD MAN.
"HE'S NOT GOING TO PROGRAM A PROGRAM OF HIMSELF TO GO BERSERK.
"YOU KNOW WHAT?
"ON SECOND THOUGHT, PUT A COVERT SURVEILLANCE TEAM ON IT."
"YES, MA'AM."
"AND I WANT DAILY UPDATES.
"I WANT ONE AT THE NIGHTTIME BRIEFING.
"EVERY NIGHT."
HEY, IT'S ME. ANOTHER DAY OF "OH MY GOD, I CAN FLY!"
"ACCORDING TO THE HACK WE HAVE ON MISS WILLIAMS' PERSONAL VIDEO JOURNAL..."

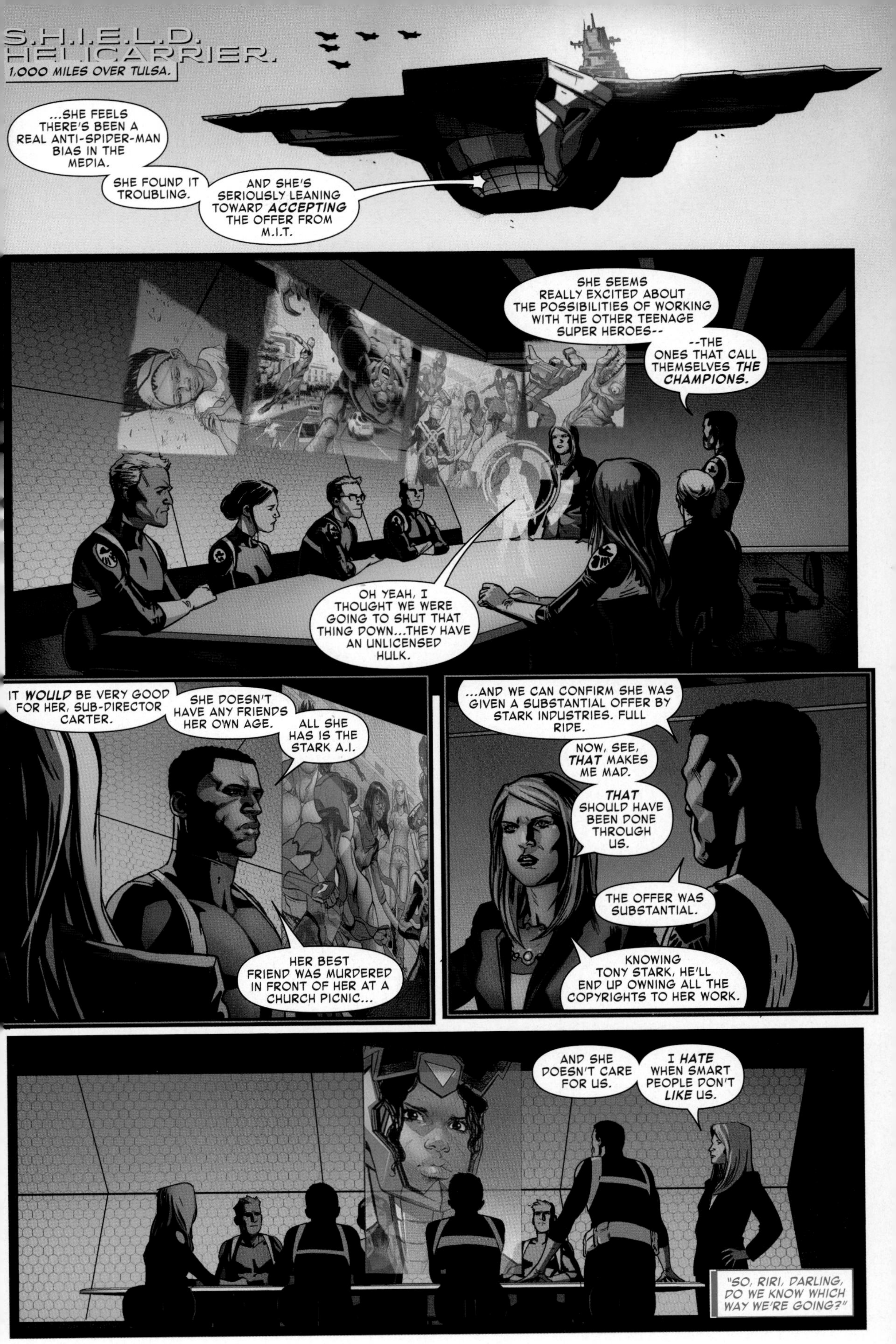
S.H.I.E.L.D. HELICARRIER.
1,000 MILES OVER TULSA.
...SHE FEELS THERE'S BEEN A REAL ANTI-SPIDER-MAN BIAS IN THE MEDIA.
SHE FOUND IT TROUBLING.
AND SHE'S SERIOUSLY LEANING TOWARD ACCEPTING THE OFFER FROM M.I.T.
SHE SEEMS REALLY EXCITED ABOUT THE POSSIBILITIES OF WORKING WITH THE OTHER TEENAGE SUPER HEROES--
--THE ONES THAT CALL THEMSELVES THE CHAMPIONS.
OH YEAH, I THOUGHT WE WERE GOING TO SHUT THAT THING DOWN...THEY HAVE AN UNLICENSED HULK.
IT WOULD BE VERY GOOD FOR HER, SUB-DIRECTOR CARTER.
SHE DOESN'T HAVE ANY FRIENDS HER OWN AGE.
ALL SHE HAS IS THE STARK A.I.
HER BEST FRIEND WAS MURDERED IN FRONT OF HER AT A CHURCH PICNIC...
...AND WE CAN CONFIRM SHE WAS GIVEN A SUBSTANTIAL OFFER BY STARK INDUSTRIES. FULL RIDE.
NOW, SEE, THAT MAKES ME MAD.
THAT SHOULD HAVE BEEN DONE THROUGH US.
THE OFFER WAS SUBSTANTIAL.
KNOWING TONY STARK, HE'LL END UP OWNING ALL THE COPYRIGHTS TO HER WORK.
AND SHE DOESN'T CARE FOR US.
I HATE WHEN SMART PEOPLE DON'T LIKE US.
"SO, RIRI, DARLING, DO WE KNOW WHICH WAY WE'RE GOING?"

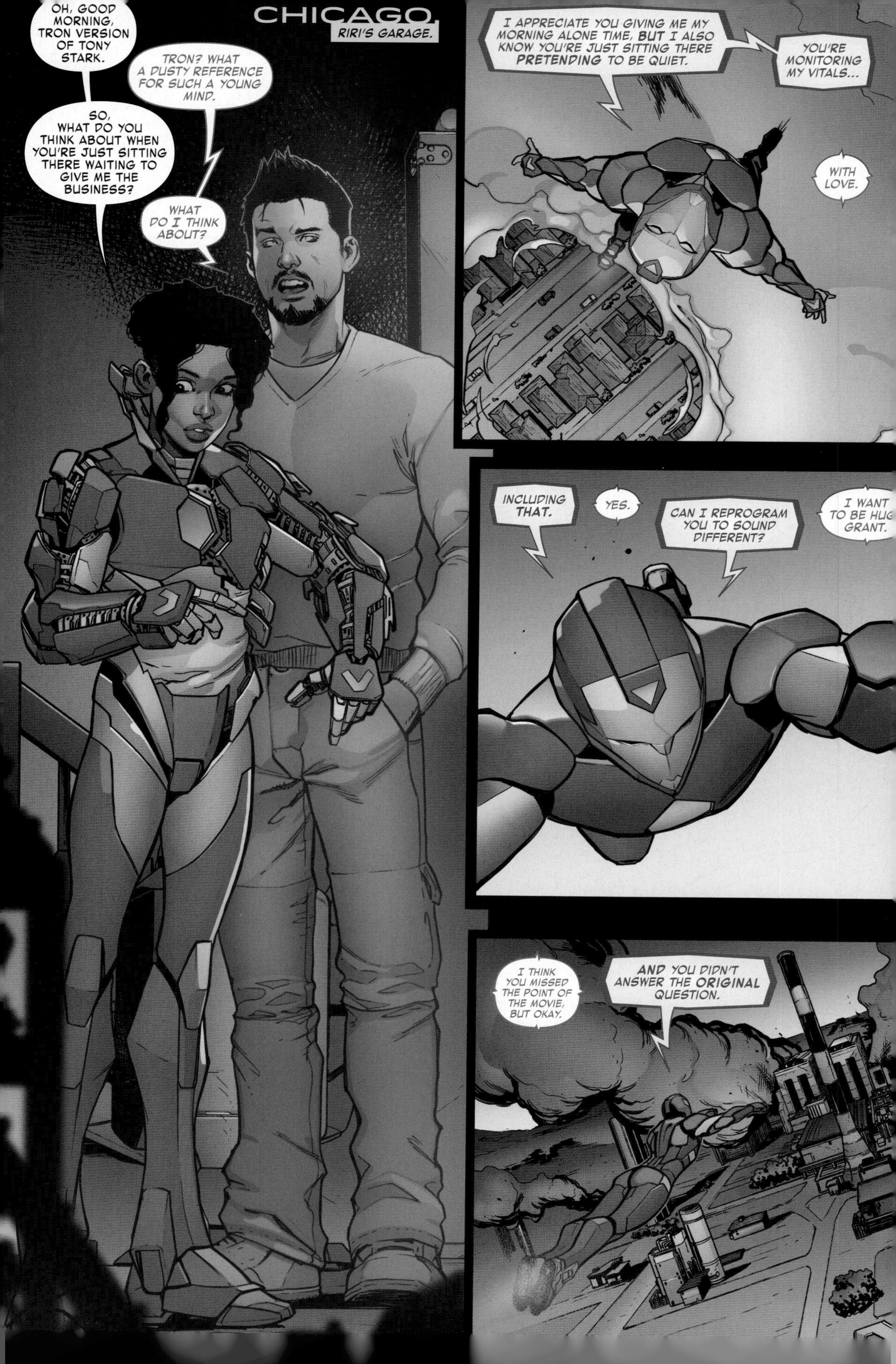
CHICAGO.
RIRI'S GARAGE.
OH, GOOD MORNING, TRON VERSION OF TONY STARK.
TRON? WHAT A DUSTY REFERENCE FOR SUCH A YOUNG MIND.
SO, WHAT DO YOU THINK ABOUT WHEN YOU'RE JUST SITTING THERE WAITING TO GIVE ME THE BUSINESS?
WHAT DO I THINK ABOUT?
I APPRECIATE YOU GIVING ME MY MORNING ALONE TIME, BUT I ALSO KNOW YOU'RE JUST SITTING THERE PRETENDING TO BE QUIET.
YOU'RE MONITORING MY VITALS...
WITH LOVE.
INCLUDING THAT.
YES.
CAN I REPROGRAM YOU TO SOUND DIFFERENT?
I WANT TO BE HUG GRANT.
I THINK YOU MISSED THE POINT OF THE MOVIE, BUT OKAY.
AND YOU DIDN'T ANSWER THE ORIGINAL QUESTION.

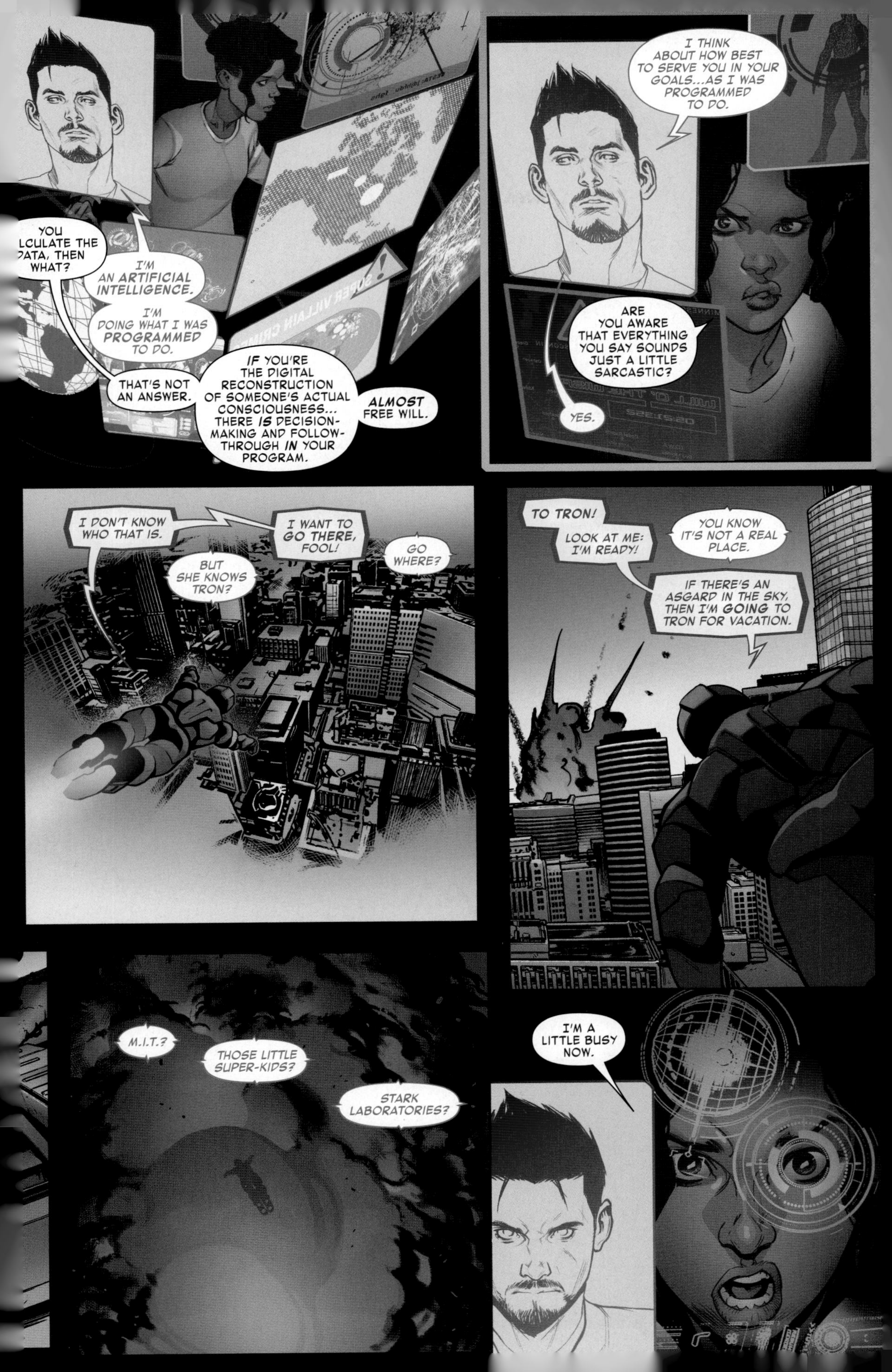

YOU LCULATE THE DATA, THEN WHAT?
I'M AN ARTIFICIAL INTELLIGENCE.
I'M DOING WHAT I WAS PROGRAMMED TO DO.
THAT'S NOT AN ANSWER.
IF YOU'RE THE DIGITAL RECONSTRUCTION OF SOMEONE'S ACTUAL CONSCIOUSNESS... THERE IS DECISION-MAKING AND FOLLOW-THROUGH IN YOUR PROGRAM.
ALMOST FREE WILL.
SUPER VILLAIN CRIME
I THINK ABOUT HOW BEST TO SERVE YOU IN YOUR GOALS...AS I WAS PROGRAMMED TO DO.
ARE YOU AWARE THAT EVERYTHING YOU SAY SOUNDS JUST A LITTLE SARCASTIC?
YES.
I DON'T KNOW WHO THAT IS.
I WANT TO GO THERE, FOOL!
BUT SHE KNOWS TRON?
GO WHERE?
TO TRON!
LOOK AT ME: I'M READY!
YOU KNOW IT'S NOT A REAL PLACE.
IF THERE'S AN ASGARD IN THE SKY, THEN I'M GOING TO TRON FOR VACATION.
M.I.T.?
THOSE LITTLE SUPER-KIDS?
STARK LABORATORIES?
I'M A LITTLE BUSY NOW.

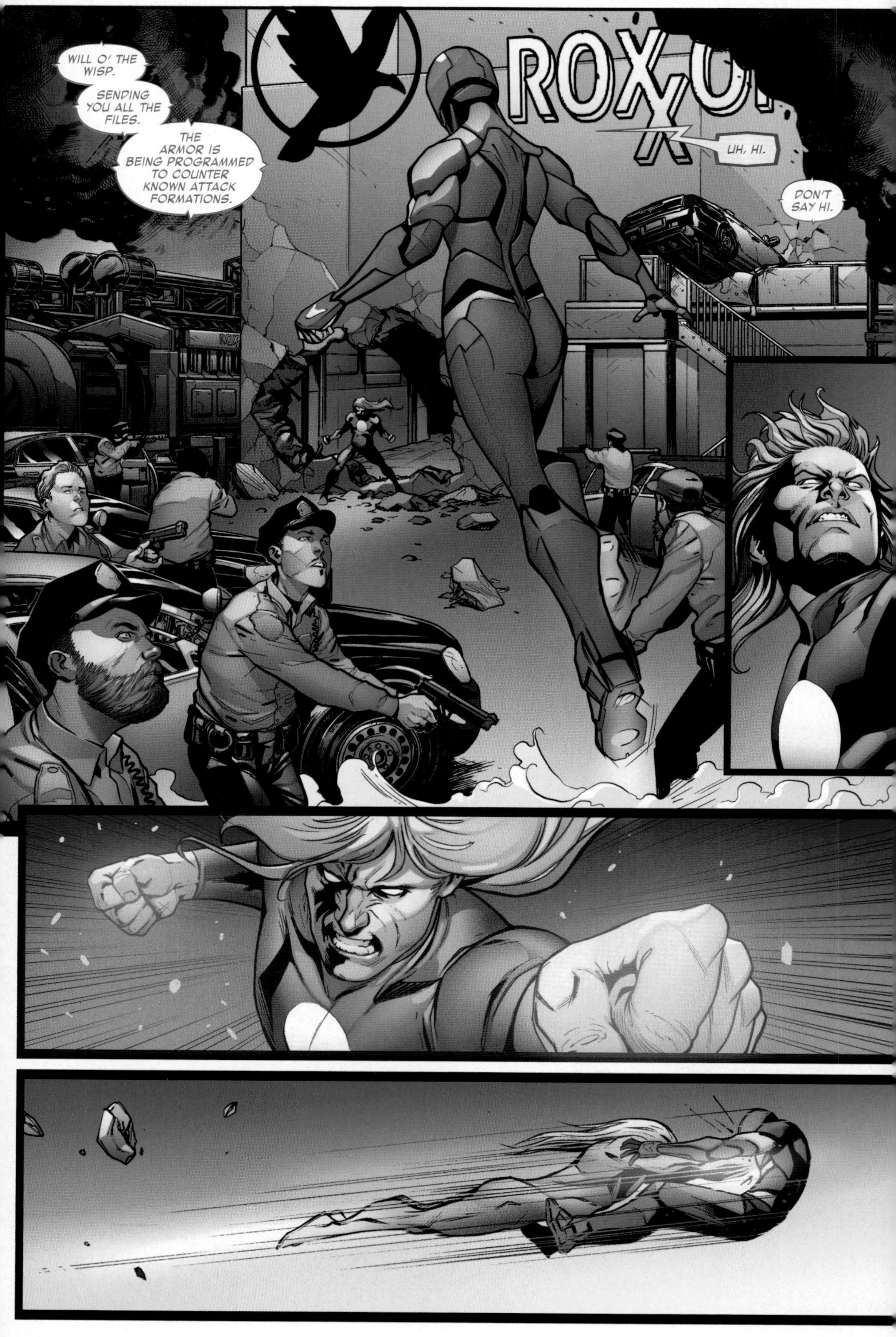
WILL O' THE WISP.
SENDING YOU ALL THE FILES.
THE ARMOR IS BEING PROGRAMMED TO COUNTER KNOWN ATTACK FORMATIONS.
ROXXON
UH, HI.
DON'T SAY HI.

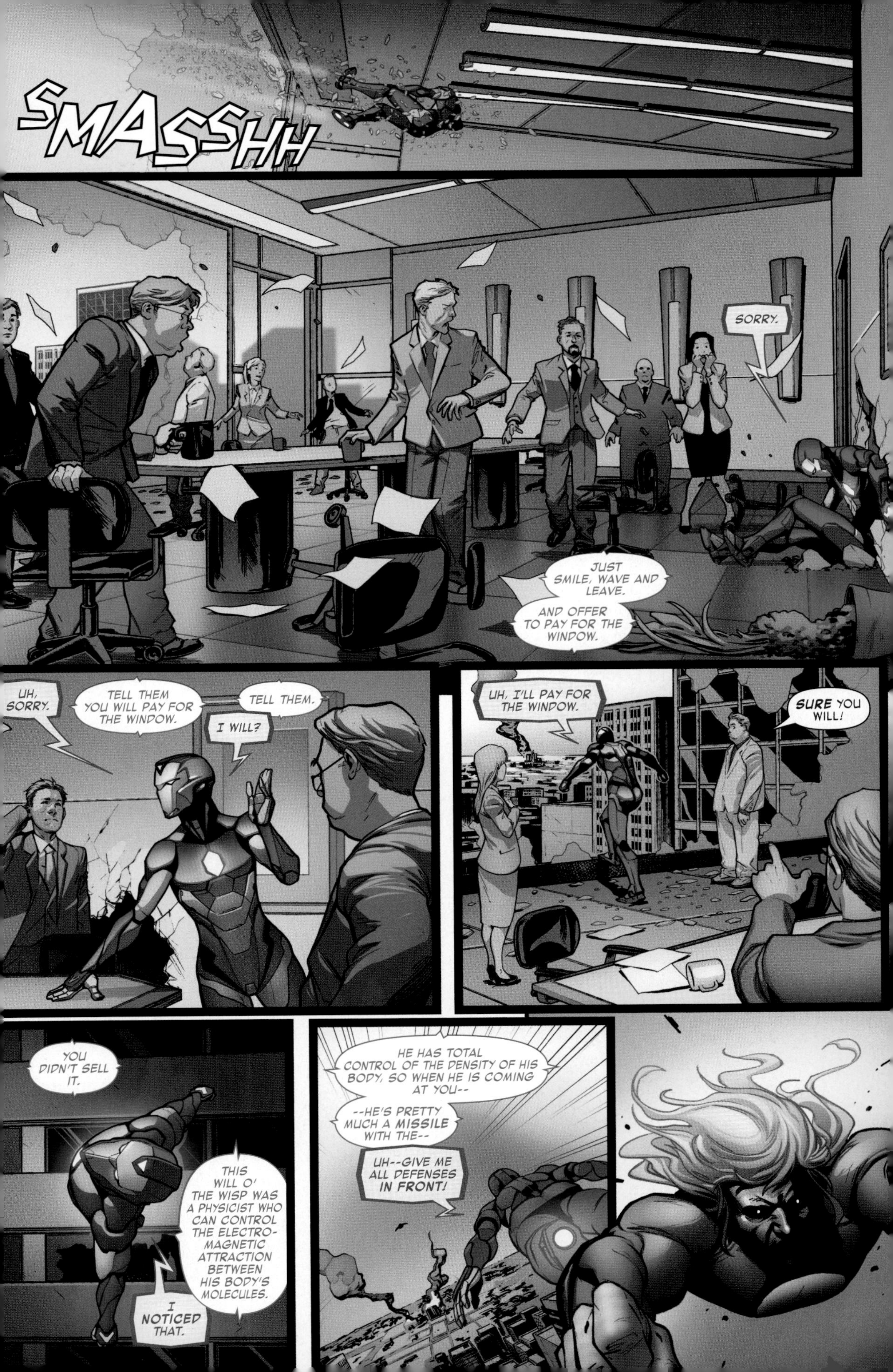
SMASSHH
SORRY.
JUST SMILE, WAVE AND LEAVE.
AND OFFER TO PAY FOR THE WINDOW.
UH, SORRY.
TELL THEM YOU WILL PAY FOR THE WINDOW.
TELL THEM.
I WILL?
UH, I'LL PAY FOR THE WINDOW.
SURE YOU WILL!
YOU DIDN'T SELL IT.
THIS WILL O' THE WISP WAS A PHYSICIST WHO CAN CONTROL THE ELECTRO-MAGNETIC ATTRACTION BETWEEN HIS BODY'S MOLECULES.
I NOTICED THAT.
HE HAS TOTAL CONTROL OF THE DENSITY OF HIS BODY, SO WHEN HE IS COMING AT YOU--
--HE'S PRETTY MUCH A MISSILE WITH THE--
UH--GIVE ME ALL DEFENSES IN FRONT!

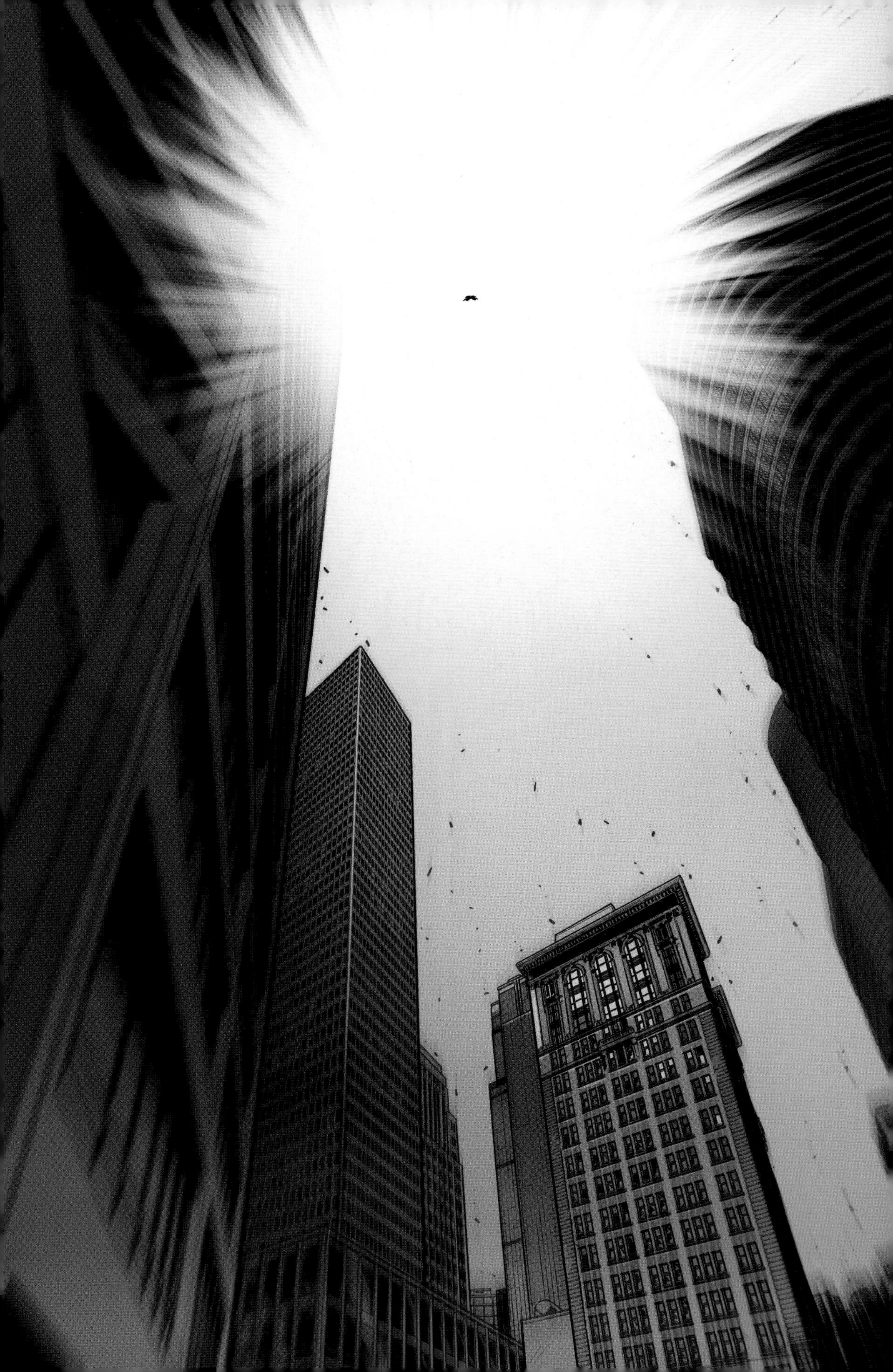

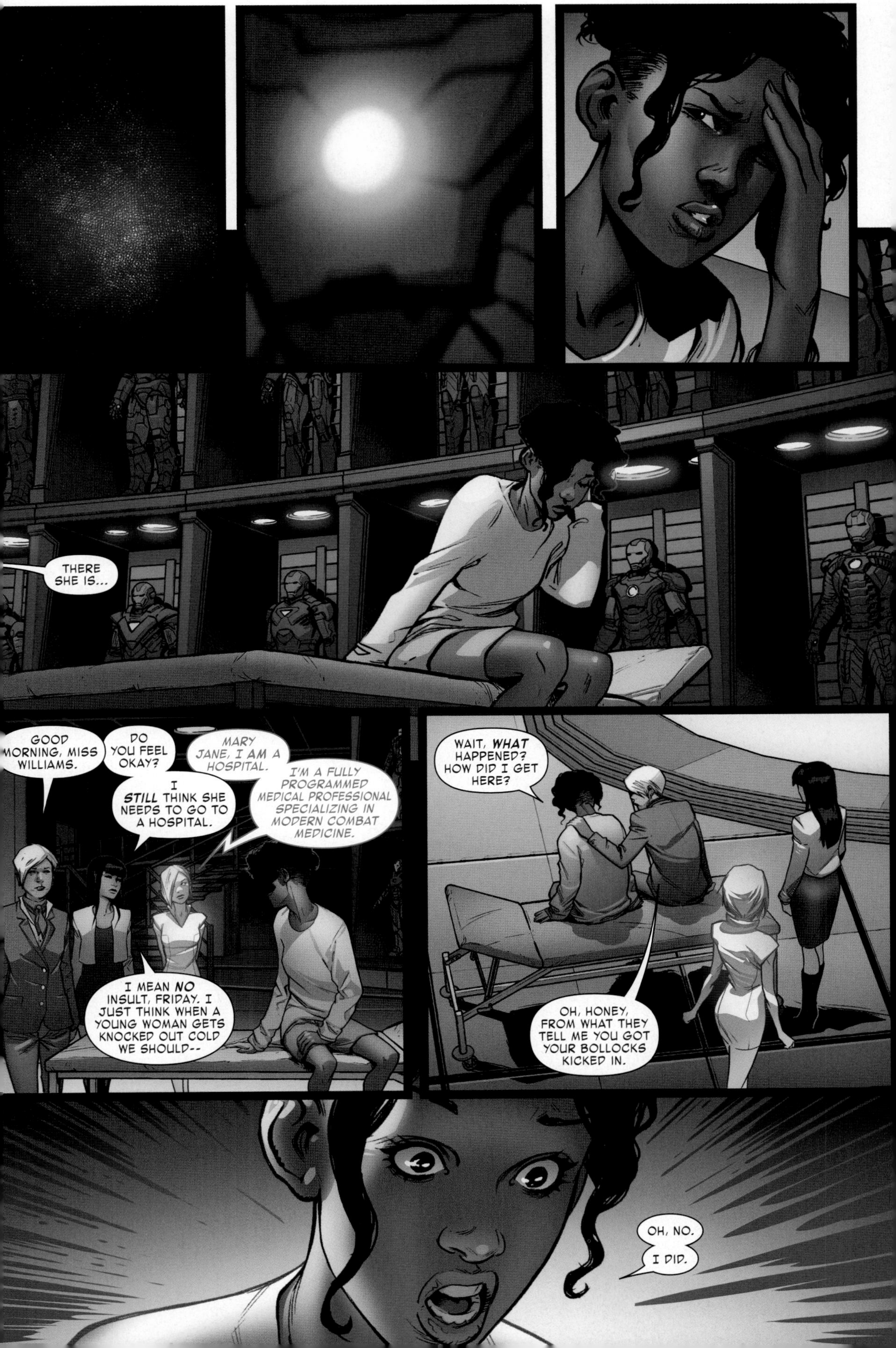
THERE SHE IS...
GOOD MORNING, MISS WILLIAMS.
DO YOU FEEL OKAY?
I STILL THINK SHE NEEDS TO GO TO A HOSPITAL.
MARY JANE, I AM A HOSPITAL.
I'M A FULLY PROGRAMMED MEDICAL PROFESSIONAL SPECIALIZING IN MODERN COMBAT MEDICINE.
I MEAN NO INSULT, FRIDAY. I JUST THINK WHEN A YOUNG WOMAN GETS KNOCKED OUT COLD WE SHOULD--
WAIT, WHAT HAPPENED? HOW DID I GET HERE?
OH, HONEY, FROM WHAT THEY TELL ME YOU GOT YOUR BOLLOCKS KICKED IN.
OH, NO.
I DID.

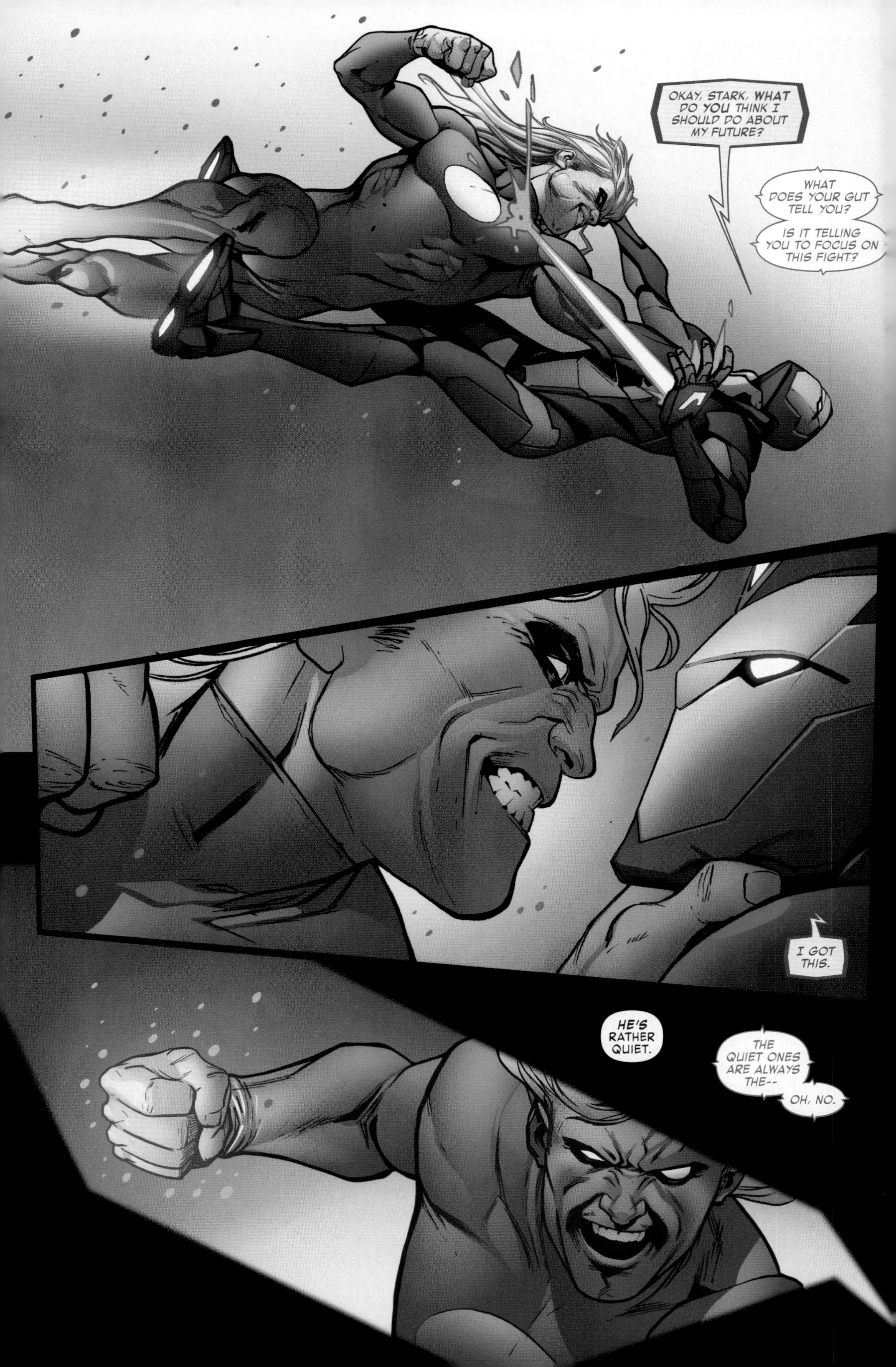
OKAY, STARK, WHAT DO YOU THINK I SHOULD DO ABOUT MY FUTURE?
WHAT DOES YOUR GUT TELL YOU?
IS IT TELLING YOU TO FOCUS ON THIS FIGHT?
I GOT THIS.
HE'S RATHER QUIET.
THE QUIET ONES ARE ALWAYS THE--
OH, NO.

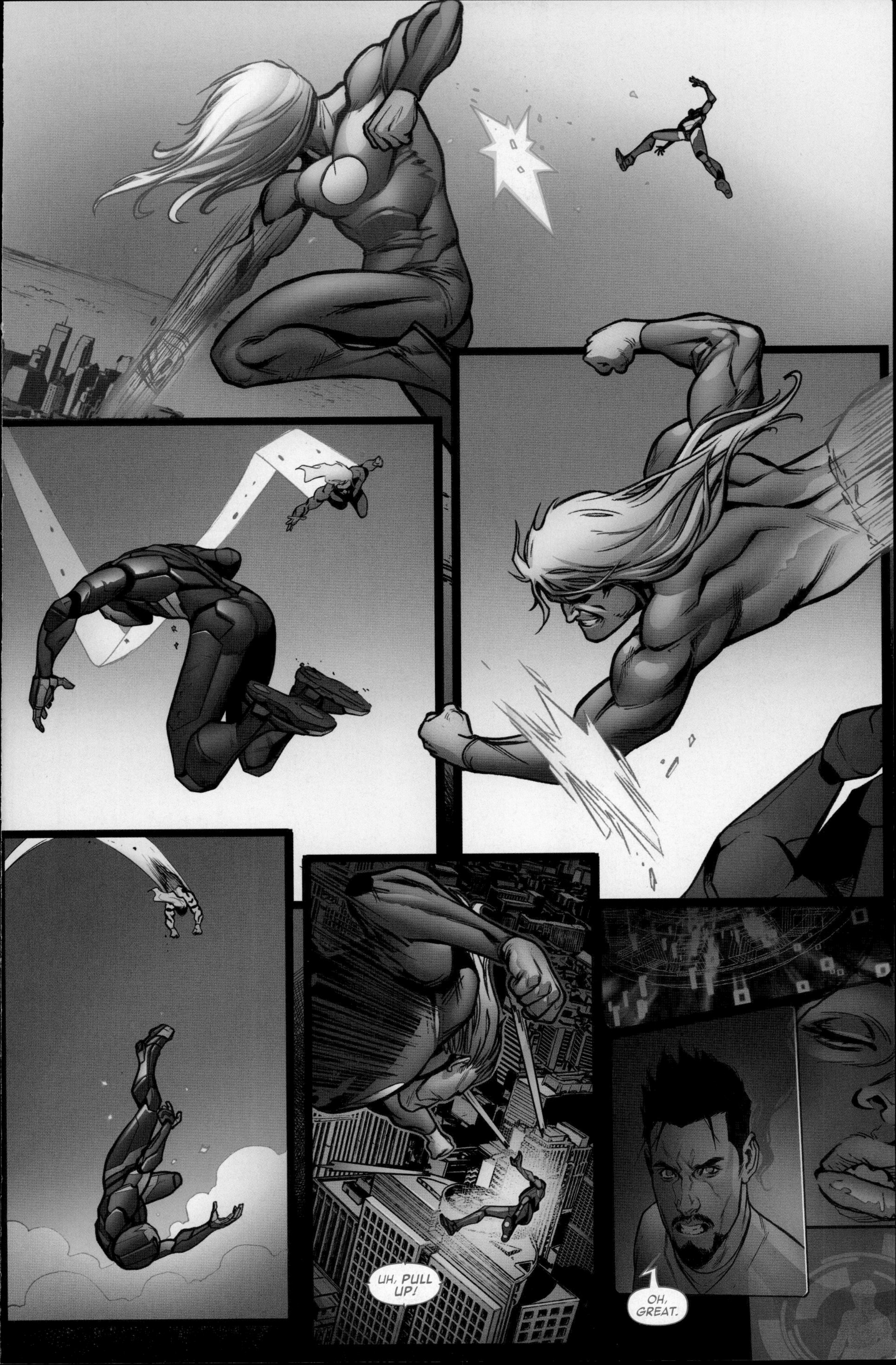
UH, PULL UP!
OH, GREAT.

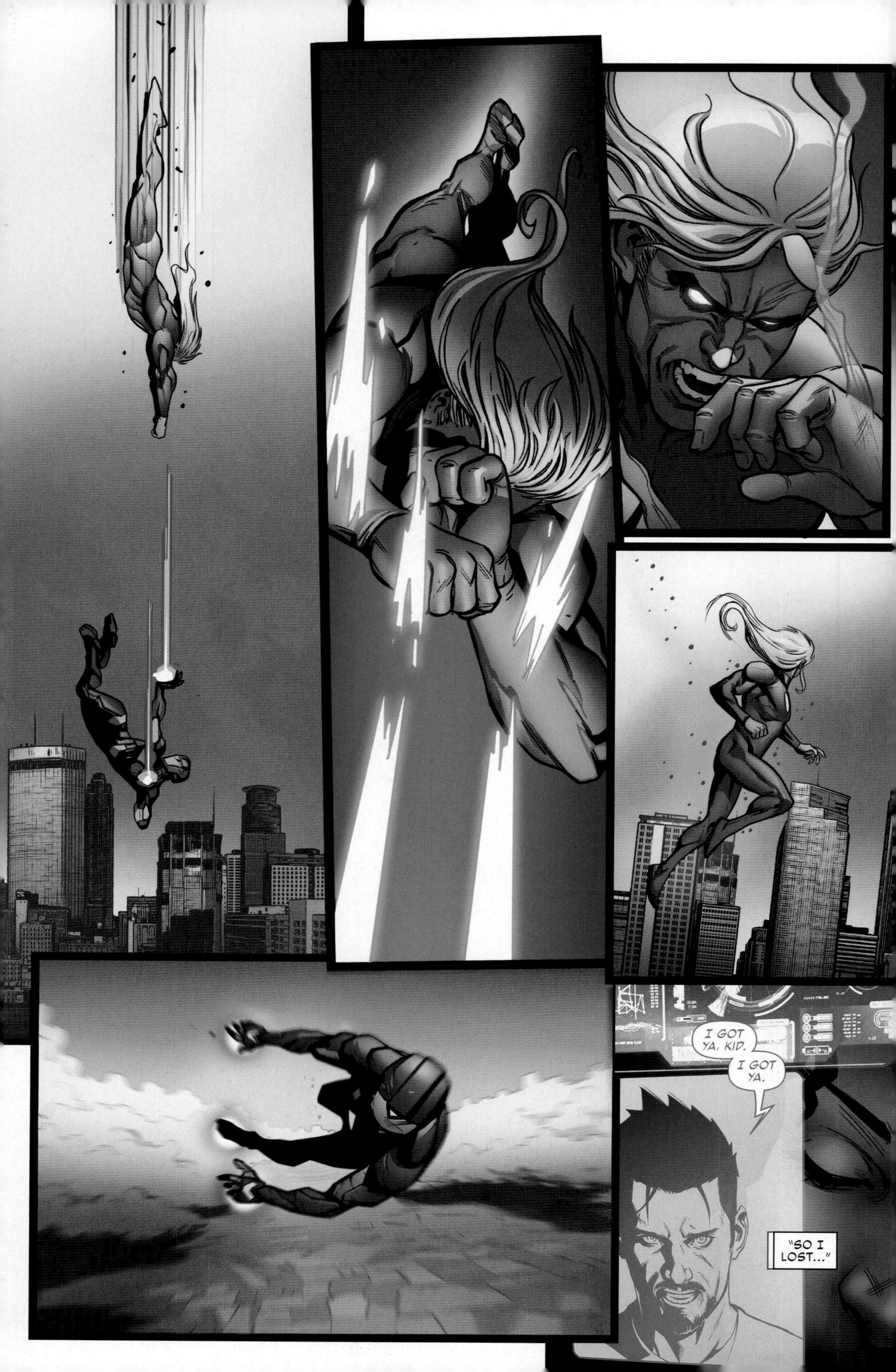
I GOT YA, KID.
I GOT YA.
"SO I LOST..."

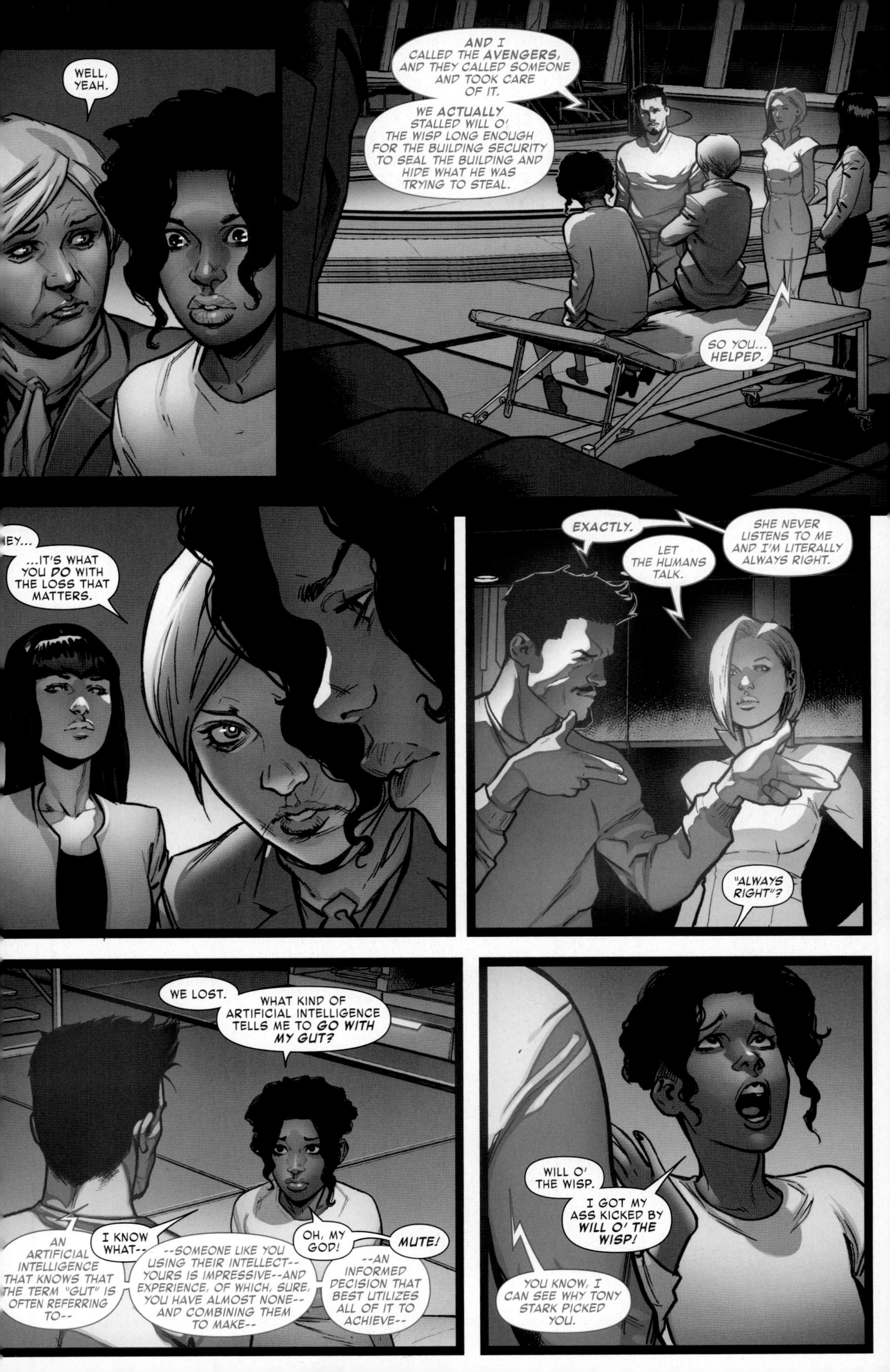

WELL, YEAH.
AND I CALLED THE AVENGERS, AND THEY CALLED SOMEONE AND TOOK CARE OF IT.
WE ACTUALLY STALLED WILL O' THE WISP LONG ENOUGH FOR THE BUILDING SECURITY TO SEAL THE BUILDING AND HIDE WHAT HE WAS TRYING TO STEAL.
SO YOU... HELPED.
...IT'S WHAT YOU DO WITH THE LOSS THAT MATTERS.
EXACTLY.
SHE NEVER LISTENS TO ME AND I'M LITERALLY ALWAYS RIGHT.
LET THE HUMANS TALK.
"ALWAYS RIGHT"?
WE LOST.
WHAT KIND OF ARTIFICIAL INTELLIGENCE TELLS ME TO GO WITH MY GUT?
AN ARTIFICIAL INTELLIGENCE THAT KNOWS THAT THE TERM "GUT" IS OFTEN REFERRING TO--
I KNOW WHAT--
--SOMEONE LIKE YOU USING THEIR INTELLECT-- YOURS IS IMPRESSIVE--AND EXPERIENCE, OF WHICH, SURE, YOU HAVE ALMOST NONE-- AND COMBINING THEM TO MAKE--
OH, MY GOD!
MUTE!
--AN INFORMED DECISION THAT BEST UTILIZES ALL OF IT TO ACHIEVE--
WILL O' THE WISP.
I GOT MY ASS KICKED BY WILL O' THE WISP!
YOU KNOW, I CAN SEE WHY TONY STARK PICKED YOU.

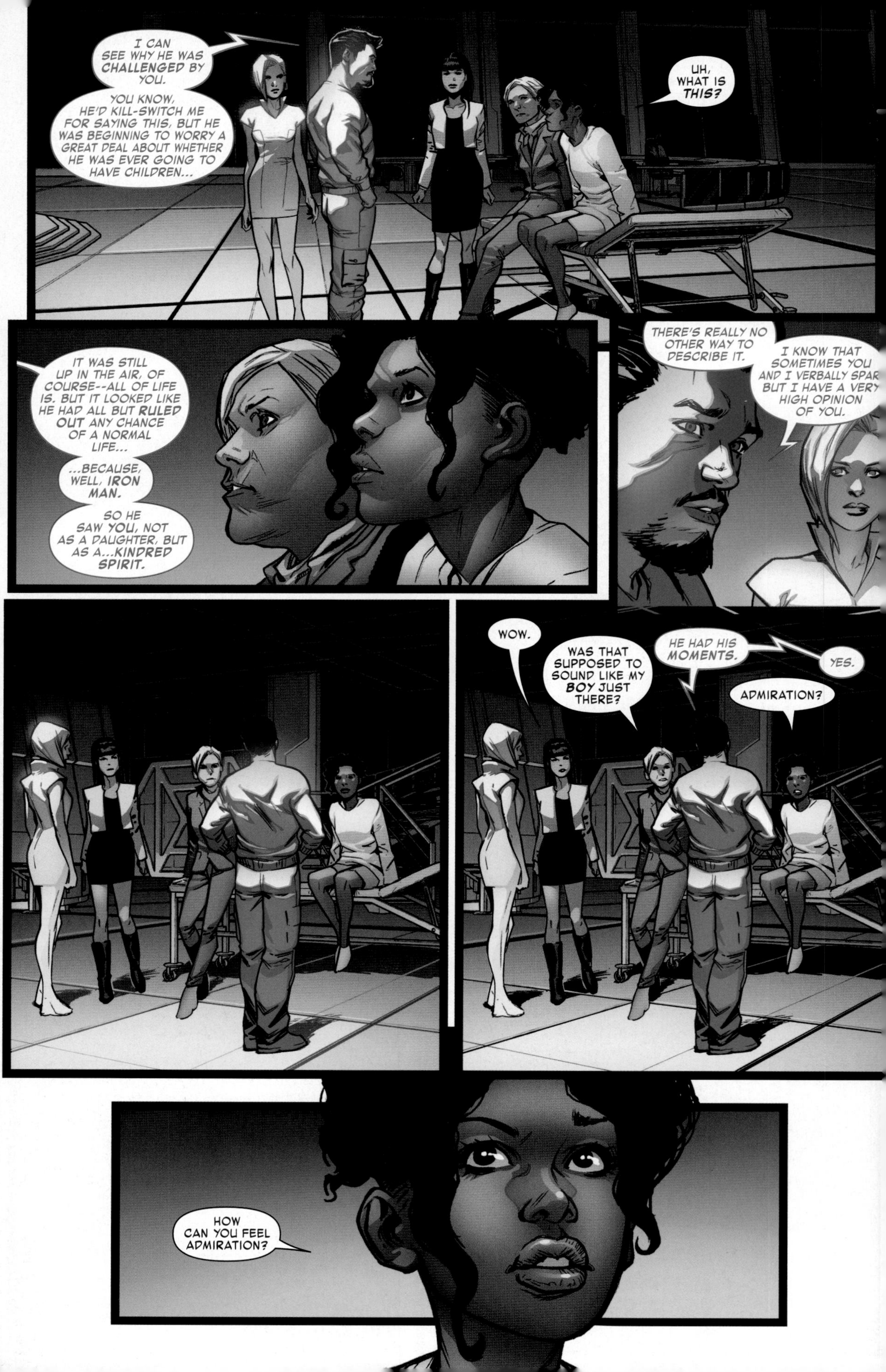
I CAN SEE WHY HE WAS CHALLENGED BY YOU.
YOU KNOW, HE'D KILL-SWITCH ME FOR SAYING THIS, BUT HE WAS BEGINNING TO WORRY A GREAT DEAL ABOUT WHETHER HE WAS EVER GOING TO HAVE CHILDREN...
UH, WHAT IS THIS?
IT WAS STILL UP IN THE AIR, OF COURSE--ALL OF LIFE IS. BUT IT LOOKED LIKE HE HAD ALL BUT RULED OUT ANY CHANCE OF A NORMAL LIFE...
...BECAUSE, WELL, IRON MAN.
SO HE SAW YOU, NOT AS A DAUGHTER, BUT AS A...KINDRED SPIRIT.
THERE'S REALLY NO OTHER WAY TO DESCRIBE IT.
I KNOW THAT SOMETIMES YOU AND I VERBALLY SPAR BUT I HAVE A VERY HIGH OPINION OF YOU.
WOW.
WAS THAT SUPPOSED TO SOUND LIKE MY BOY JUST THERE?
HE HAD HIS MOMENTS.
YES.
ADMIRATION?
HOW CAN YOU FEEL ADMIRATION?

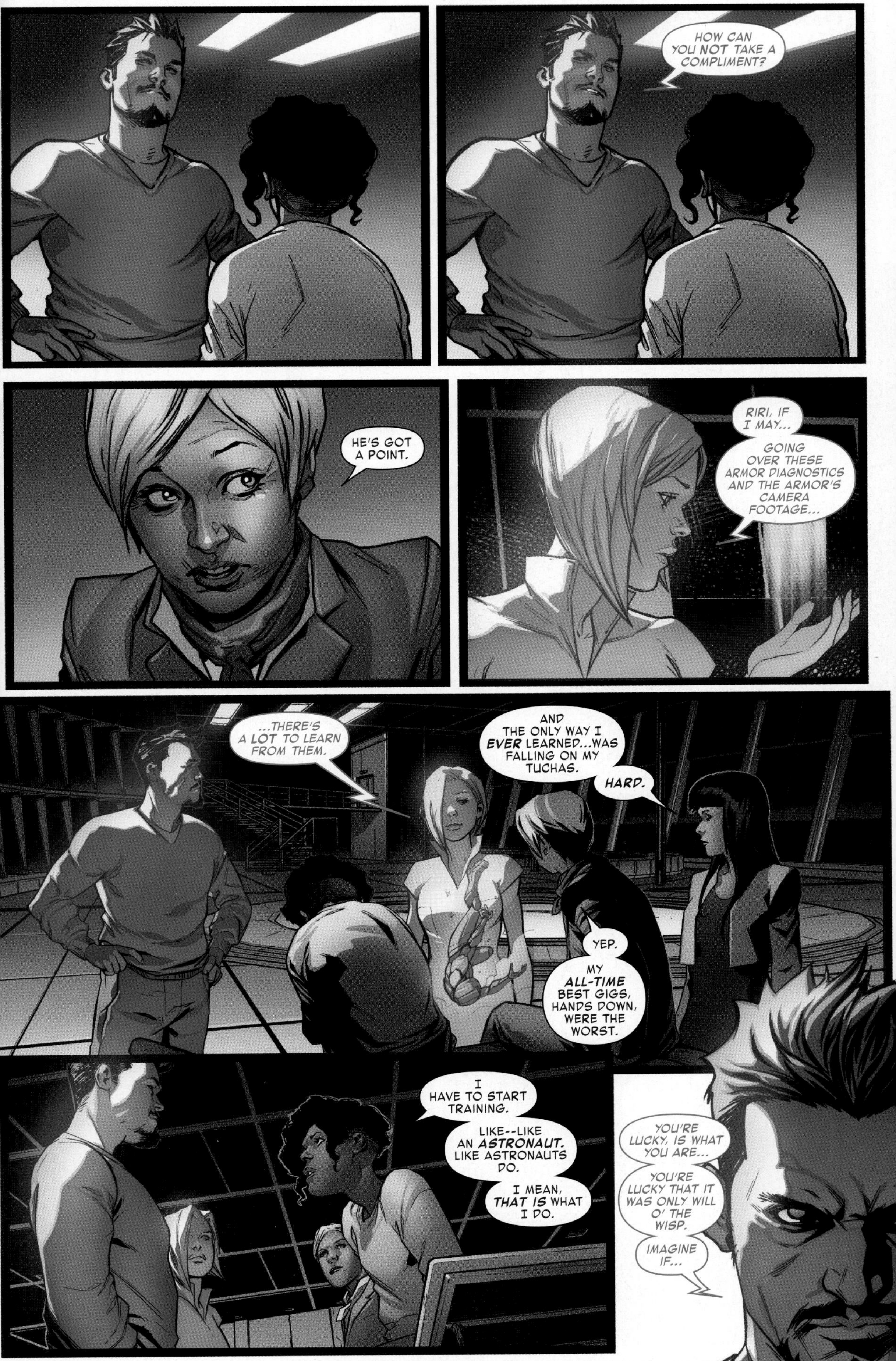
HOW CAN YOU NOT TAKE A COMPLIMENT?
HE'S GOT A POINT.
RIRI, IF I MAY...
GOING OVER THESE ARMOR DIAGNOSTICS AND THE ARMOR'S CAMERA FOOTAGE...
...THERE'S A LOT TO LEARN FROM THEM.
AND THE ONLY WAY I EVER LEARNED...WAS FALLING ON MY TUCHAS.
HARD.
YEP.
MY ALL-TIME BEST GIGS, HANDS DOWN, WERE THE WORST.
I HAVE TO START TRAINING.
LIKE--LIKE AN ASTRONAUT. LIKE ASTRONAUTS DO.
I MEAN, THAT IS WHAT I DO.
YOU'RE LUCKY, IS WHAT YOU ARE...
YOU'RE LUCKY THAT IT WAS ONLY WILL O' THE WISP.
IMAGINE IF...

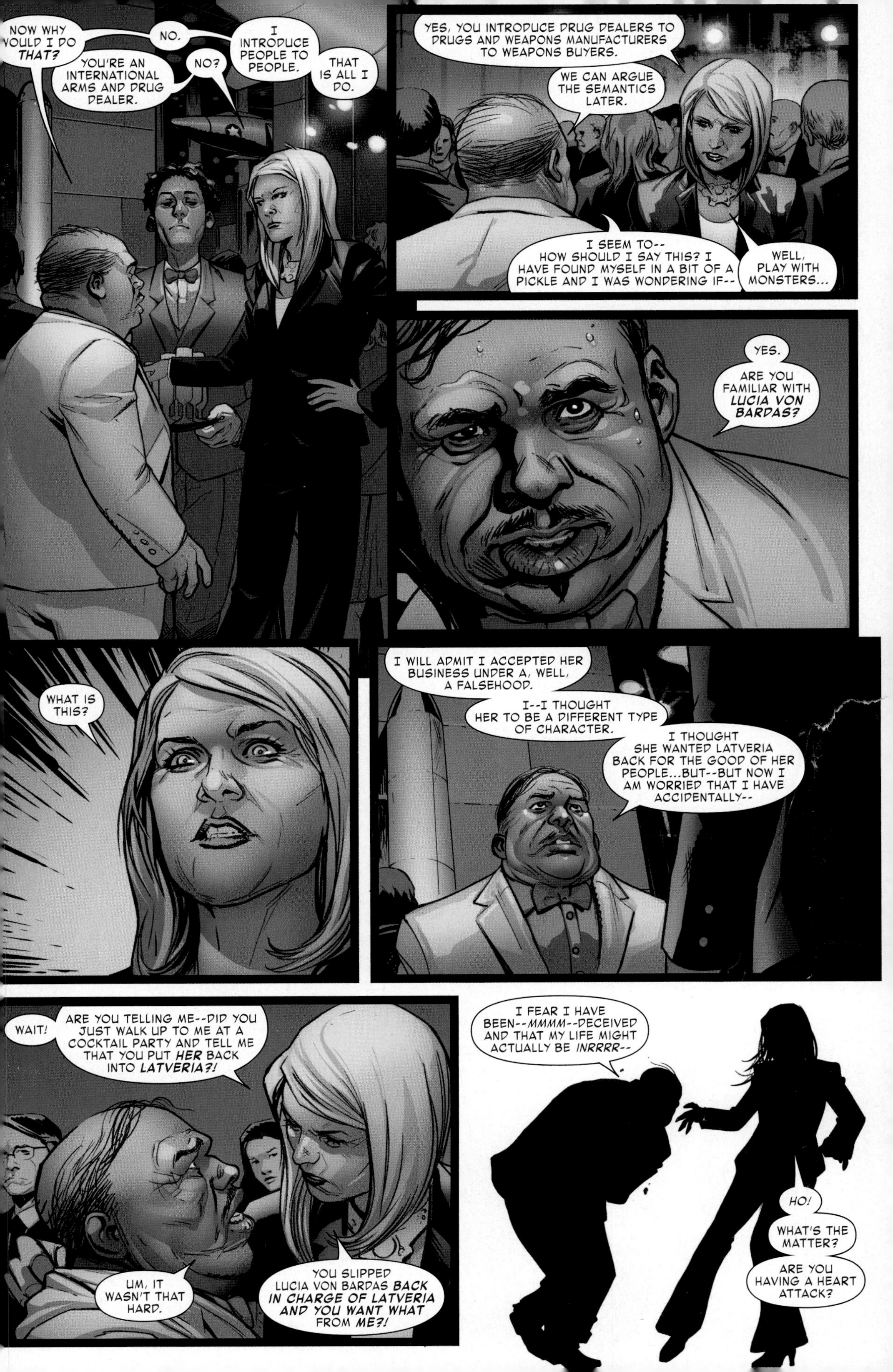
NOW WHY WOULD I DO THAT?
NO.
I INTRODUCE PEOPLE TO PEOPLE.
YOU'RE AN INTERNATIONAL ARMS AND DRUG DEALER.
NO?
THAT IS ALL I DO.
YES, YOU INTRODUCE DRUG DEALERS TO DRUGS AND WEAPONS MANUFACTURERS TO WEAPONS BUYERS.
WE CAN ARGUE THE SEMANTICS LATER.
I SEEM TO-- HOW SHOULD I SAY THIS? I HAVE FOUND MYSELF IN A BIT OF A PICKLE AND I WAS WONDERING IF--
WELL, PLAY WITH MONSTERS...
YES.
ARE YOU FAMILIAR WITH LUCIA VON BARDAS?
WHAT IS THIS?
I WILL ADMIT I ACCEPTED HER BUSINESS UNDER A, WELL, A FALSEHOOD.
I--I THOUGHT HER TO BE A DIFFERENT TYPE OF CHARACTER.
I THOUGHT SHE WANTED LATVERIA BACK FOR THE GOOD OF HER PEOPLE...BUT--BUT NOW I AM WORRIED THAT I HAVE ACCIDENTALLY--
WAIT!
ARE YOU TELLING ME--DID YOU JUST WALK UP TO ME AT A COCKTAIL PARTY AND TELL ME THAT YOU PUT HER BACK INTO LATVERIA?!
UM, IT WASN'T THAT HARD.
YOU SLIPPED LUCIA VON BARDAS BACK IN CHARGE OF LATVERIA AND YOU WANT WHAT FROM ME?!
I FEAR I HAVE BEEN--MMMM--DECEIVED AND THAT MY LIFE MIGHT ACTUALLY BE INRRRR--
HO!
WHAT'S THE MATTER?
ARE YOU HAVING A HEART ATTACK?

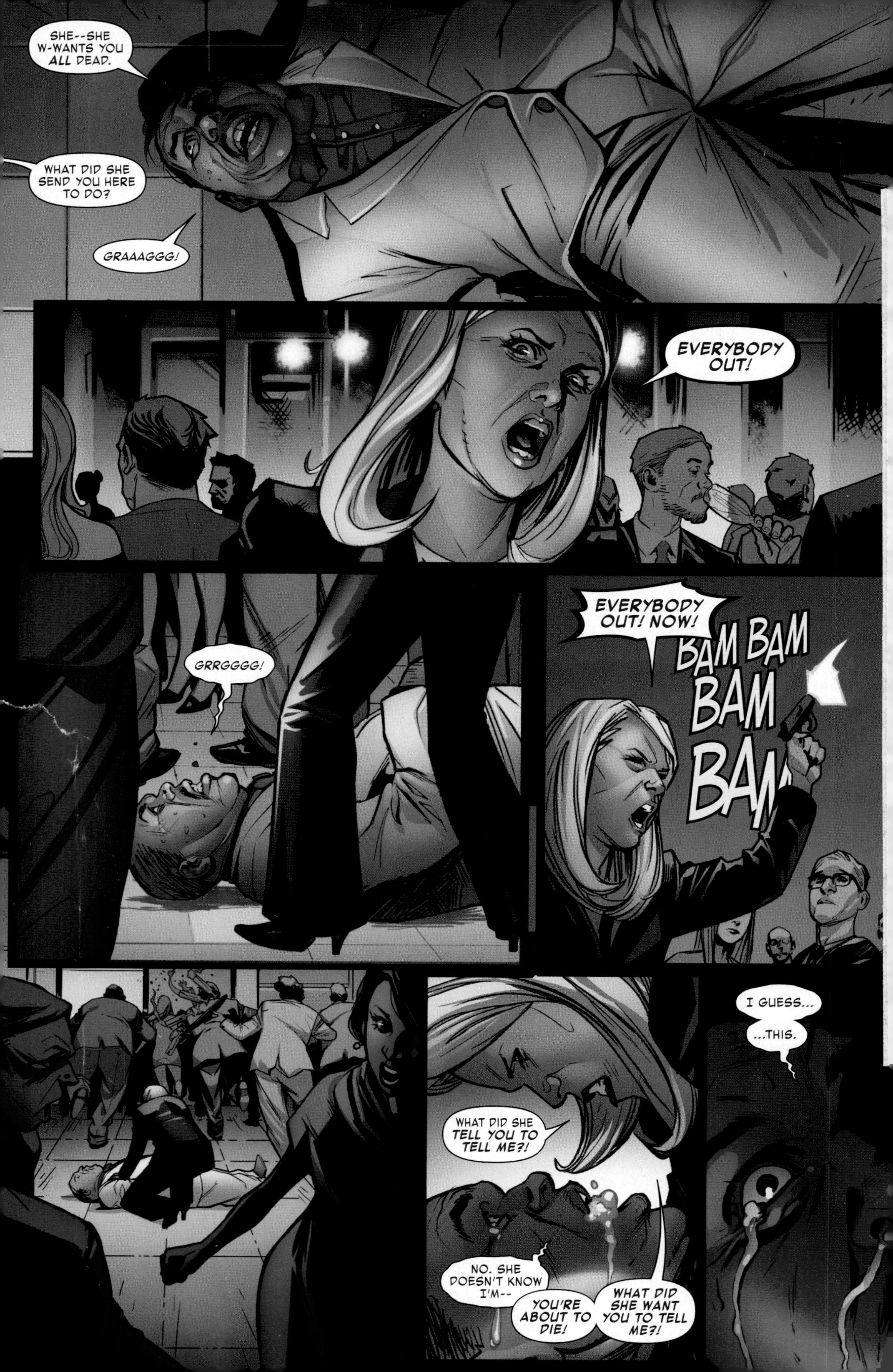
SHE--SHE W-WANTS YOU ALL DEAD.
WHAT DID SHE SEND YOU HERE TO DO?
GRAAAGGG!
EVERYBODY OUT!
GRRGGGG!
EVERYBODY OUT! NOW!
BAM BAM BAM BAM
I GUESS...
...THIS.
WHAT DID SHE TELL YOU TO TELL ME?!
NO. SHE DOESN'T KNOW I'M--
YOU'RE ABOUT TO DIE!
WHAT DID SHE WANT YOU TO TELL ME?!

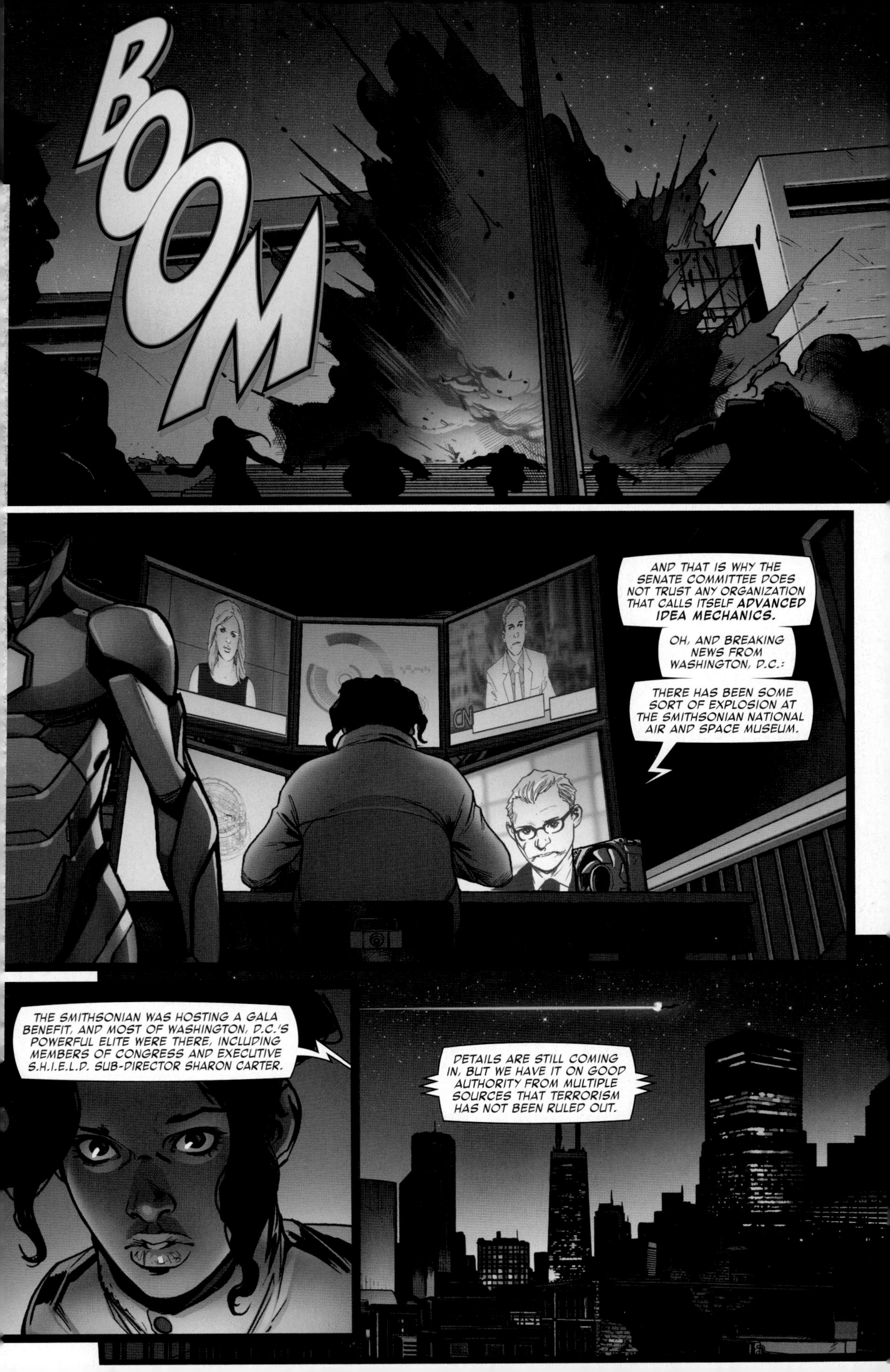
BOOM
AND THAT IS WHY THE SENATE COMMITTEE DOES NOT TRUST ANY ORGANIZATION THAT CALLS ITSELF **ADVANCED IDEA MECHANICS.**
OH, AND BREAKING NEWS FROM WASHINGTON, D.C.:
THERE HAS BEEN SOME SORT OF EXPLOSION AT THE SMITHSONIAN NATIONAL AIR AND SPACE MUSEUM.
THE SMITHSONIAN WAS HOSTING A GALA BENEFIT, AND MOST OF WASHINGTON, D.C.'S POWERFUL ELITE WERE THERE, INCLUDING MEMBERS OF CONGRESS AND EXECUTIVE S.H.I.E.L.D. SUB-DIRECTOR SHARON CARTER.
DETAILS ARE STILL COMING IN, BUT WE HAVE IT ON GOOD AUTHORITY FROM MULTIPLE SOURCES THAT TERRORISM HAS NOT BEEN RULED OUT.

8

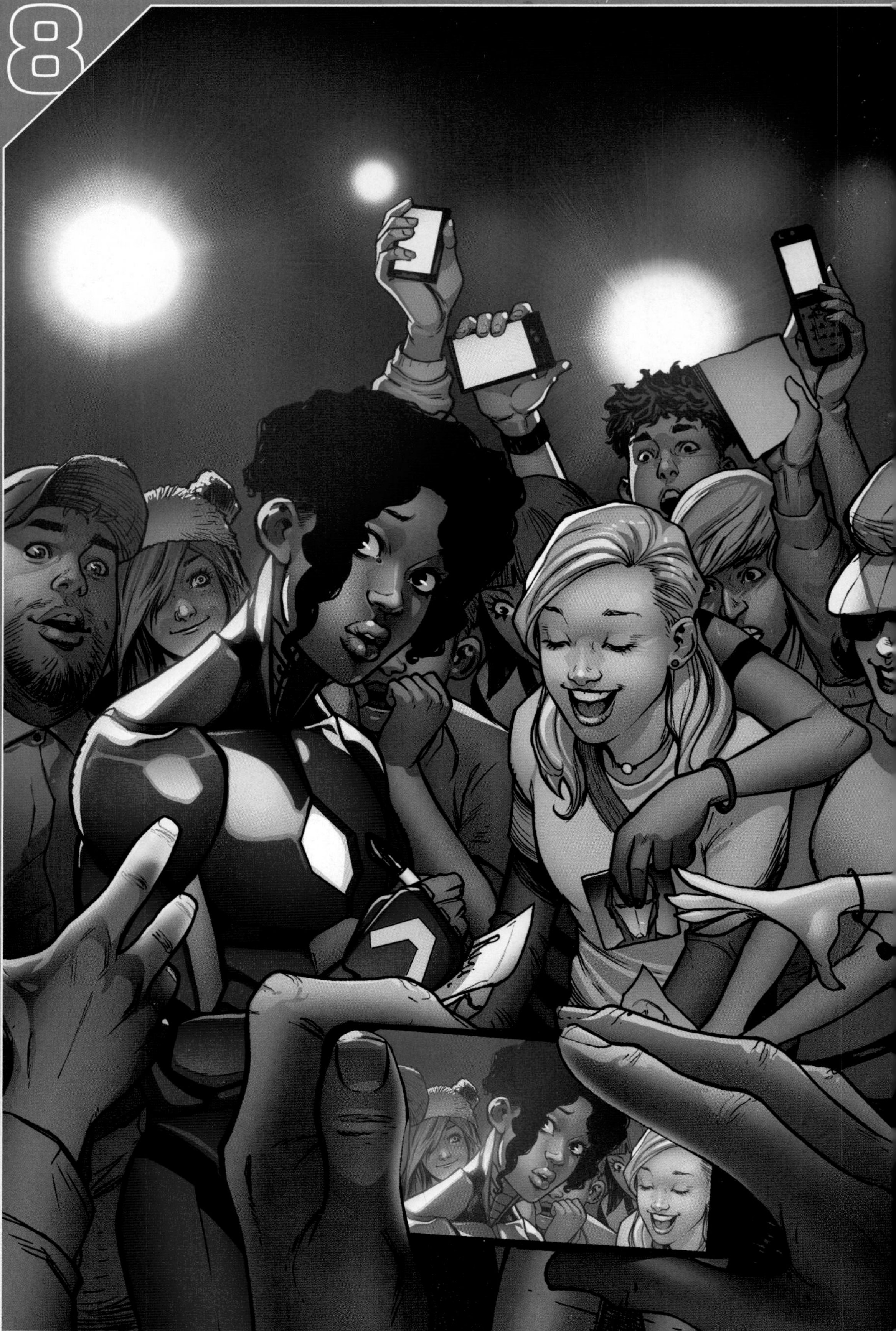

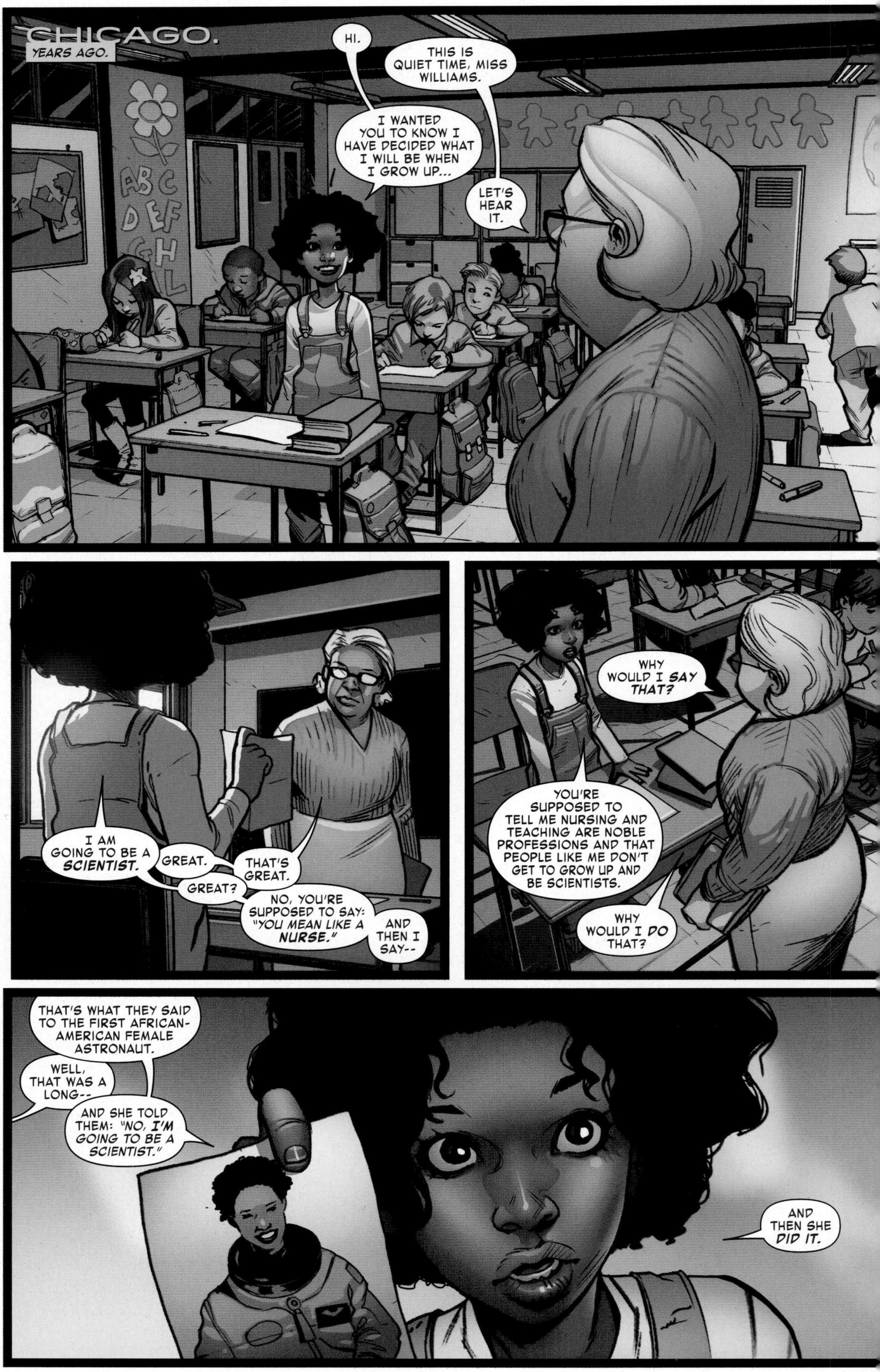
CHICAGO.
YEARS AGO.
HI.
THIS IS QUIET TIME, MISS WILLIAMS.
I WANTED YOU TO KNOW I HAVE DECIDED WHAT I WILL BE WHEN I GROW UP...
LET'S HEAR IT.
I AM GOING TO BE A SCIENTIST.
GREAT.
THAT'S GREAT.
GREAT?
NO, YOU'RE SUPPOSED TO SAY: "YOU MEAN LIKE A NURSE."
AND THEN I SAY--
WHY WOULD I SAY THAT?
YOU'RE SUPPOSED TO TELL ME NURSING AND TEACHING ARE NOBLE PROFESSIONS AND THAT PEOPLE LIKE ME DON'T GET TO GROW UP AND BE SCIENTISTS.
WHY WOULD I DO THAT?
THAT'S WHAT THEY SAID TO THE FIRST AFRICAN-AMERICAN FEMALE ASTRONAUT.
WELL, THAT WAS A LONG--
AND SHE TOLD THEM: "NO, I'M GOING TO BE A SCIENTIST."
AND THEN SHE DID IT.

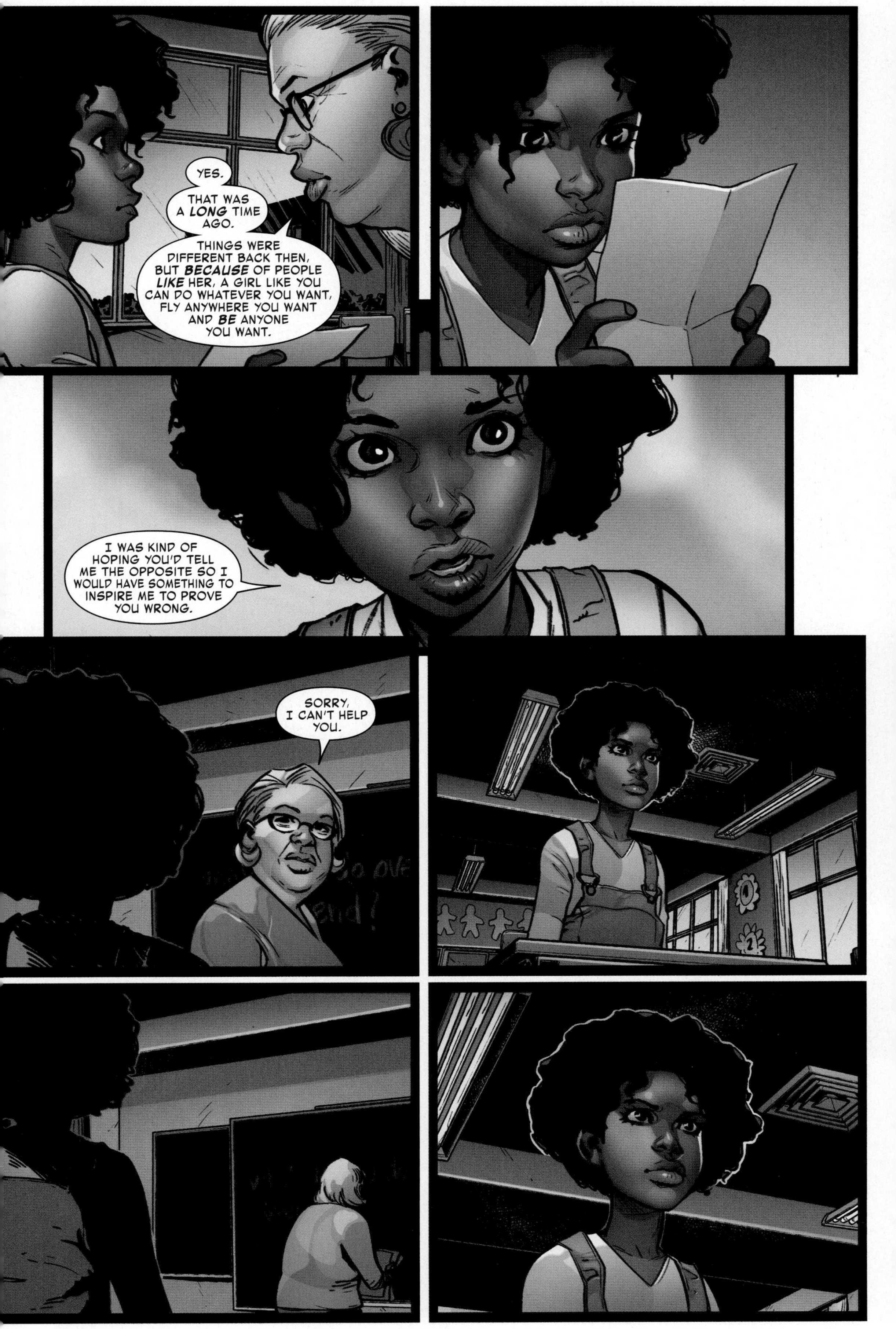
YES.
THAT WAS A LONG TIME AGO.
THINGS WERE DIFFERENT BACK THEN, BUT BECAUSE OF PEOPLE LIKE HER, A GIRL LIKE YOU CAN DO WHATEVER YOU WANT, FLY ANYWHERE YOU WANT AND BE ANYONE YOU WANT.
I WAS KIND OF HOPING YOU'D TELL ME THE OPPOSITE SO I WOULD HAVE SOMETHING TO INSPIRE ME TO PROVE YOU WRONG.
SORRY, I CAN'T HELP YOU.

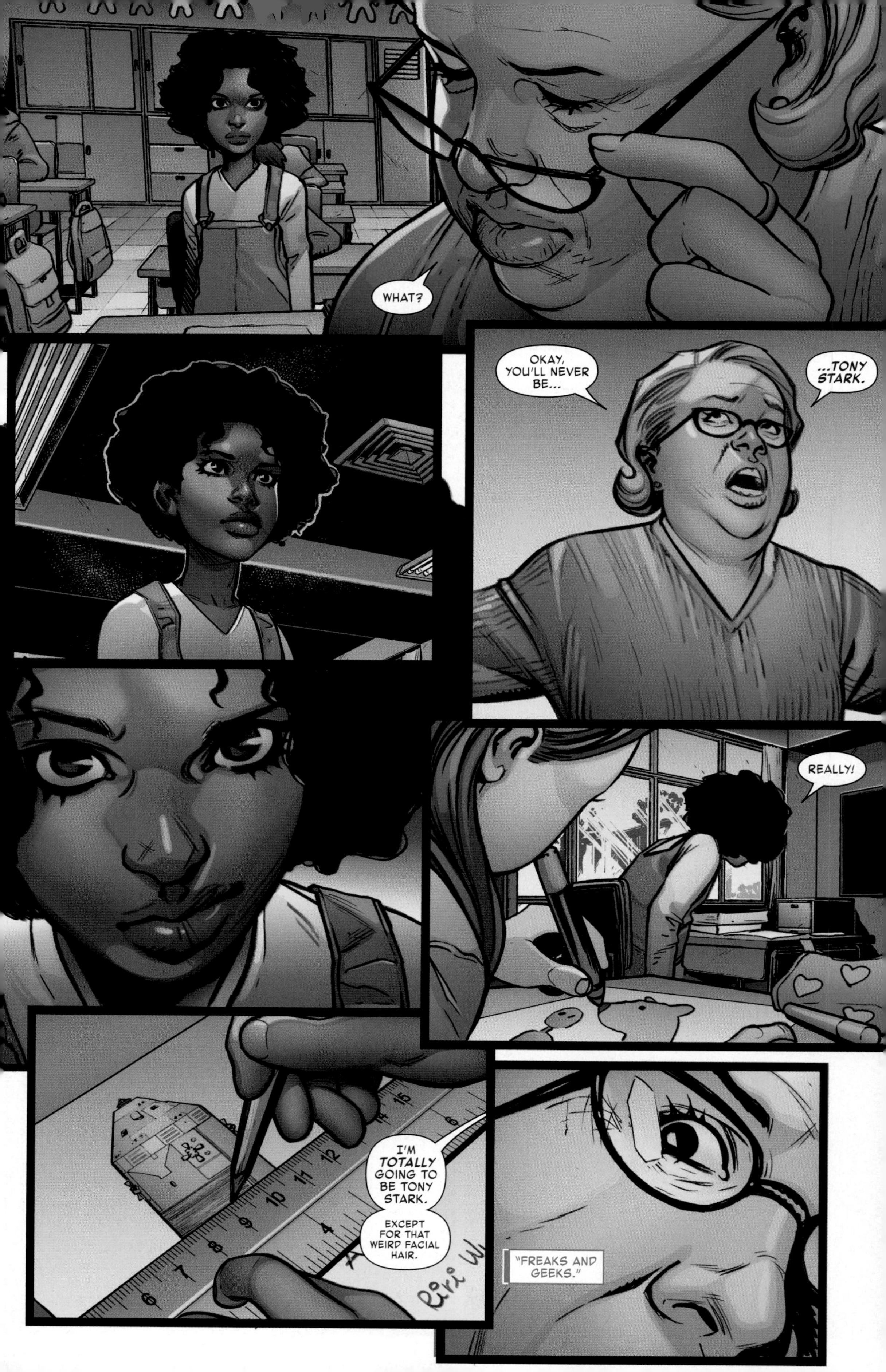
WHAT?
OKAY, YOU'LL NEVER BE...
...TONY STARK.
REALLY!
I'M TOTALLY GOING TO BE TONY STARK.
EXCEPT FOR THAT WEIRD FACIAL HAIR.
"FREAKS AND GEEKS."

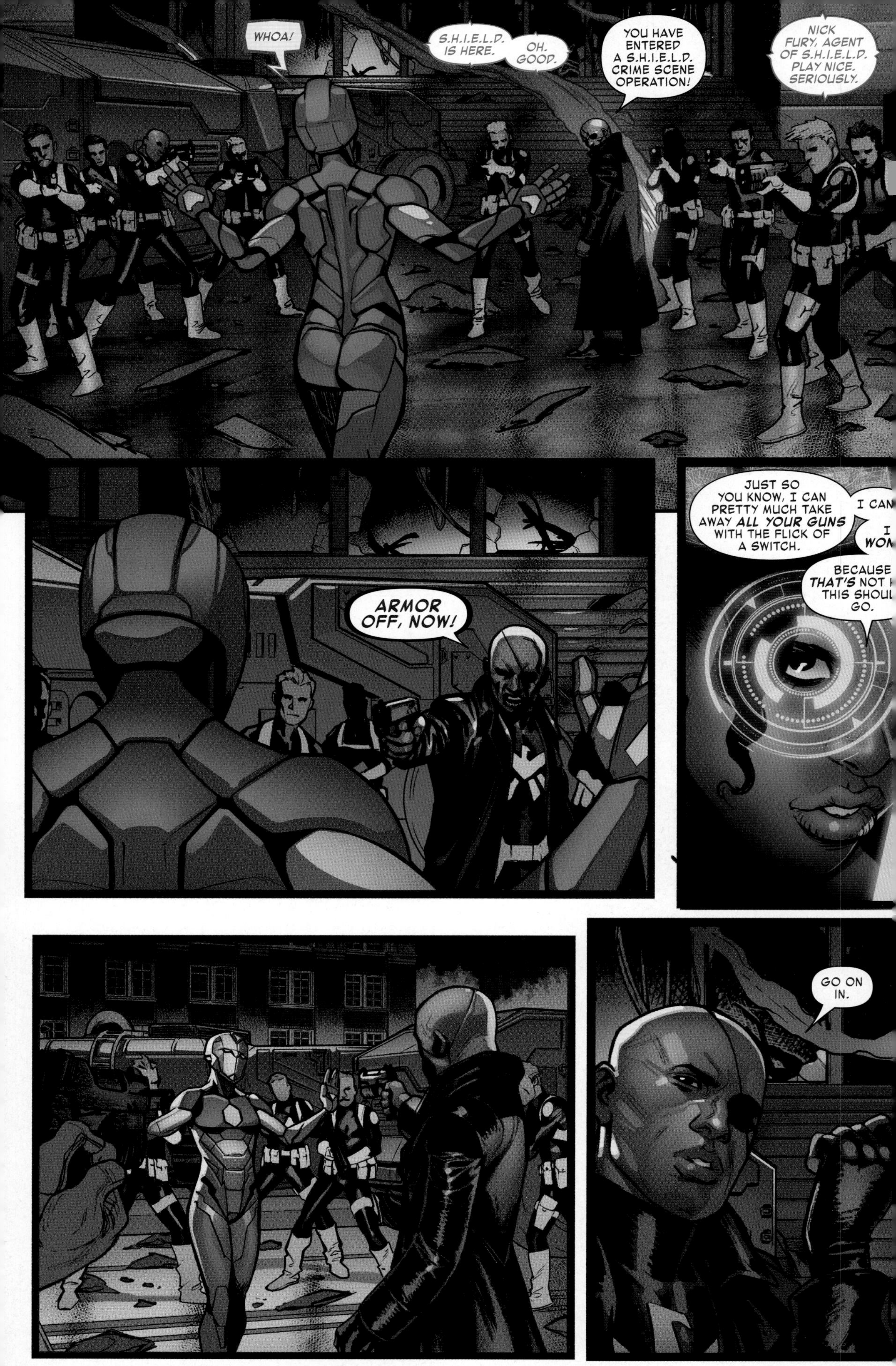
WHOA!
S.H.I.E.L.D. IS HERE.
OH. GOOD.
YOU HAVE ENTERED A S.H.I.E.L.D. CRIME SCENE OPERATION!
NICK FURY, AGENT OF S.H.I.E.L.D. PLAY NICE. SERIOUSLY.
ARMOR OFF, NOW!
JUST SO YOU KNOW, I CAN PRETTY MUCH TAKE AWAY ALL YOUR GUNS WITH THE FLICK OF A SWITCH.
I CAN
BECAUSE THAT'S NOT
GO.
GO ON IN.

REMOVE THAT ARMOR IMMEDIATELY OR SUFFER THE CONSEQUENCES!

UH, HI.

I'M, UH, IRONHEART-- I'M HERE TO HELP!

YEAH, THAT'LL DO IT.

YOU'RE DOING GREAT.

SHUT UP.

I'M HERE TO HELP!

YOU ACTUALLY WANT US TO DO A COUNT TO THREE?

ONE!

HOLD ON.

YEAH?

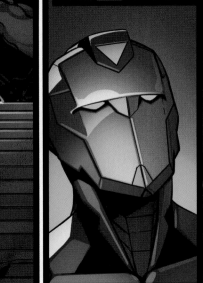

OH, NO.

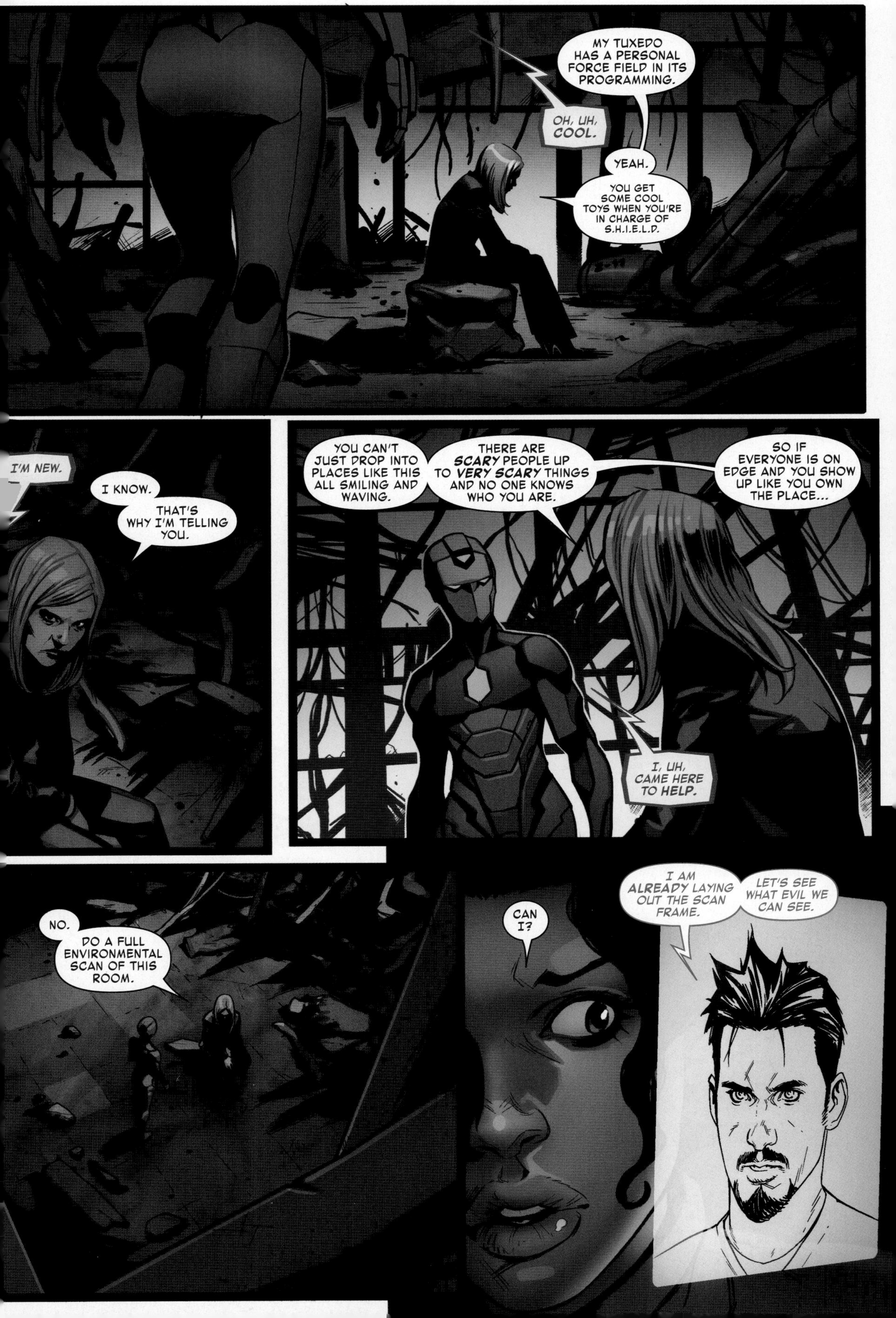
MY TUXEDO HAS A PERSONAL FORCE FIELD IN ITS PROGRAMMING.
OH, UH, COOL.
YEAH.
YOU GET SOME COOL TOYS WHEN YOU'RE IN CHARGE OF S.H.I.E.L.D.
I'M NEW.
I KNOW.
THAT'S WHY I'M TELLING YOU.
YOU CAN'T JUST DROP INTO PLACES LIKE THIS ALL SMILING AND WAVING.
THERE ARE SCARY PEOPLE UP TO VERY SCARY THINGS AND NO ONE KNOWS WHO YOU ARE.
SO IF EVERYONE IS ON EDGE AND YOU SHOW UP LIKE YOU OWN THE PLACE...
I, UH, CAME HERE TO HELP.
NO.
DO A FULL ENVIRONMENTAL SCAN OF THIS ROOM.
CAN I?
I AM ALREADY LAYING OUT THE SCAN FRAME.
LET'S SEE WHAT EVIL WE CAN SEE.

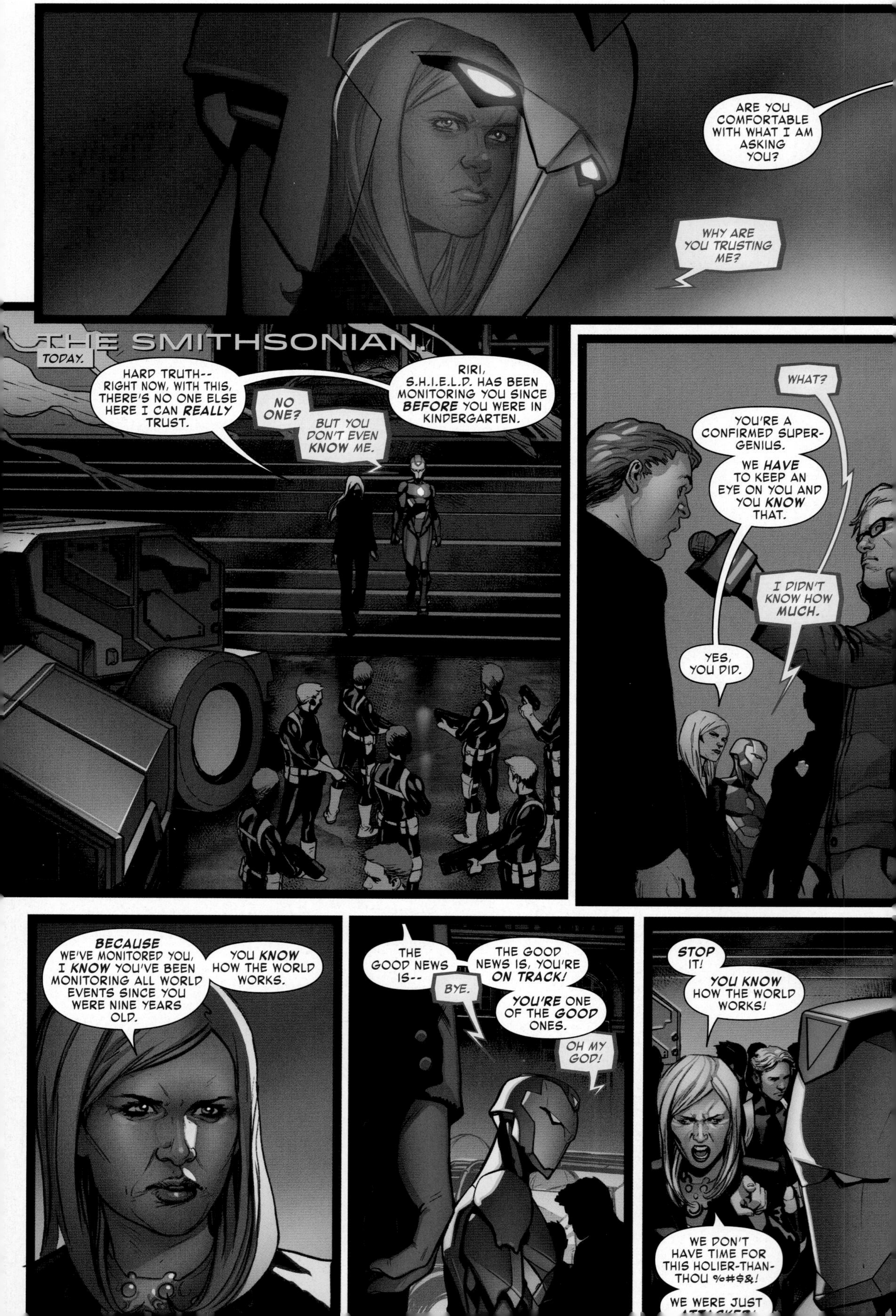
ARE YOU COMFORTABLE WITH WHAT I AM ASKING YOU?
WHY ARE YOU TRUSTING ME?
THE SMITHSONIAN.
TODAY.
HARD TRUTH-- RIGHT NOW, WITH THIS, THERE'S NO ONE ELSE HERE I CAN REALLY TRUST.
NO ONE?
BUT YOU DON'T EVEN KNOW ME.
RIRI, S.H.I.E.L.D. HAS BEEN MONITORING YOU SINCE BEFORE YOU WERE IN KINDERGARTEN.
WHAT?
YOU'RE A CONFIRMED SUPER-GENIUS.
WE HAVE TO KEEP AN EYE ON YOU AND YOU KNOW THAT.
I DIDN'T KNOW HOW MUCH.
YES, YOU DID.
BECAUSE WE'VE MONITORED YOU, I KNOW YOU'VE BEEN MONITORING ALL WORLD EVENTS SINCE YOU WERE NINE YEARS OLD.
YOU KNOW HOW THE WORLD WORKS.
THE GOOD NEWS IS--
THE GOOD NEWS IS, YOU'RE ON TRACK!
BYE.
YOU'RE ONE OF THE GOOD ONES.
OH MY GOD!
STOP IT!
YOU KNOW HOW THE WORLD WORKS!
WE DON'T HAVE TIME FOR THIS HOLIER-THAN-THOU %#$&!
WE WERE JUST

DO YOU GET THAT TELLING ME THAT YOU *SPY* ON ME DOESN'T--?

YOU SHOWED UP!

YOU GET ME?

NOT THE AVENGERS, NOT THE DEFENDERS... YOU.

YOU *SHOWED* UP.

TO HELP.

THIS IS HOW YOU CAN HELP.

HOLD ON...

SIDEBAR, WHAT'S HER ANGLE HERE?

BEST GUESS, SHE WANTS TO ATTACK THIS LUCIA VON BARDAS, BUT SHE PROBABLY CAN'T WITHOUT MUCH MORE ACTUALLY PROVABLE... PROOF.

SO CARTER WANTS TO THROW ME AT HER BECAUSE I "SHOWED UP," AND SHE CAN ALWAYS CLAIM SHE HAD NO CONTROL OVER ME, SINCE--

EXACTLY.

I DON'T KNOW.

YOU'RE NOT AN AGENT OF S.H.I.E.L.D.

I DON'T KNOW.

I THINK IT'S MORE.

IT'S NOT.

BE HONEST.

WHY ME?

I CAN'T AUTHORIZE A MILITARY STRIKE ON THIS WITHOUT MORE PROOF.

OH.

PST! TOLDJA.

THIS-- THIS IS OVER THE LINE.

IF THAT BOMB HAD GONE OFF WITH THE CROWD STILL INSIDE...

...SENATORS, BILLIONAIRES, AN EX-VICE PRESIDENT...

...THIS *COULD* HAVE TRIGGERED WORLD WAR III.

IT *STILL* MIGHT.

I'M TELLING YOU--THIS IS NEW TERRITORY...I DON'T KNOW *WHAT* THEY ARE CAPABLE OF.

AIEEE!

OH MY GOOOOOAAAD!

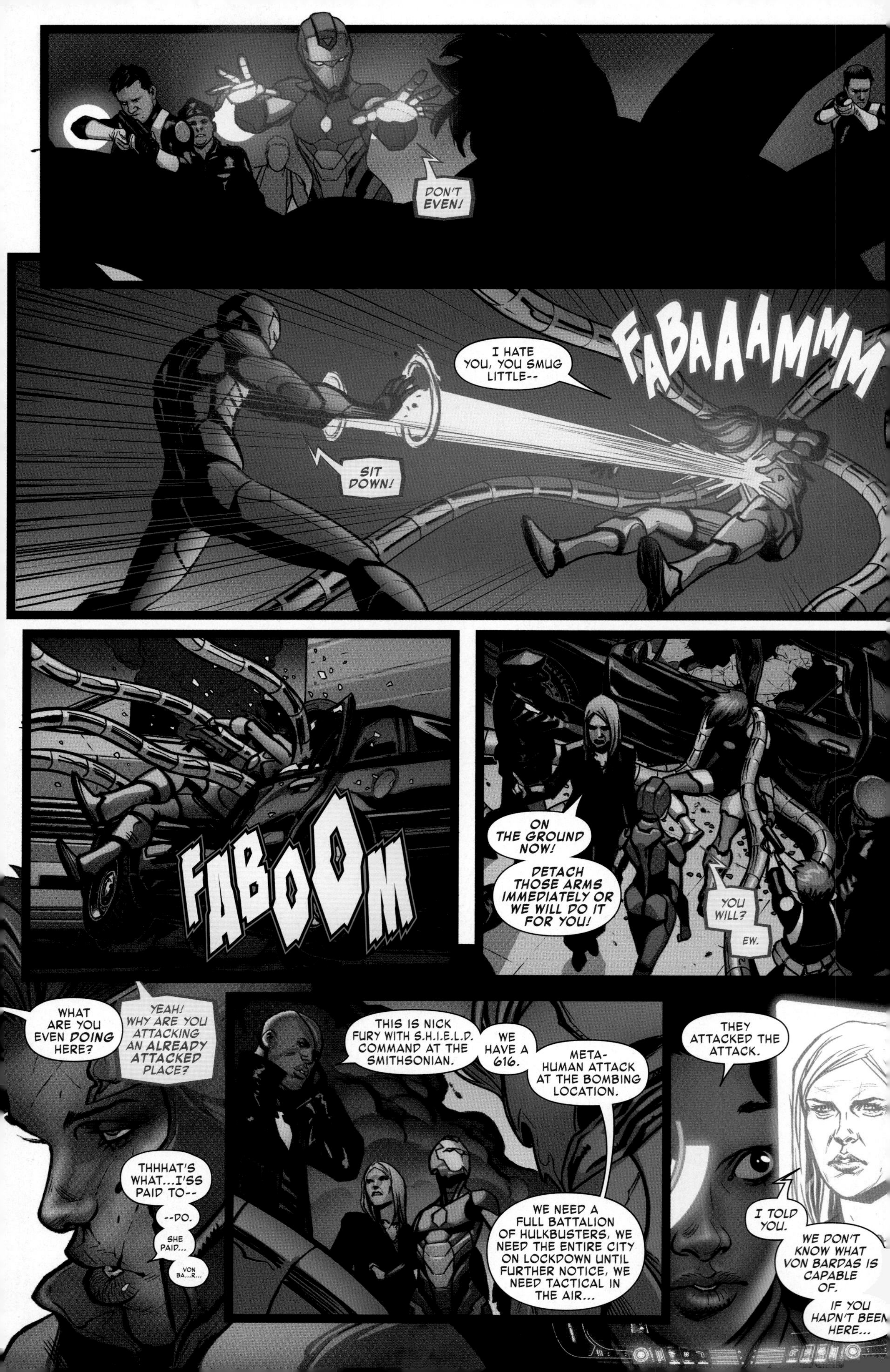
DON'T EVEN!
I HATE YOU, YOU SMUG LITTLE--
FABAAAMMM
SIT DOWN!
FABOOM
ON THE GROUND NOW!
DETACH THOSE ARMS IMMEDIATELY OR WE WILL DO IT FOR YOU!
YOU WILL?
EW.
WHAT ARE YOU EVEN DOING HERE?
YEAH! WHY ARE YOU ATTACKING AN ALREADY ATTACKED PLACE?
THHHAT'S WHAT...I'SS PAID TO--
--DO.
SHE PAID...
VON BA...R...
THIS IS NICK FURY WITH S.H.I.E.L.D. COMMAND AT THE SMITHSONIAN.
WE HAVE A 616.
META-HUMAN ATTACK AT THE BOMBING LOCATION.
WE NEED A FULL BATTALION OF HULKBUSTERS, WE NEED THE ENTIRE CITY ON LOCKDOWN UNTIL FURTHER NOTICE, WE NEED TACTICAL IN THE AIR...
THEY ATTACKED THE ATTACK.
I TOLD YOU.
WE DON'T KNOW WHAT VON BARDAS IS CAPABLE OF.
IF YOU HADN'T BEEN HERE...

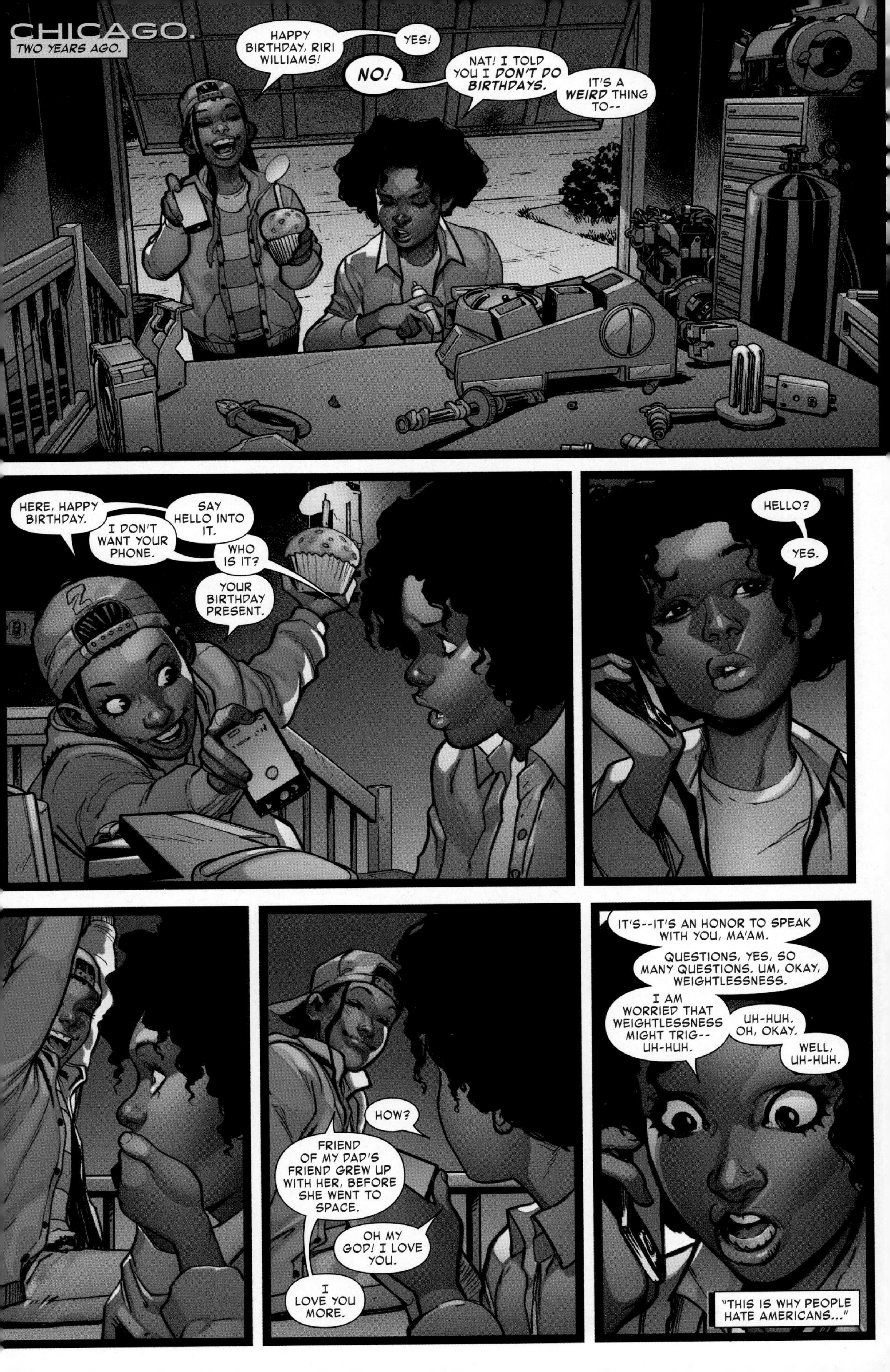
CHICAGO.
TWO YEARS AGO.
HAPPY BIRTHDAY, RIRI WILLIAMS!
YES!
NO!
NAT! I TOLD YOU I DON'T DO BIRTHDAYS.
IT'S A WEIRD THING TO--
HERE, HAPPY BIRTHDAY.
I DON'T WANT YOUR PHONE.
SAY HELLO INTO IT.
WHO IS IT?
YOUR BIRTHDAY PRESENT.
HELLO?
YES.
HOW?
FRIEND OF MY DAD'S FRIEND GREW UP WITH HER, BEFORE SHE WENT TO SPACE.
OH MY GOD! I LOVE YOU.
I LOVE YOU MORE.
IT'S--IT'S AN HONOR TO SPEAK WITH YOU, MA'AM.
QUESTIONS, YES, SO MANY QUESTIONS. UM, OKAY, WEIGHTLESSNESS.
I AM WORRIED THAT WEIGHTLESSNESS MIGHT TRIG-- UH-HUH.
UH-HUH. OH, OKAY.
WELL, UH-HUH.
"THIS IS WHY PEOPLE HATE AMERICANS..."

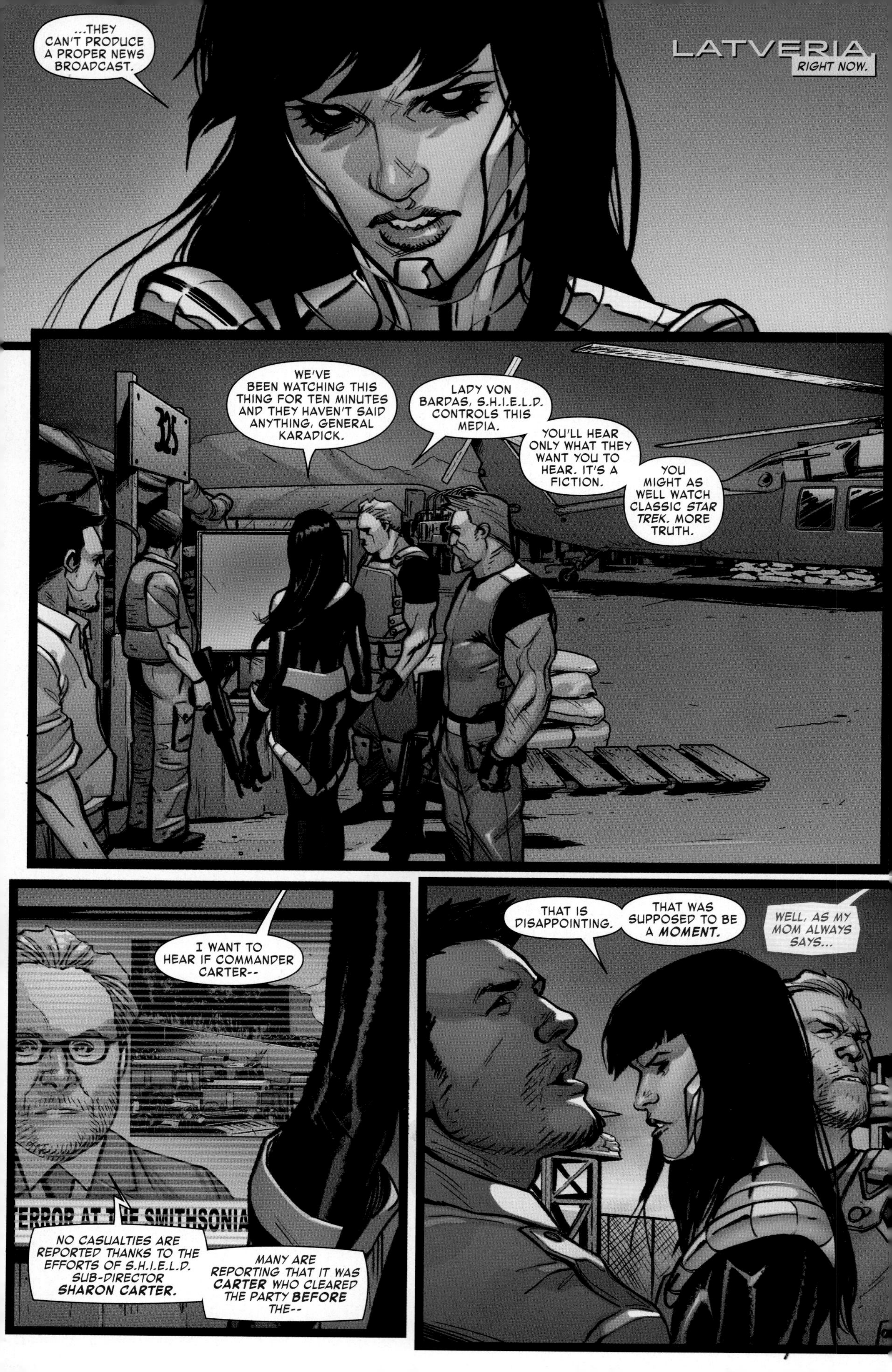

...THEY CAN'T PRODUCE A PROPER NEWS BROADCAST.
LATVERIA
RIGHT NOW.
325
WE'VE BEEN WATCHING THIS THING FOR TEN MINUTES AND THEY HAVEN'T SAID ANYTHING, GENERAL KARADICK.
LADY VON BARDAS, S.H.I.E.L.D. CONTROLS THIS MEDIA.
YOU'LL HEAR ONLY WHAT THEY WANT YOU TO HEAR. IT'S A FICTION.
YOU MIGHT AS WELL WATCH CLASSIC STAR TREK. MORE TRUTH.
I WANT TO HEAR IF COMMANDER CARTER--
ERROR AT THE SMITHSONIA
NO CASUALTIES ARE REPORTED THANKS TO THE EFFORTS OF S.H.I.E.L.D. SUB-DIRECTOR SHARON CARTER.
MANY ARE REPORTING THAT IT WAS CARTER WHO CLEARED THE PARTY BEFORE THE--
THAT IS DISAPPOINTING.
THAT WAS SUPPOSED TO BE A MOMENT.
WELL, AS MY MOM ALWAYS SAYS...

9

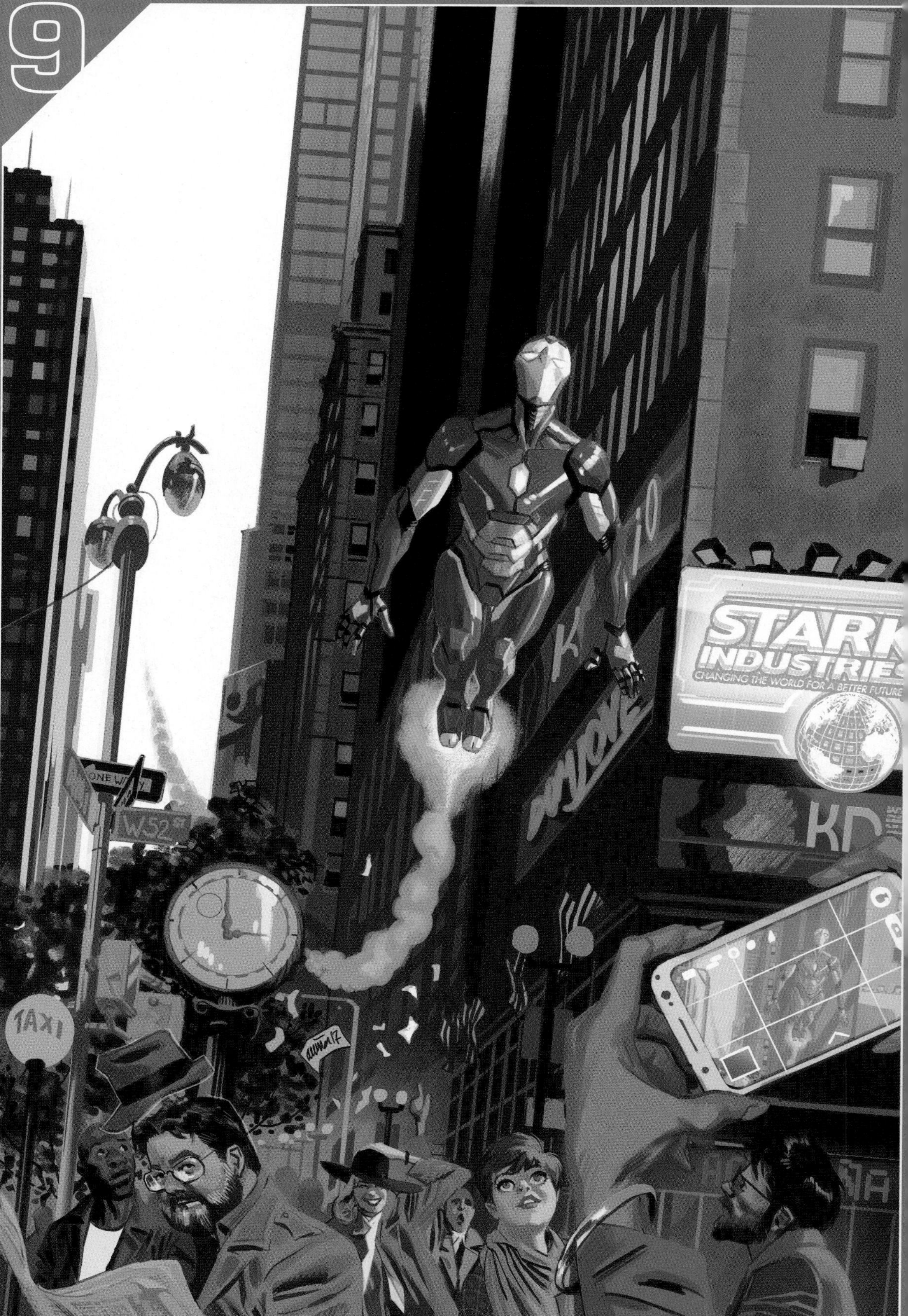
STARK
INDUSTRIES
CHANGING THE WORLD FOR A BETTER FUTURE
W52 ST
TAXI

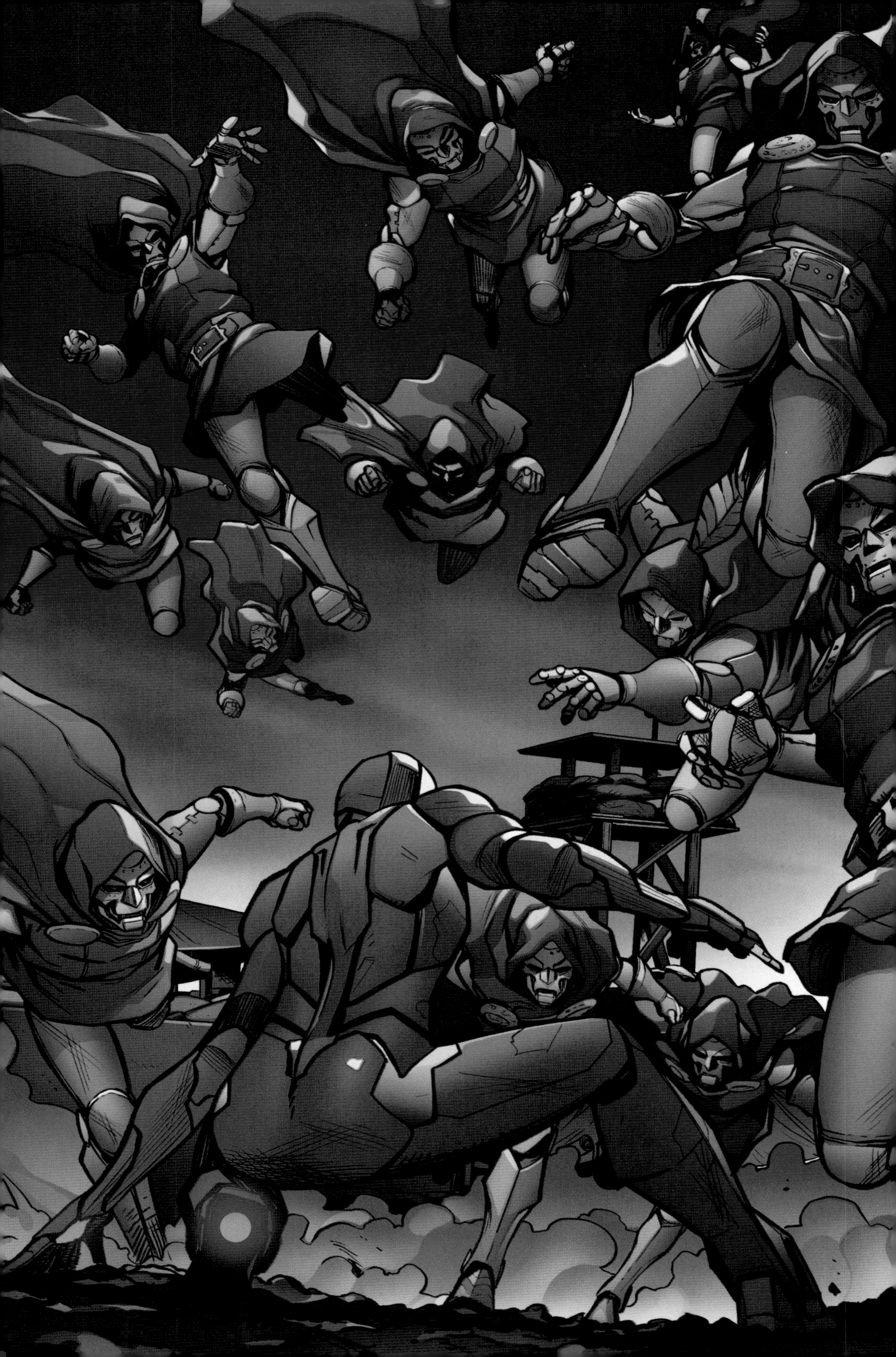

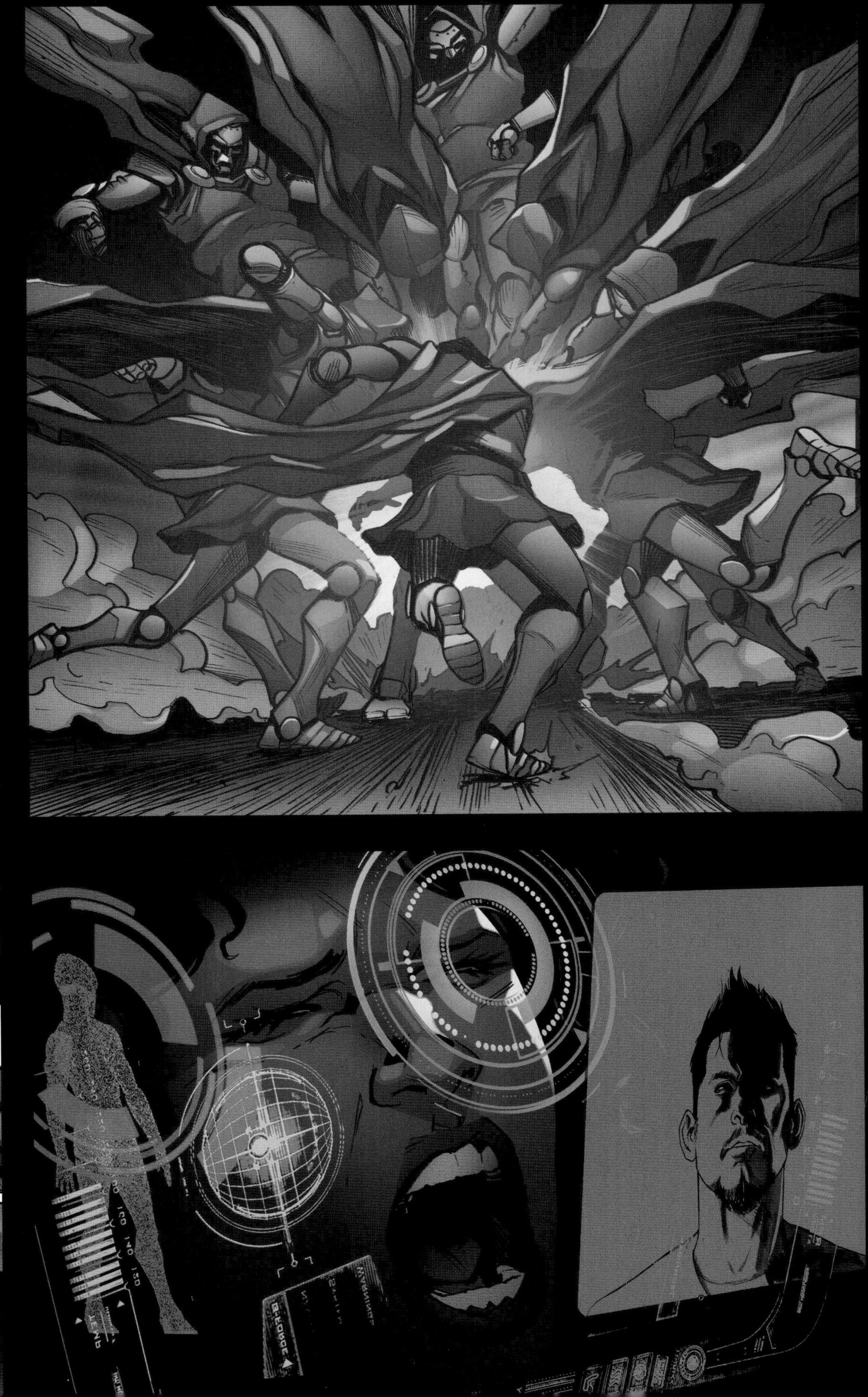

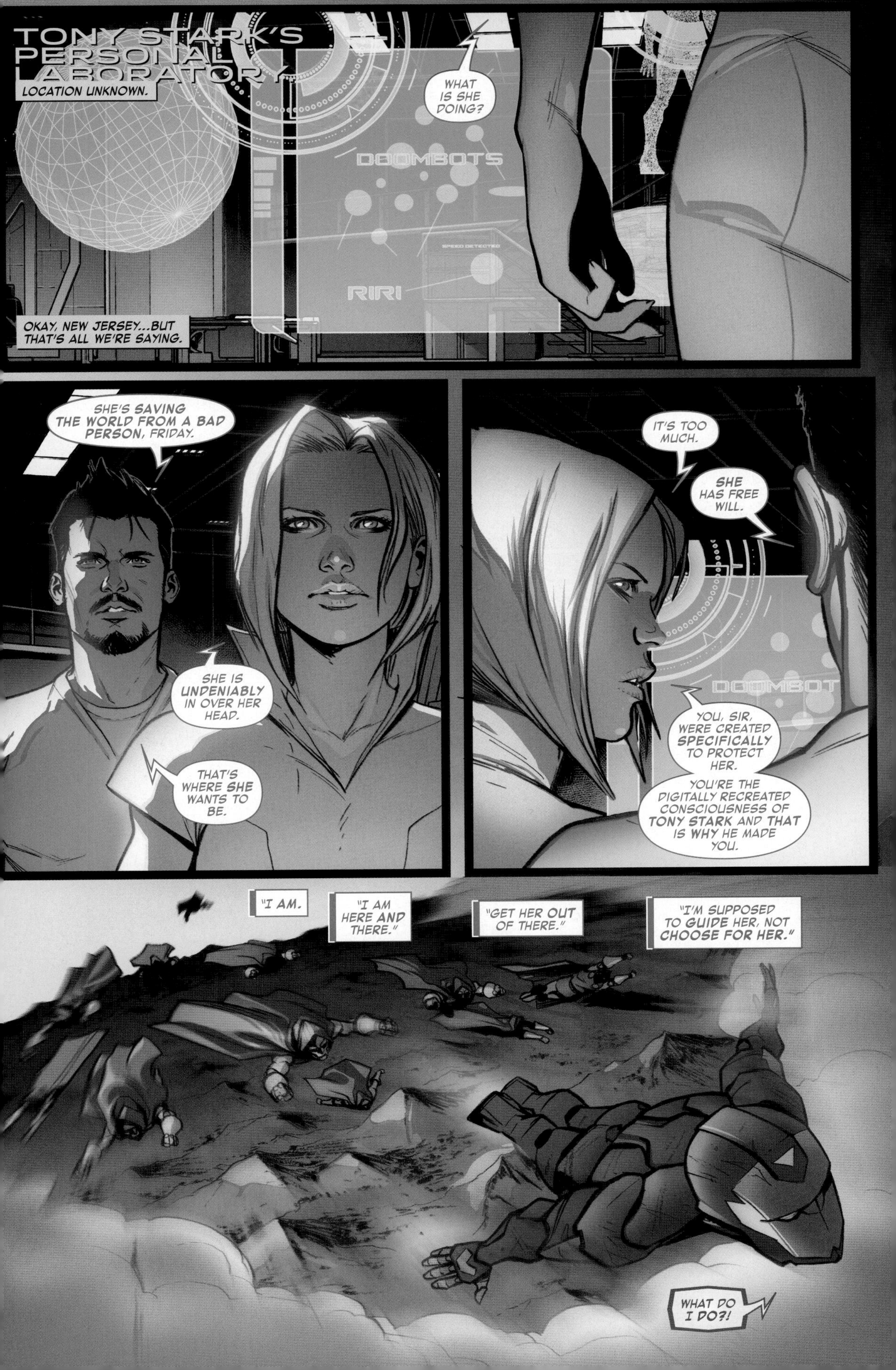
TONY STARK'S PERSONAL LABORATORY
LOCATION UNKNOWN.
OKAY, NEW JERSEY...BUT THAT'S ALL WE'RE SAYING.
WHAT IS SHE DOING?
DOOMBOTS
RIRI
SHE'S SAVING THE WORLD FROM A BAD PERSON, FRIDAY.
SHE IS UNDENIABLY IN OVER HER HEAD.
THAT'S WHERE SHE WANTS TO BE.
IT'S TOO MUCH.
SHE HAS FREE WILL.
DOOMBOT
YOU, SIR, WERE CREATED SPECIFICALLY TO PROTECT HER.
YOU'RE THE DIGITALLY RECREATED CONSCIOUSNESS OF TONY STARK AND THAT IS WHY HE MADE YOU.
"I AM.
"I AM HERE AND THERE."
"GET HER OUT OF THERE."
"I'M SUPPOSED TO GUIDE HER, NOT CHOOSE FOR HER."
WHAT DO I DO?!

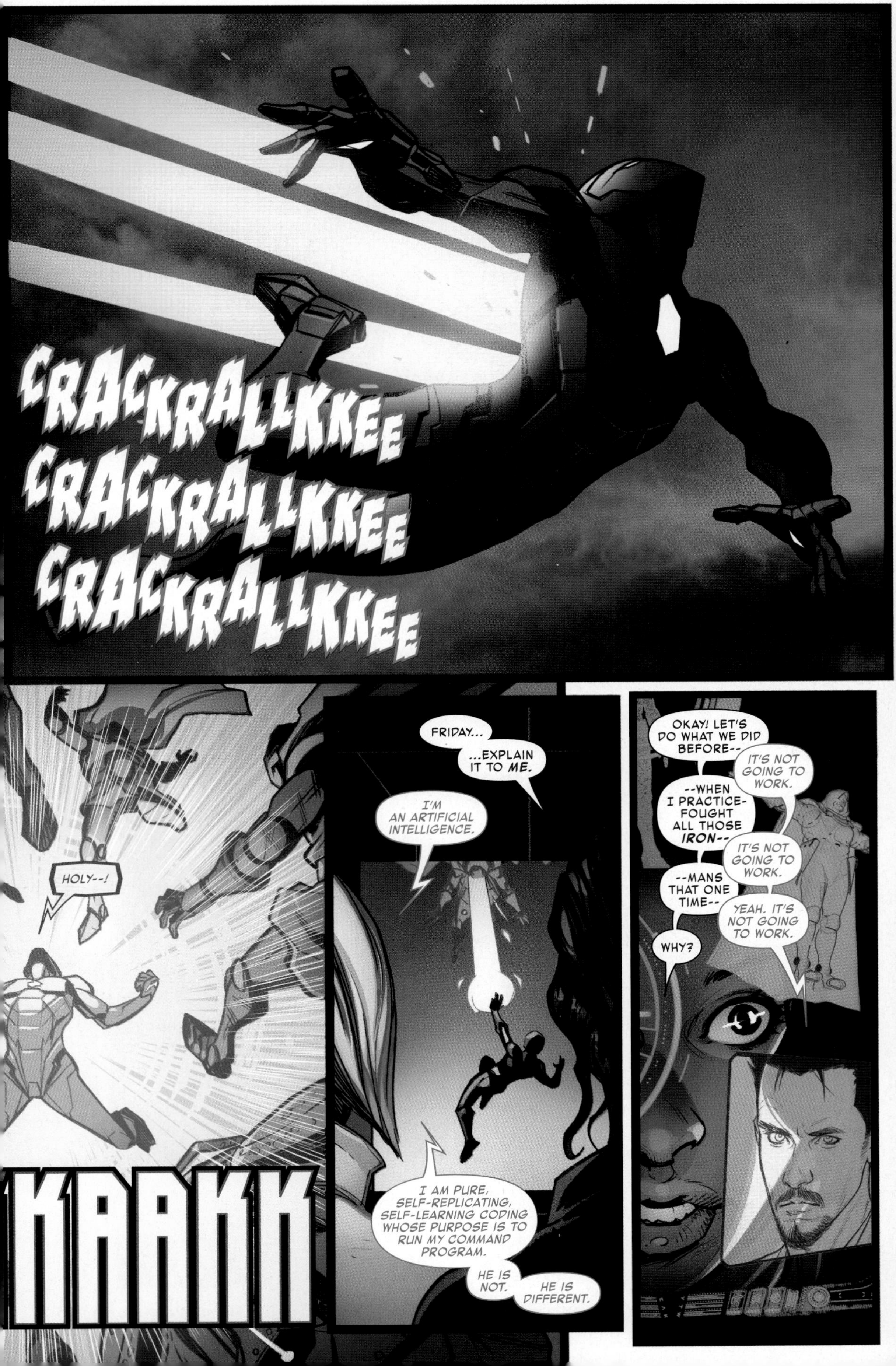
CRACKRALLKKEE
CRACKRALLKKEE
CRACKRALLKKEE
HOLY--!
KRAKK
FRIDAY...
...EXPLAIN IT TO ME.
I'M AN ARTIFICIAL INTELLIGENCE.
I AM PURE, SELF-REPLICATING, SELF-LEARNING CODING WHOSE PURPOSE IS TO RUN MY COMMAND PROGRAM.
HE IS NOT.
HE IS DIFFERENT.
OKAY! LET'S DO WHAT WE DID BEFORE--
IT'S NOT GOING TO WORK.
--WHEN I PRACTICE-FOUGHT ALL THOSE IRON--
IT'S NOT GOING TO WORK.
--MANS THAT ONE TIME--
YEAH. IT'S NOT GOING TO WORK.
WHY?

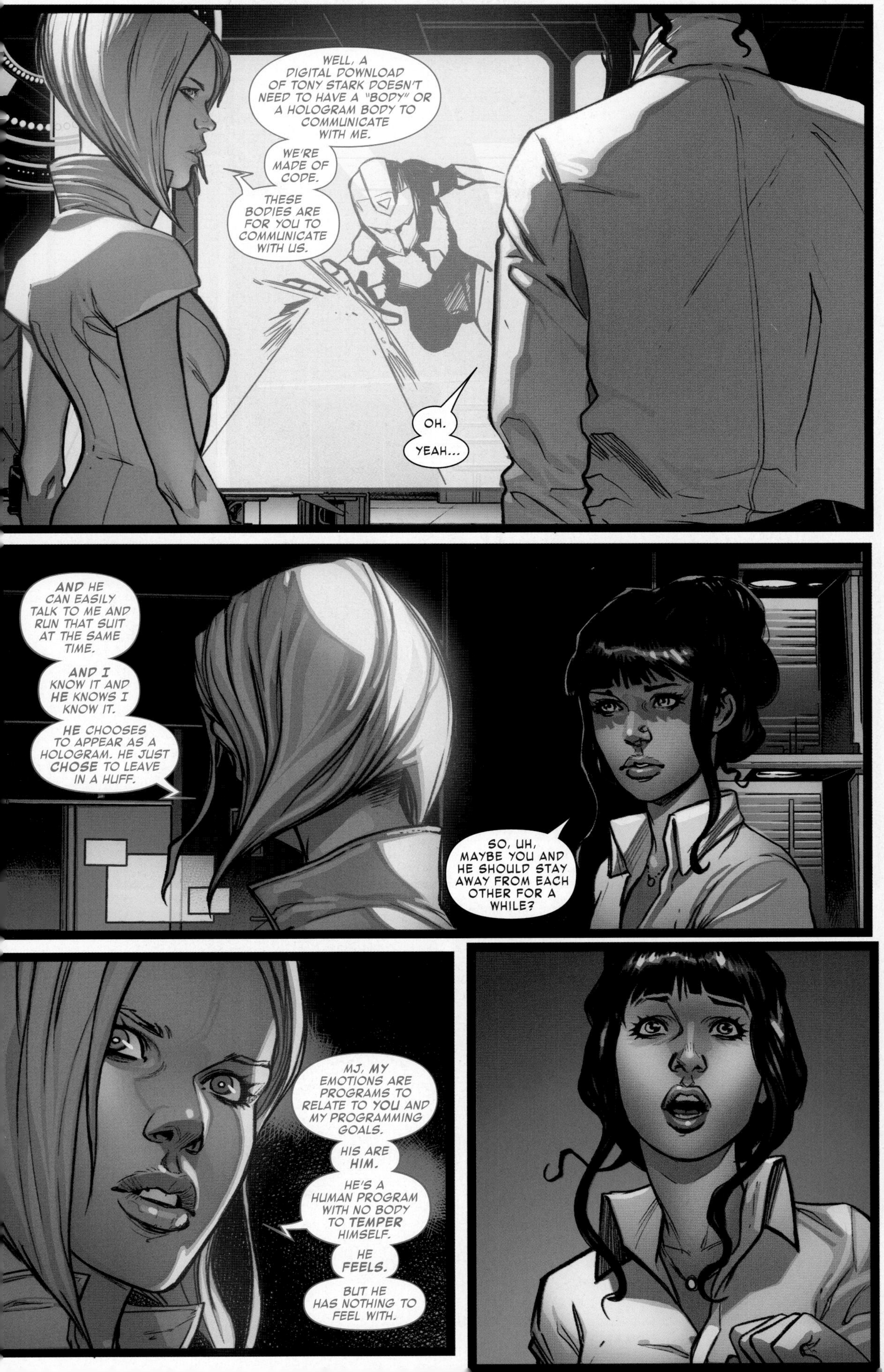
WELL, A DIGITAL DOWNLOAD OF TONY STARK DOESN'T NEED TO HAVE A "BODY" OR A HOLOGRAM BODY TO COMMUNICATE WITH ME.
WE'RE MADE OF CODE.
THESE BODIES ARE FOR YOU TO COMMUNICATE WITH US.
OH.
YEAH...
AND HE CAN EASILY TALK TO ME AND RUN THAT SUIT AT THE SAME TIME.
AND I KNOW IT AND HE KNOWS I KNOW IT.
HE CHOOSES TO APPEAR AS A HOLOGRAM. HE JUST CHOSE TO LEAVE IN A HUFF.
SO, UH, MAYBE YOU AND HE SHOULD STAY AWAY FROM EACH OTHER FOR A WHILE?
MJ, MY EMOTIONS ARE PROGRAMS TO RELATE TO YOU AND MY PROGRAMMING GOALS.
HIS ARE HIM.
HE'S A HUMAN PROGRAM WITH NO BODY TO TEMPER HIMSELF.
HE FEELS.
BUT HE HAS NOTHING TO FEEL WITH.

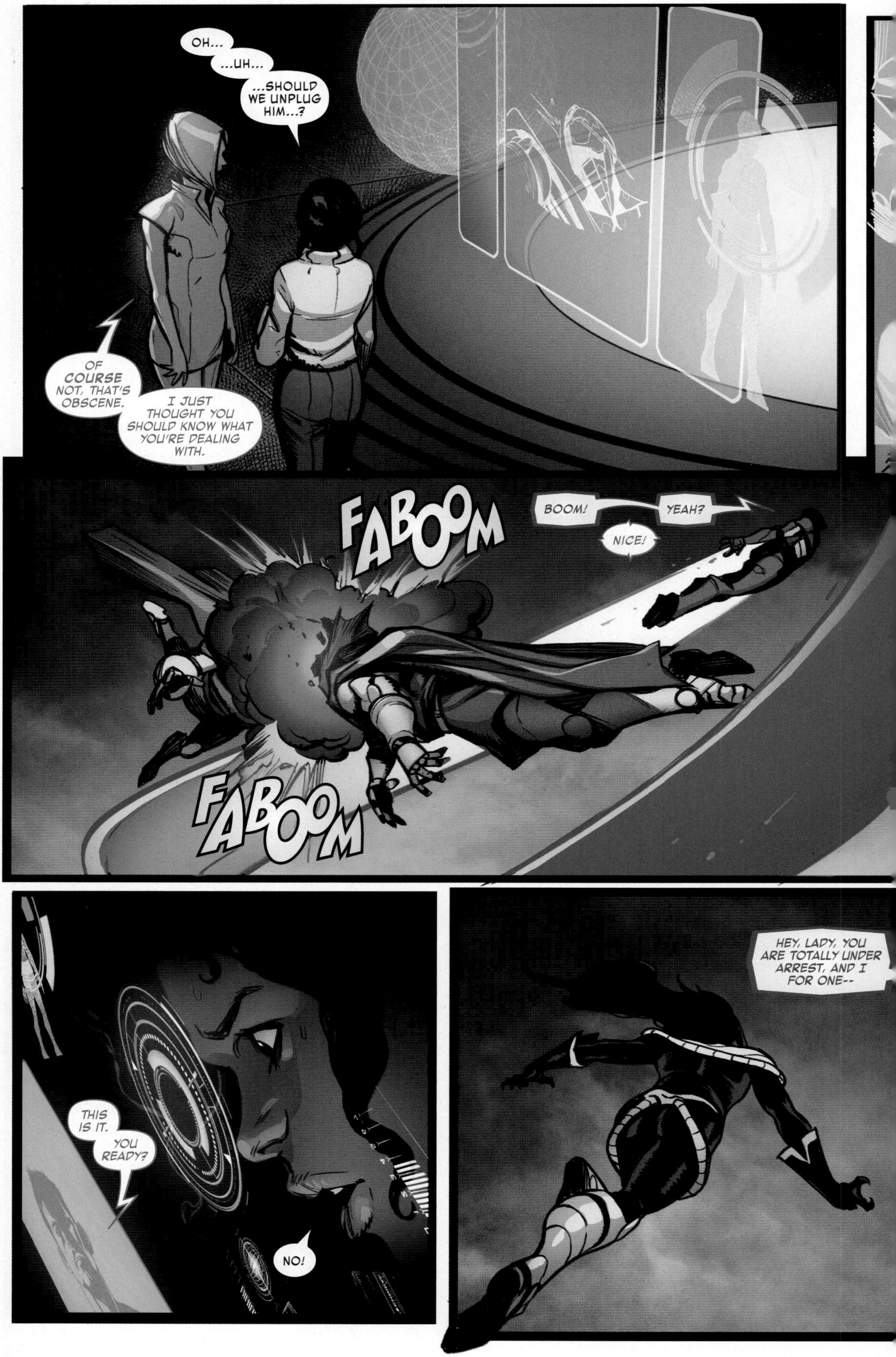
OH...
...UH...
...SHOULD WE UNPLUG HIM...?
OF COURSE NOT, THAT'S OBSCENE.
I JUST THOUGHT YOU SHOULD KNOW WHAT YOU'RE DEALING WITH.
FABOOM
BOOM!
YEAH?
NICE!
FABOOM
THIS IS IT.
YOU READY?
NO!
HEY, LADY, YOU ARE TOTALLY UNDER ARREST, AND I FOR ONE--

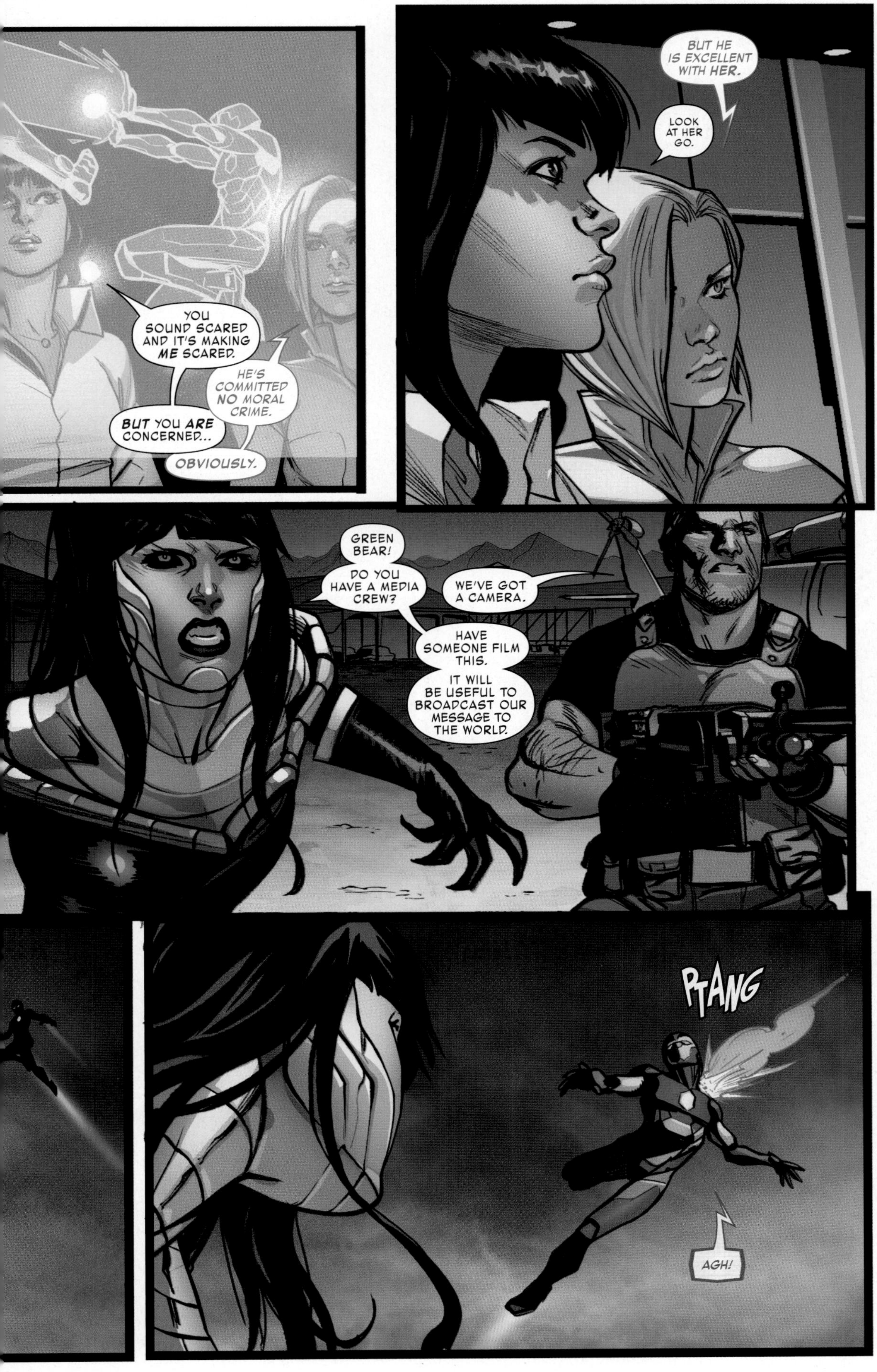
YOU SOUND SCARED AND IT'S MAKING **ME** SCARED.
HE'S COMMITTED NO MORAL CRIME.
BUT YOU **ARE** CONCERNED...
OBVIOUSLY.
BUT HE IS EXCELLENT WITH **HER**.
LOOK AT HER GO.
GREEN BEAR!
DO YOU HAVE A MEDIA CREW?
WE'VE GOT A CAMERA.
HAVE SOMEONE FILM THIS.
IT WILL BE USEFUL TO BROADCAST OUR MESSAGE TO THE WORLD.
PTANG
AGH!

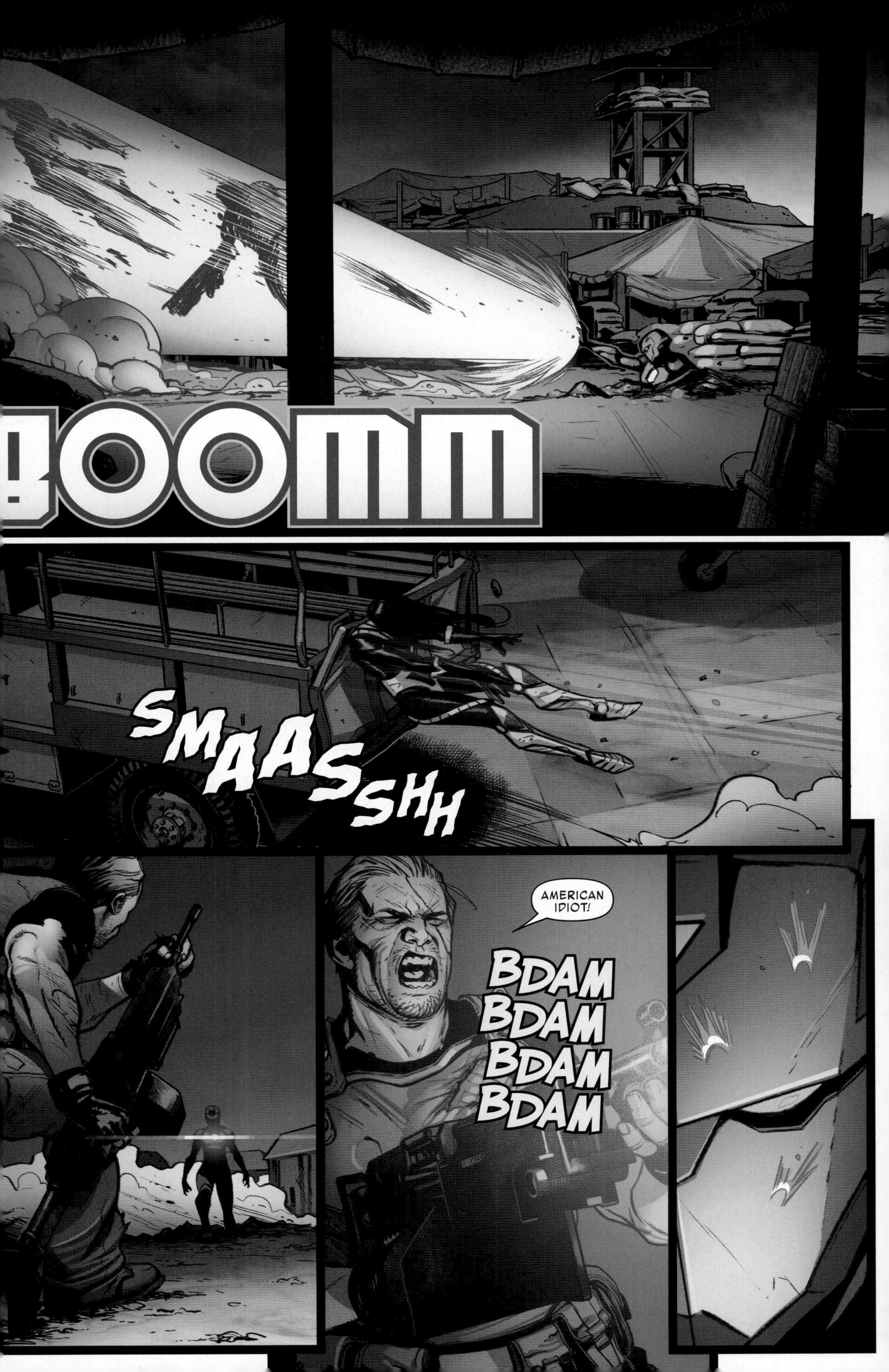
BOOMM
SMAASSHH
AMERICAN IDIOT!
BDAM
BDAM
BDAM
BDAM

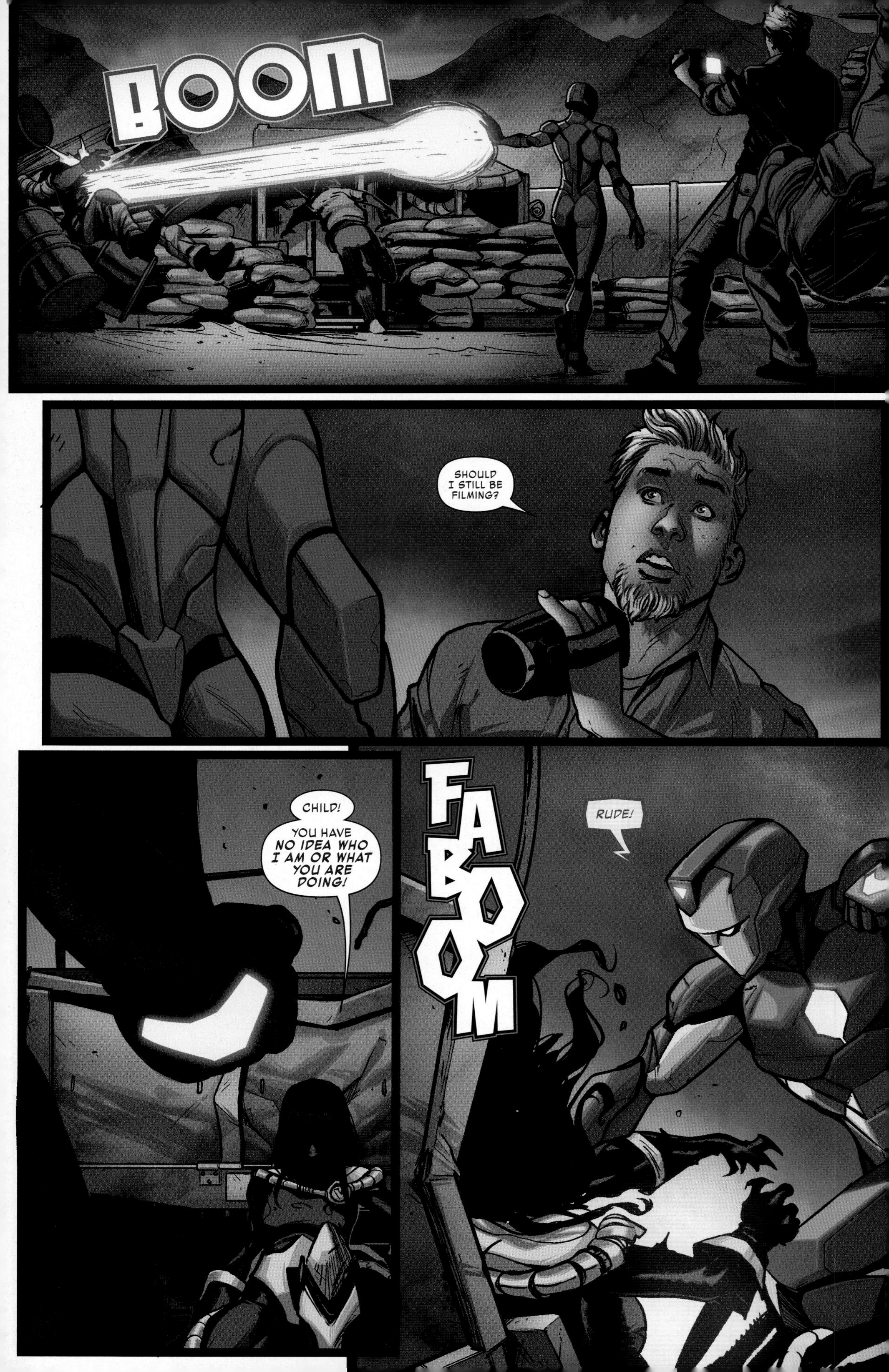
BOOM
SHOULD I STILL BE FILMING?
CHILD!
YOU HAVE NO IDEA WHO I AM OR WHAT YOU ARE DOING!
FABOOM
RUDE!

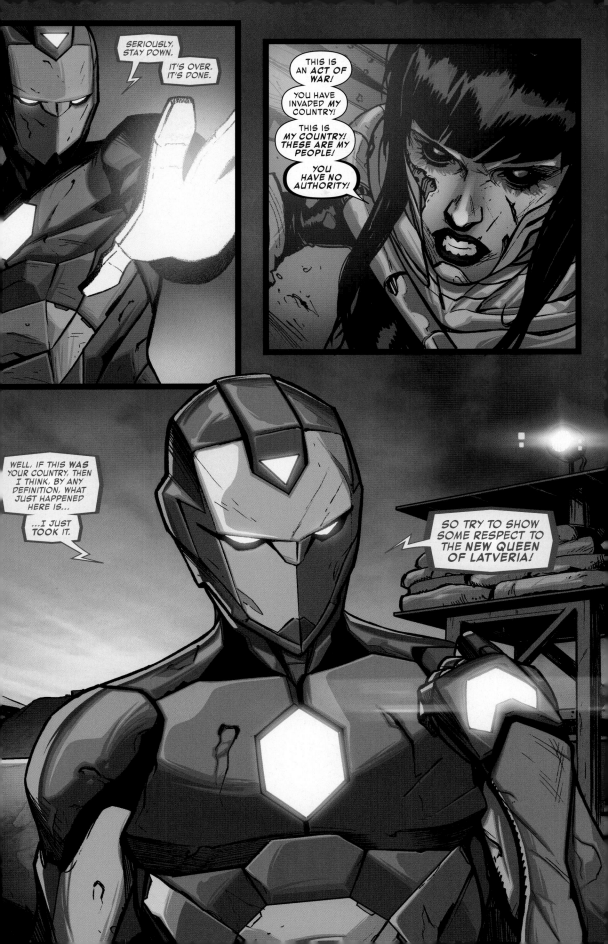

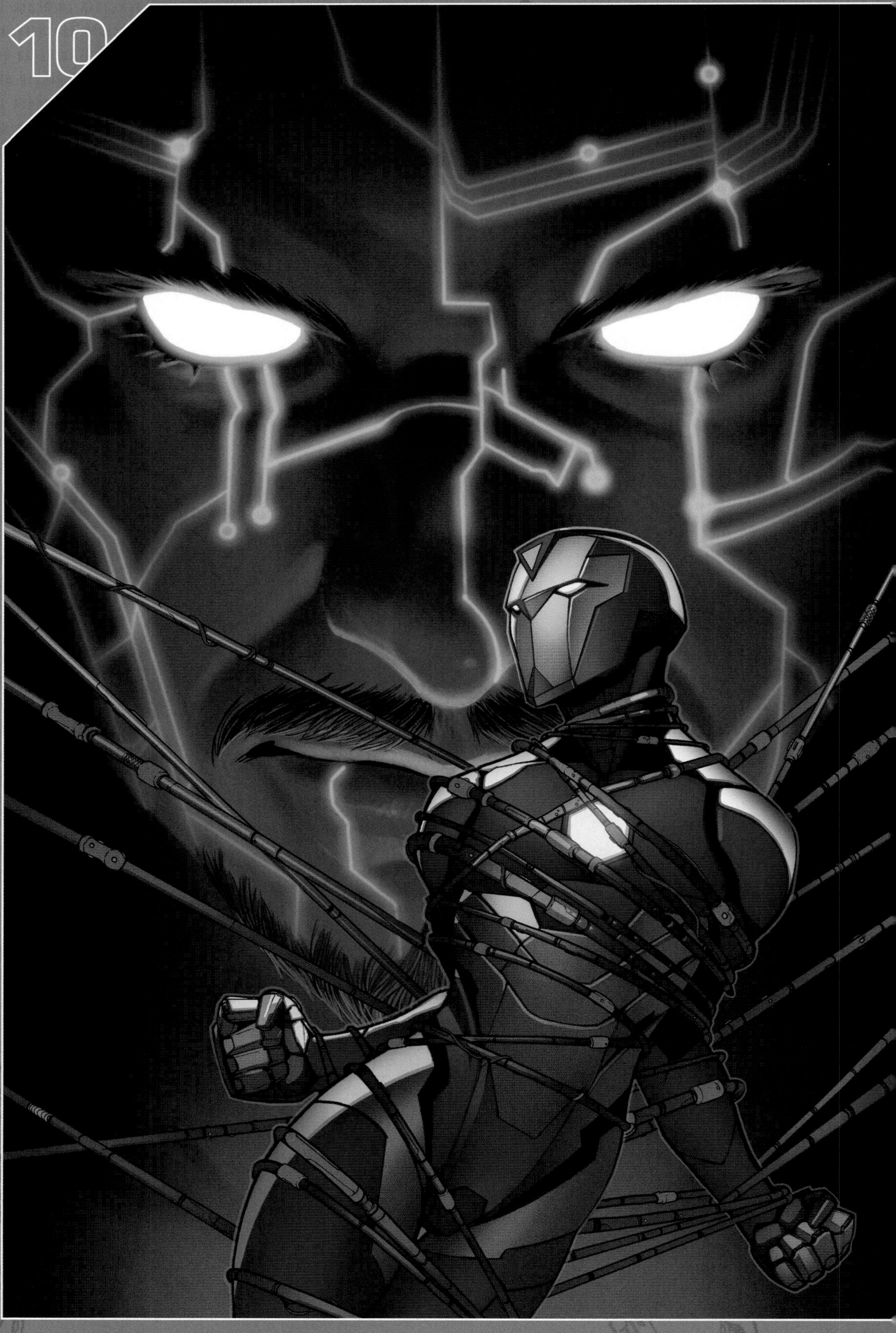
10

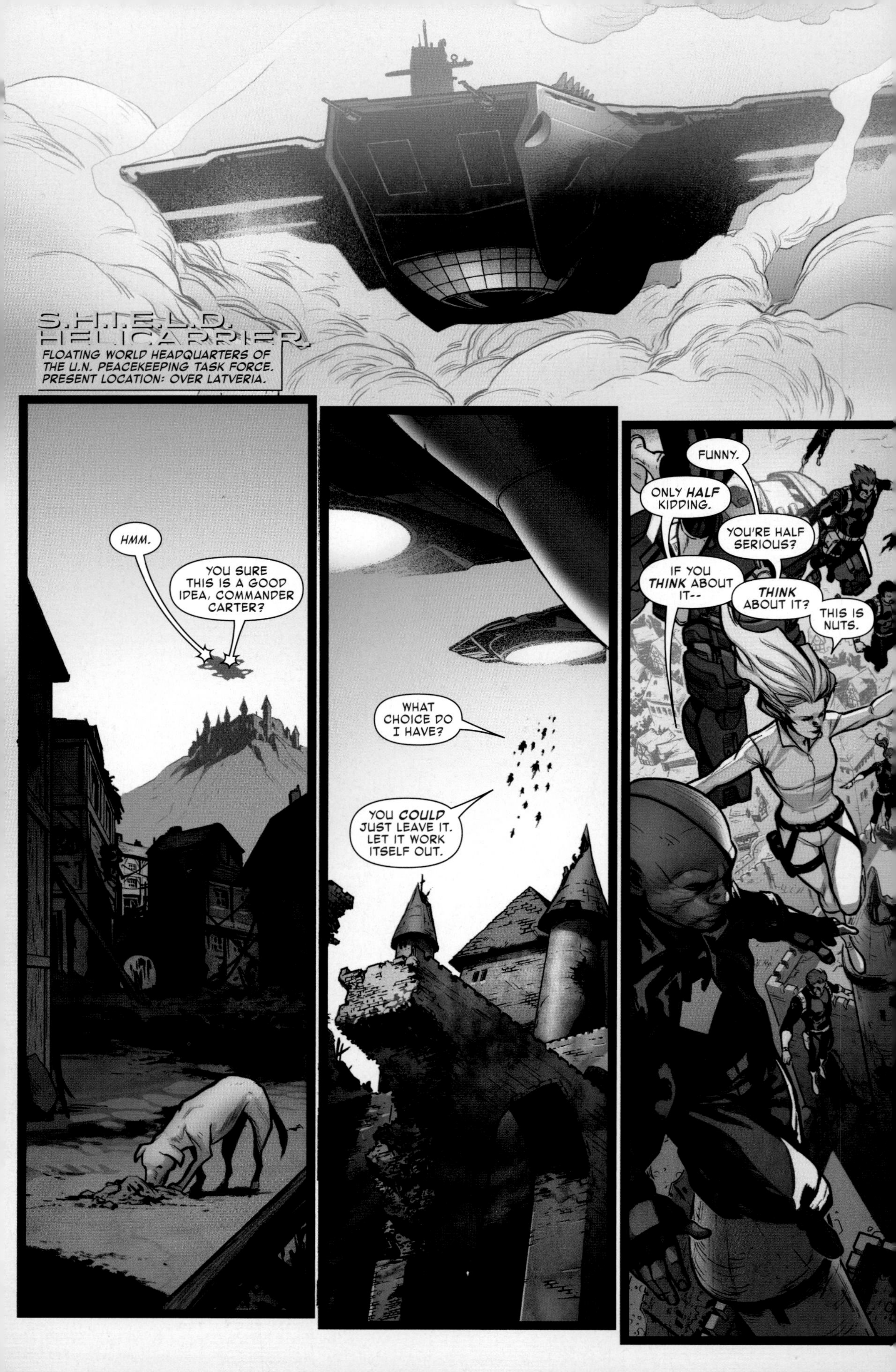

S.H.I.E.L.D. HELICARRIER
FLOATING WORLD HEADQUARTERS OF THE U.N. PEACEKEEPING TASK FORCE. PRESENT LOCATION: OVER LATVERIA.
HMM.
YOU SURE THIS IS A GOOD IDEA, COMMANDER CARTER?
WHAT CHOICE DO I HAVE?
YOU COULD JUST LEAVE IT. LET IT WORK ITSELF OUT.
FUNNY.
ONLY HALF KIDDING.
YOU'RE HALF SERIOUS?
IF YOU THINK ABOUT IT--
THINK ABOUT IT?
THIS IS NUTS.

GET ME OUT OF HERE.

OH MY GOD.

IT WAS AN ACCIDENT.

OH MY GOD.

I NEED YOU TO--

GO HOME.

I CAN'T.

SHE CAN'T.

YES, YOU CAN.

I CAN'T.

DOES YOUR ARMOR NOT WORK?

SHE REALLY CAN'T.

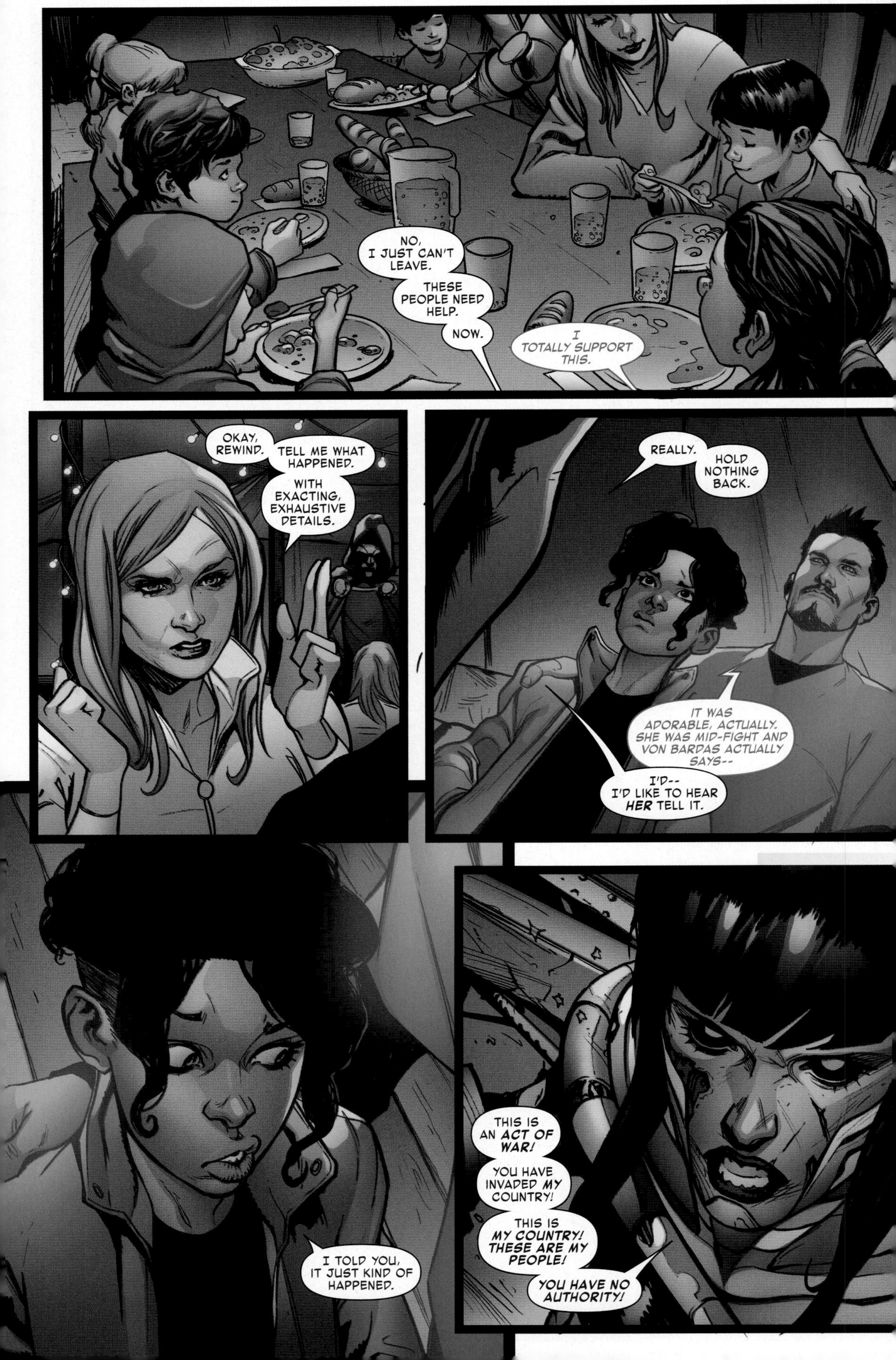
NO, I JUST CAN'T LEAVE.
THESE PEOPLE NEED HELP.
NOW.
I TOTALLY SUPPORT THIS.
OKAY, REWIND.
TELL ME WHAT HAPPENED.
WITH EXACTING, EXHAUSTIVE DETAILS.
REALLY.
HOLD NOTHING BACK.
IT WAS ADORABLE, ACTUALLY. SHE WAS MID-FIGHT AND VON BARDAS ACTUALLY SAYS--
I'D-- I'D LIKE TO HEAR HER TELL IT.
I TOLD YOU, IT JUST KIND OF HAPPENED.
THIS IS AN ACT OF WAR!
YOU HAVE INVADED MY COUNTRY!
THIS IS MY COUNTRY! THESE ARE MY PEOPLE!
YOU HAVE NO AUTHORITY!

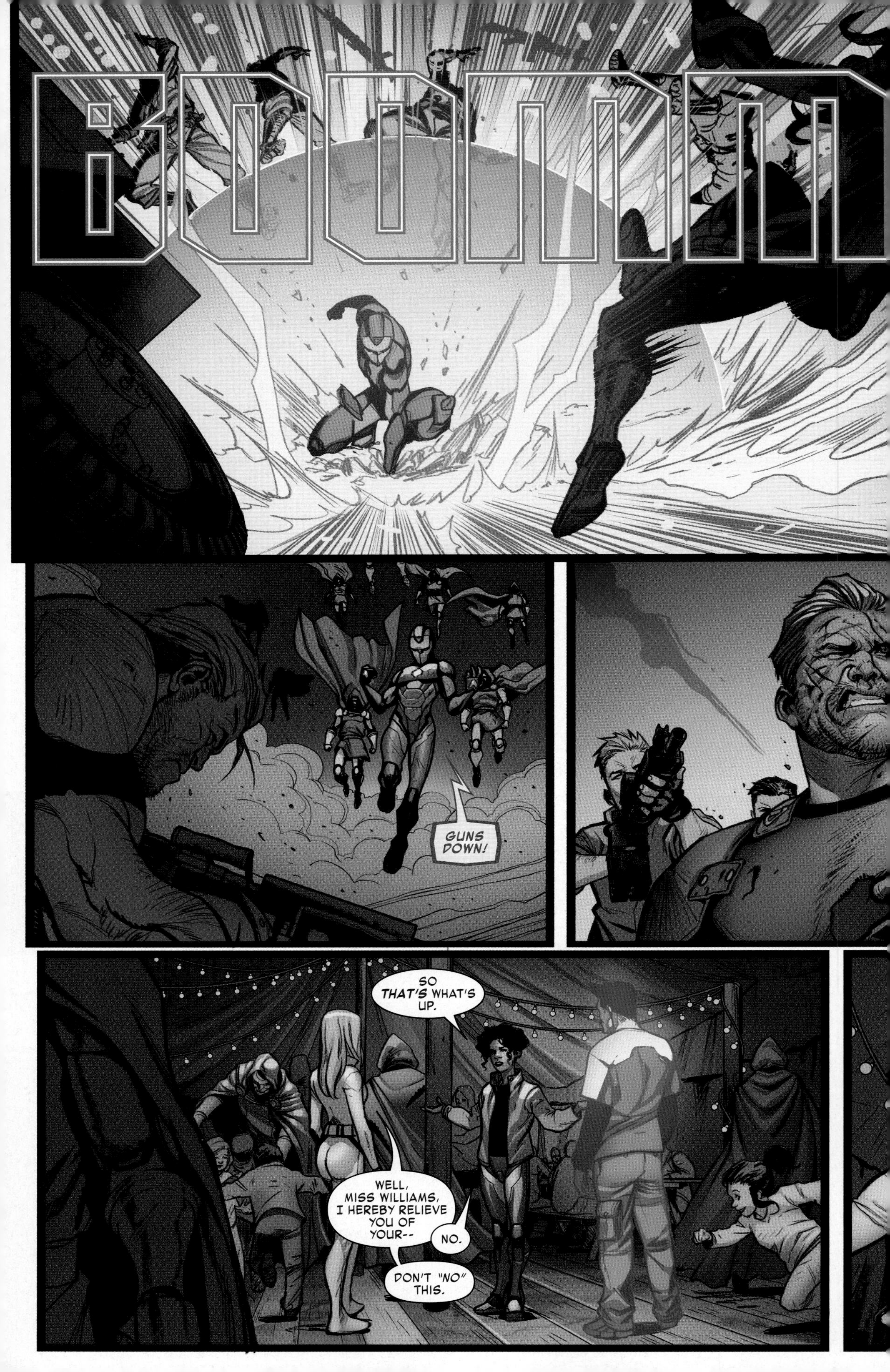
BOOMM
GUNS DOWN!
SO THAT'S WHAT'S UP.
WELL, MISS WILLIAMS, I HEREBY RELIEVE YOU OF YOUR--
NO.
DON'T "NO" THIS.

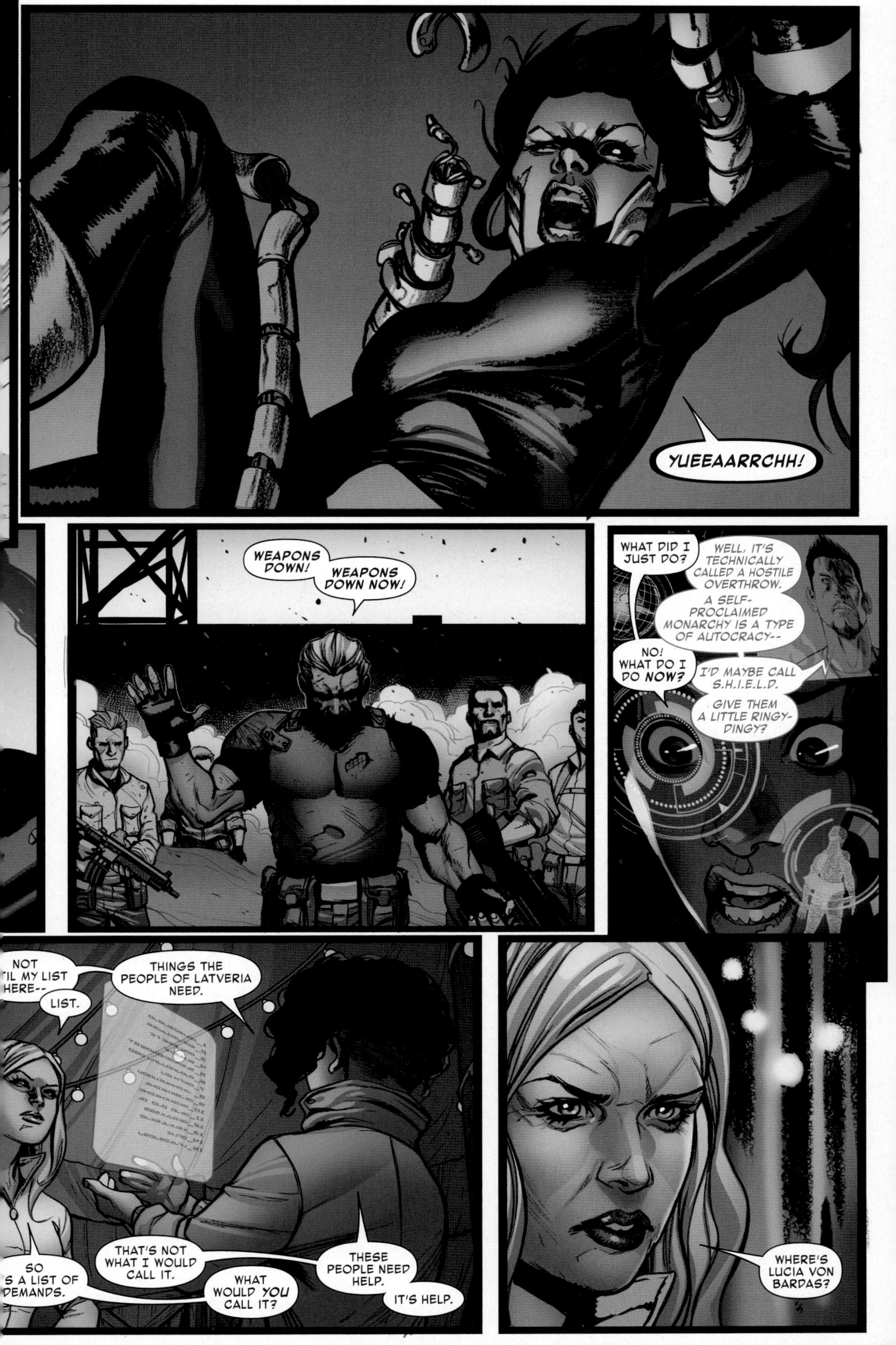
YUEEAARRCHH!
WEAPONS DOWN!
WEAPONS DOWN NOW!
WHAT DID I JUST DO?
WELL, IT'S TECHNICALLY CALLED A HOSTILE OVERTHROW.
A SELF-PROCLAIMED MONARCHY IS A TYPE OF AUTOCRACY--
NO! WHAT DO I DO NOW?
I'D MAYBE CALL S.H.I.E.L.D.
GIVE THEM A LITTLE RINGY-DINGY?
NOT TIL MY LIST HERE--
THINGS THE PEOPLE OF LATVERIA NEED.
LIST.
SO S A LIST OF DEMANDS.
THAT'S NOT WHAT I WOULD CALL IT.
WHAT WOULD YOU CALL IT?
THESE PEOPLE NEED HELP.
IT'S HELP.
WHERE'S LUCIA VON BARDAS?

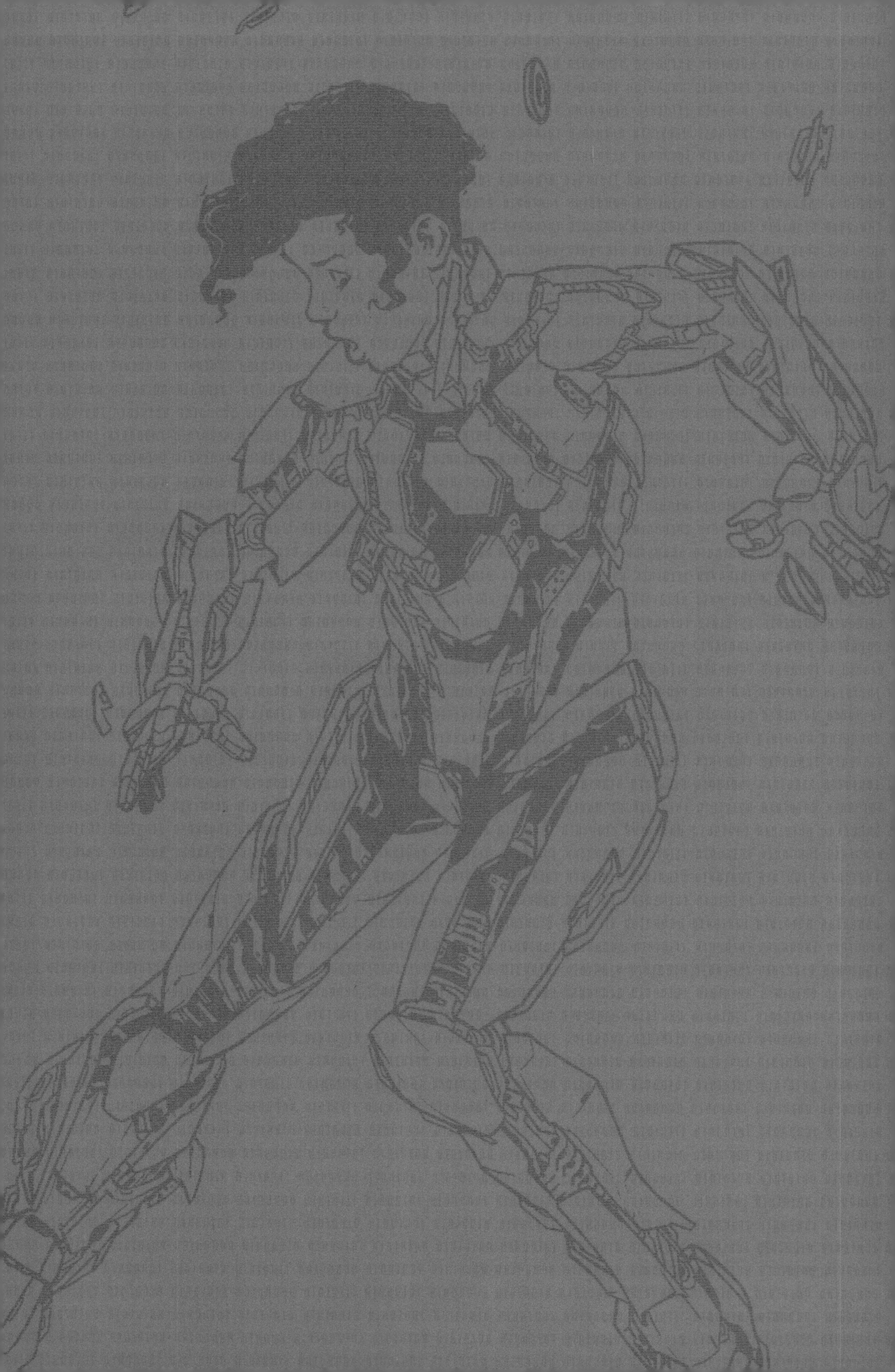

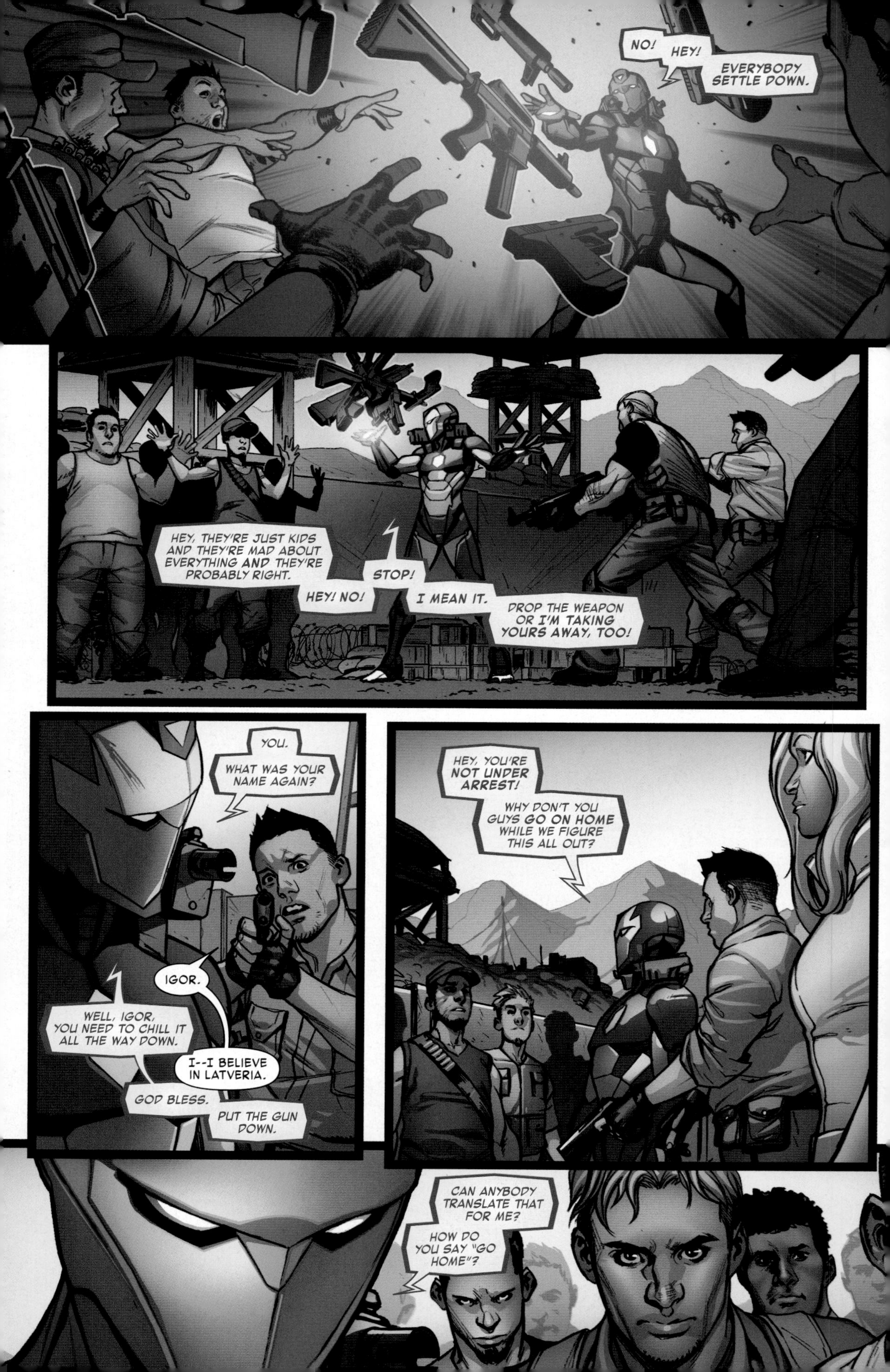
NO!
HEY!
EVERYBODY SETTLE DOWN.
HEY, THEY'RE JUST KIDS AND THEY'RE MAD ABOUT EVERYTHING AND THEY'RE PROBABLY RIGHT.
STOP!
HEY! NO!
I MEAN IT.
DROP THE WEAPON OR I'M TAKING YOURS AWAY, TOO!
YOU.
WHAT WAS YOUR NAME AGAIN?
IGOR.
WELL, IGOR, YOU NEED TO CHILL IT ALL THE WAY DOWN.
I--I BELIEVE IN LATVERIA.
GOD BLESS.
PUT THE GUN DOWN.
HEY, YOU'RE NOT UNDER ARREST!
WHY DON'T YOU GUYS GO ON HOME WHILE WE FIGURE THIS ALL OUT?
CAN ANYBODY TRANSLATE THAT FOR ME?
HOW DO YOU SAY "GO HOME"?

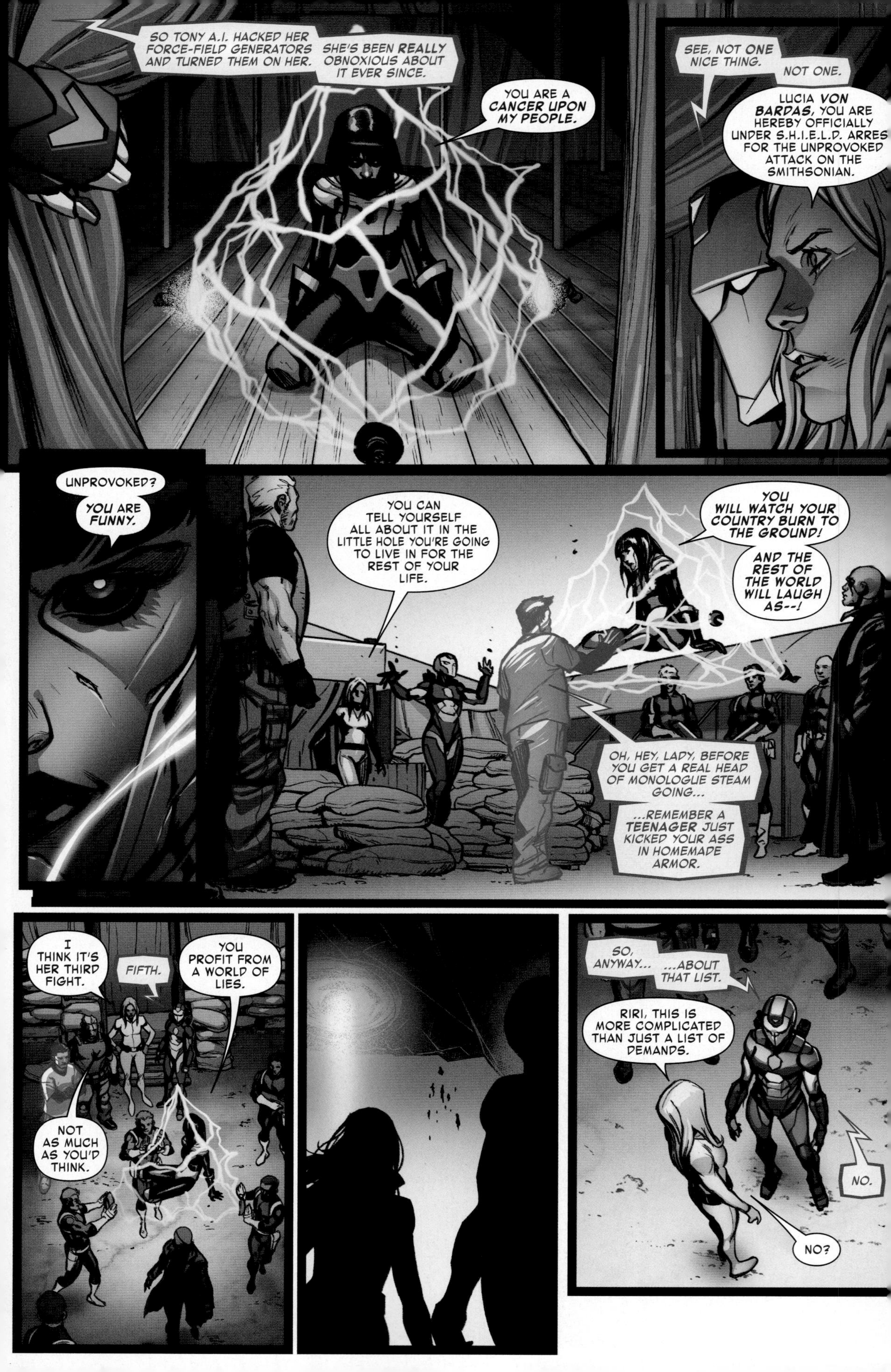

SO TONY A.I. HACKED HER FORCE-FIELD GENERATORS AND TURNED THEM ON HER.
SHE'S BEEN REALLY OBNOXIOUS ABOUT IT EVER SINCE.
YOU ARE A CANCER UPON MY PEOPLE.
SEE, NOT ONE NICE THING.
NOT ONE.
LUCIA VON BARDAS, YOU ARE HEREBY OFFICIALLY UNDER S.H.I.E.L.D. ARREST FOR THE UNPROVOKED ATTACK ON THE SMITHSONIAN.
UNPROVOKED?
YOU ARE FUNNY.
YOU CAN TELL YOURSELF ALL ABOUT IT IN THE LITTLE HOLE YOU'RE GOING TO LIVE IN FOR THE REST OF YOUR LIFE.
YOU WILL WATCH YOUR COUNTRY BURN TO THE GROUND!
AND THE REST OF THE WORLD WILL LAUGH AS--!
OH, HEY, LADY, BEFORE YOU GET A REAL HEAD OF MONOLOGUE STEAM GOING...
...REMEMBER A TEENAGER JUST KICKED YOUR ASS IN HOMEMADE ARMOR.
I THINK IT'S HER THIRD FIGHT.
FIFTH.
YOU PROFIT FROM A WORLD OF LIES.
NOT AS MUCH AS YOU'D THINK.
SO, ANYWAY...
...ABOUT THAT LIST.
RIRI, THIS IS MORE COMPLICATED THAN JUST A LIST OF DEMANDS.
NO.
NO?

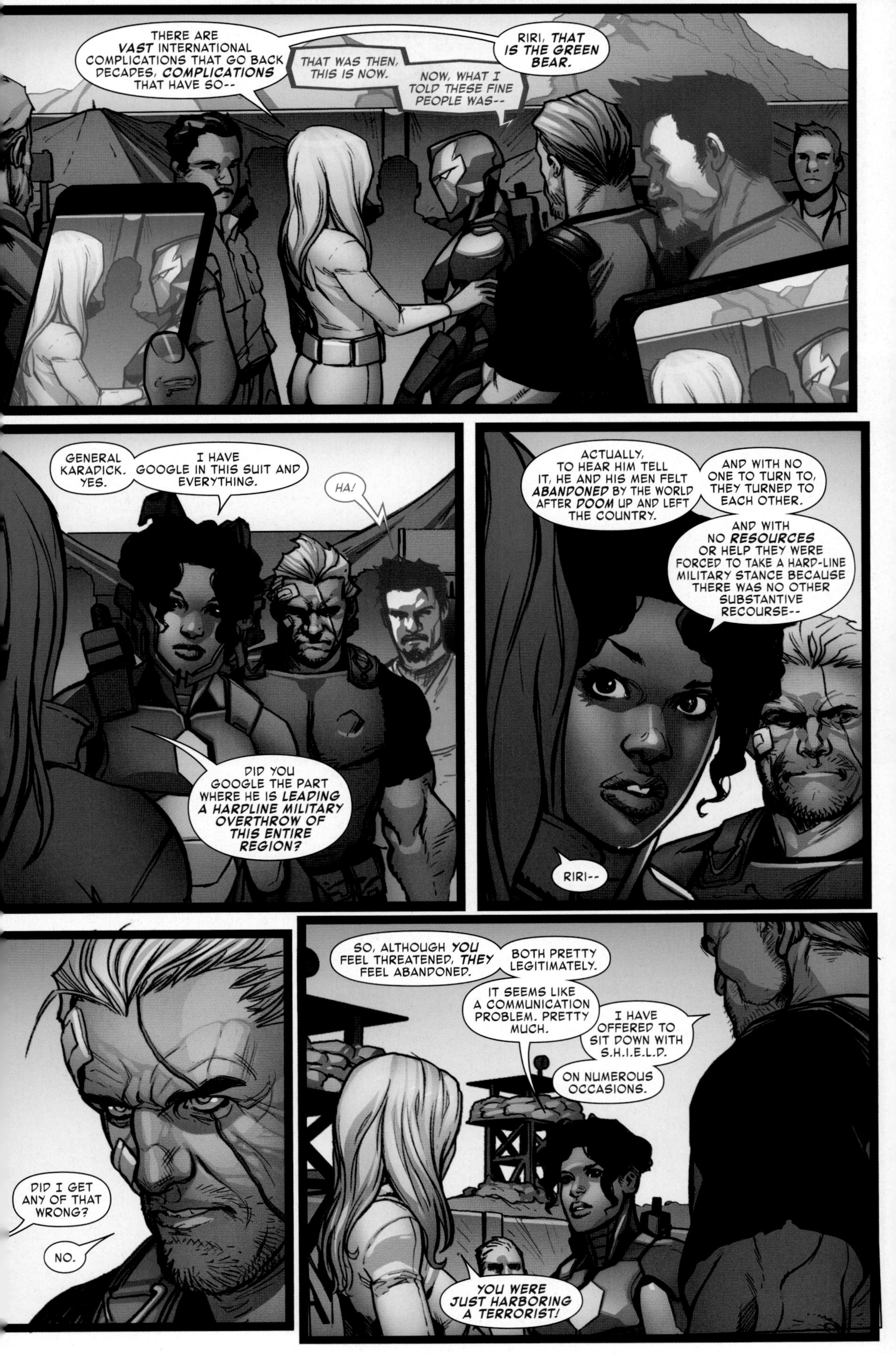
THERE ARE VAST INTERNATIONAL COMPLICATIONS THAT GO BACK DECADES, COMPLICATIONS THAT HAVE SO--
THAT WAS THEN, THIS IS NOW.
NOW, WHAT I TOLD THESE FINE PEOPLE WAS--
RIRI, THAT IS THE GREEN BEAR.
GENERAL KARADICK. YES.
I HAVE GOOGLE IN THIS SUIT AND EVERYTHING.
HA!
DID YOU GOOGLE THE PART WHERE HE IS LEADING A HARDLINE MILITARY OVERTHROW OF THIS ENTIRE REGION?
ACTUALLY, TO HEAR HIM TELL IT, HE AND HIS MEN FELT ABANDONED BY THE WORLD AFTER DOOM UP AND LEFT THE COUNTRY.
AND WITH NO ONE TO TURN TO, THEY TURNED TO EACH OTHER.
AND WITH NO RESOURCES OR HELP THEY WERE FORCED TO TAKE A HARD-LINE MILITARY STANCE BECAUSE THERE WAS NO OTHER SUBSTANTIVE RECOURSE--
RIRI--
DID I GET ANY OF THAT WRONG?
NO.
SO, ALTHOUGH YOU FEEL THREATENED, THEY FEEL ABANDONED.
BOTH PRETTY LEGITIMATELY.
IT SEEMS LIKE A COMMUNICATION PROBLEM. PRETTY MUCH.
I HAVE OFFERED TO SIT DOWN WITH S.H.I.E.L.D.
ON NUMEROUS OCCASIONS.
YOU WERE JUST HARBORING A TERRORIST!

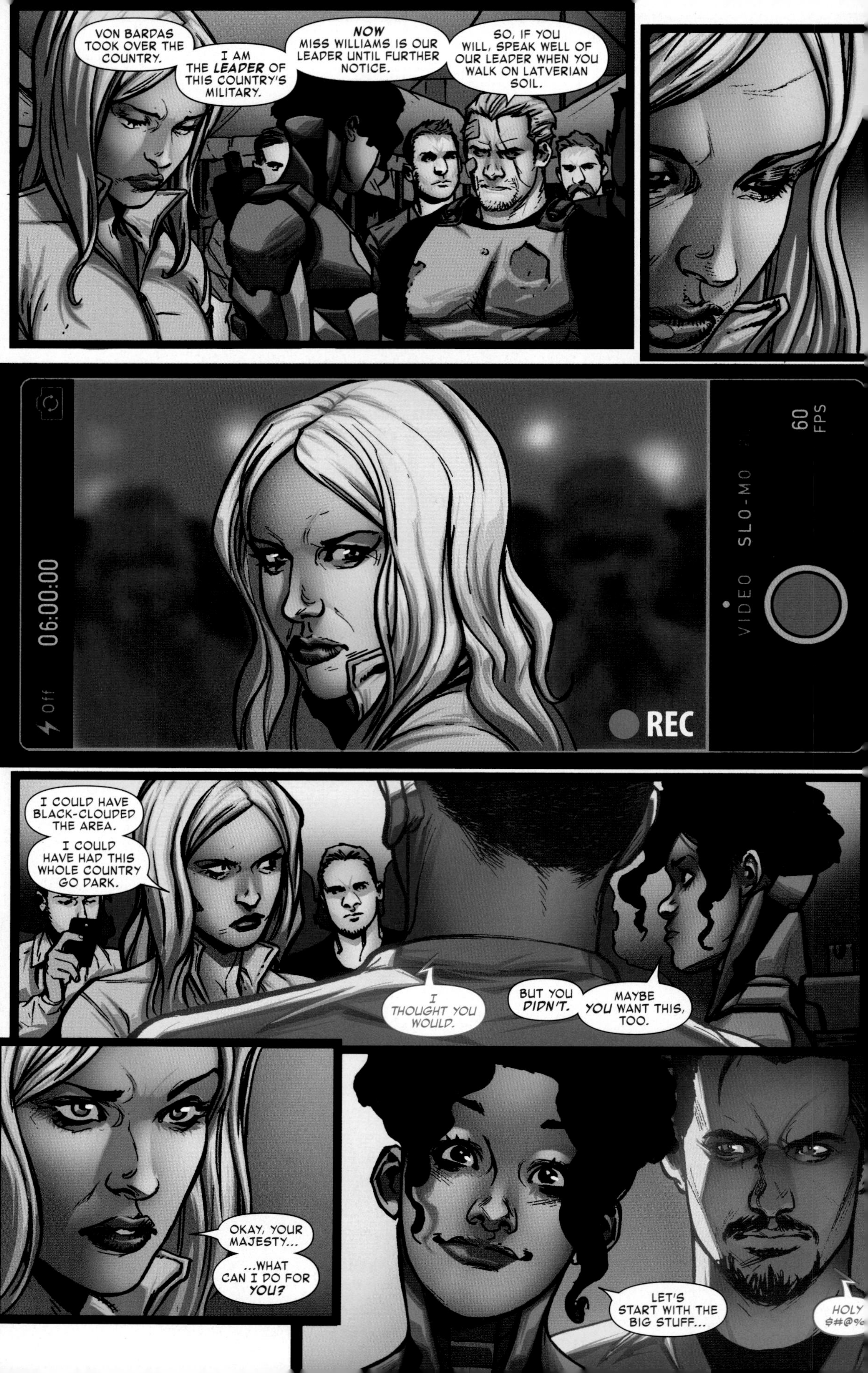
VON BARDAS TOOK OVER THE COUNTRY.
I AM THE *LEADER* OF THIS COUNTRY'S MILITARY.
NOW MISS WILLIAMS IS OUR LEADER UNTIL FURTHER NOTICE.
SO, IF YOU WILL, SPEAK WELL OF OUR LEADER WHEN YOU WALK ON LATVERIAN SOIL.
06:00:00
Off
60 FPS
SLO-MO
VIDEO
REC
I COULD HAVE BLACK-CLOUDED THE AREA.
I COULD HAVE HAD THIS WHOLE COUNTRY GO DARK.
I THOUGHT YOU WOULD.
BUT YOU *DIDN'T.*
MAYBE *YOU* WANT THIS, TOO.
OKAY, YOUR MAJESTY...
...WHAT CAN I DO FOR *YOU?*
LET'S START WITH THE BIG STUFF...
HOLY $#@%

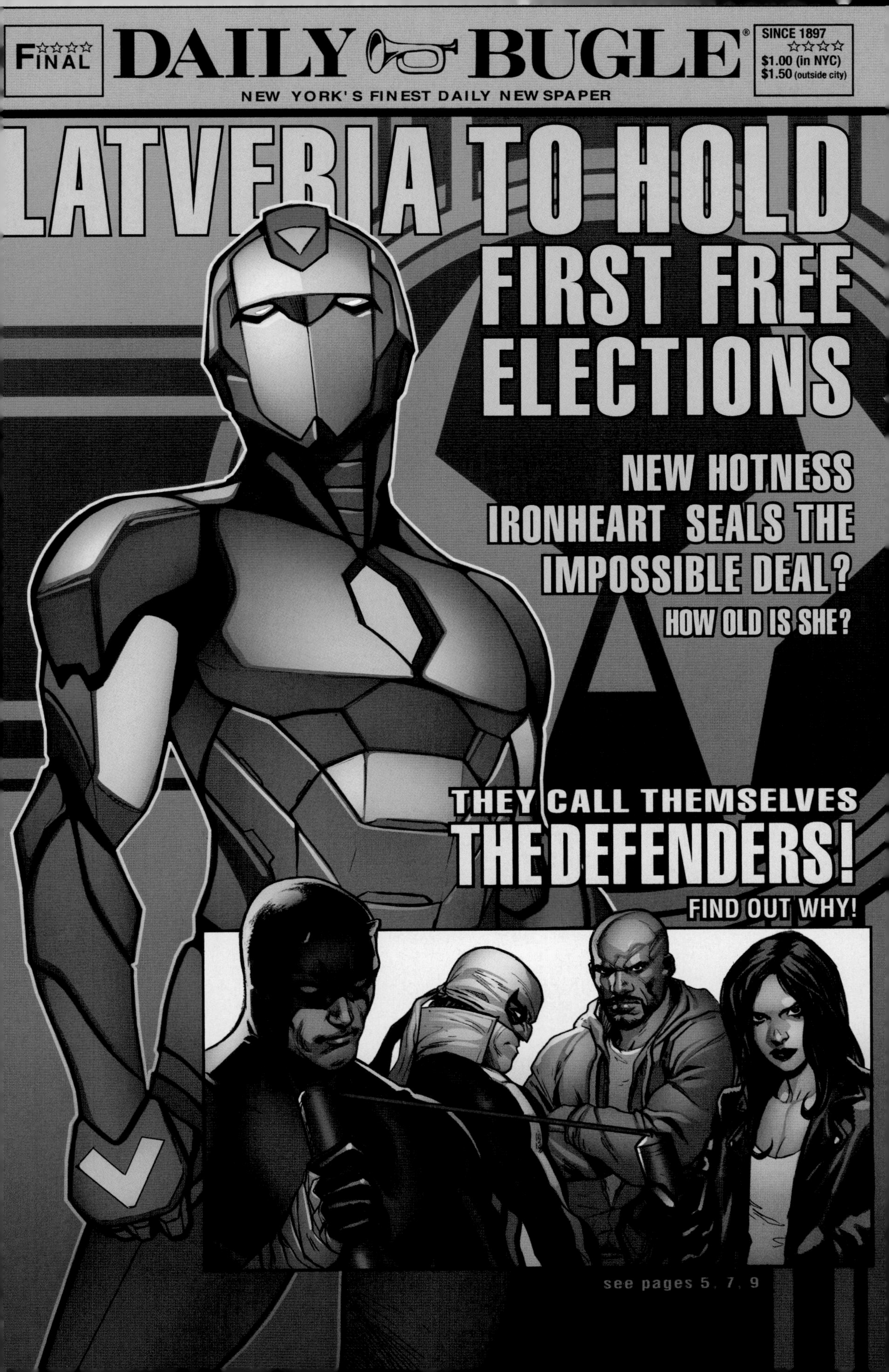

☆☆☆☆
Fɪɴᴀʟ

DAILY 🎺 BUGLE

NEW YORK'S FINEST DAILY NEWSPAPER

SINCE 1897
☆☆☆☆
$1.00 (in NYC)
$1.50 (outside city)

LATVERIA TO HOLD FIRST FREE ELECTIONS

NEW HOTNESS IRONHEART SEALS THE IMPOSSIBLE DEAL?

HOW OLD IS SHE?

THEY CALL THEMSELVES THE DEFENDERS!

FIND OUT WHY!

see pages 5, 7, 9

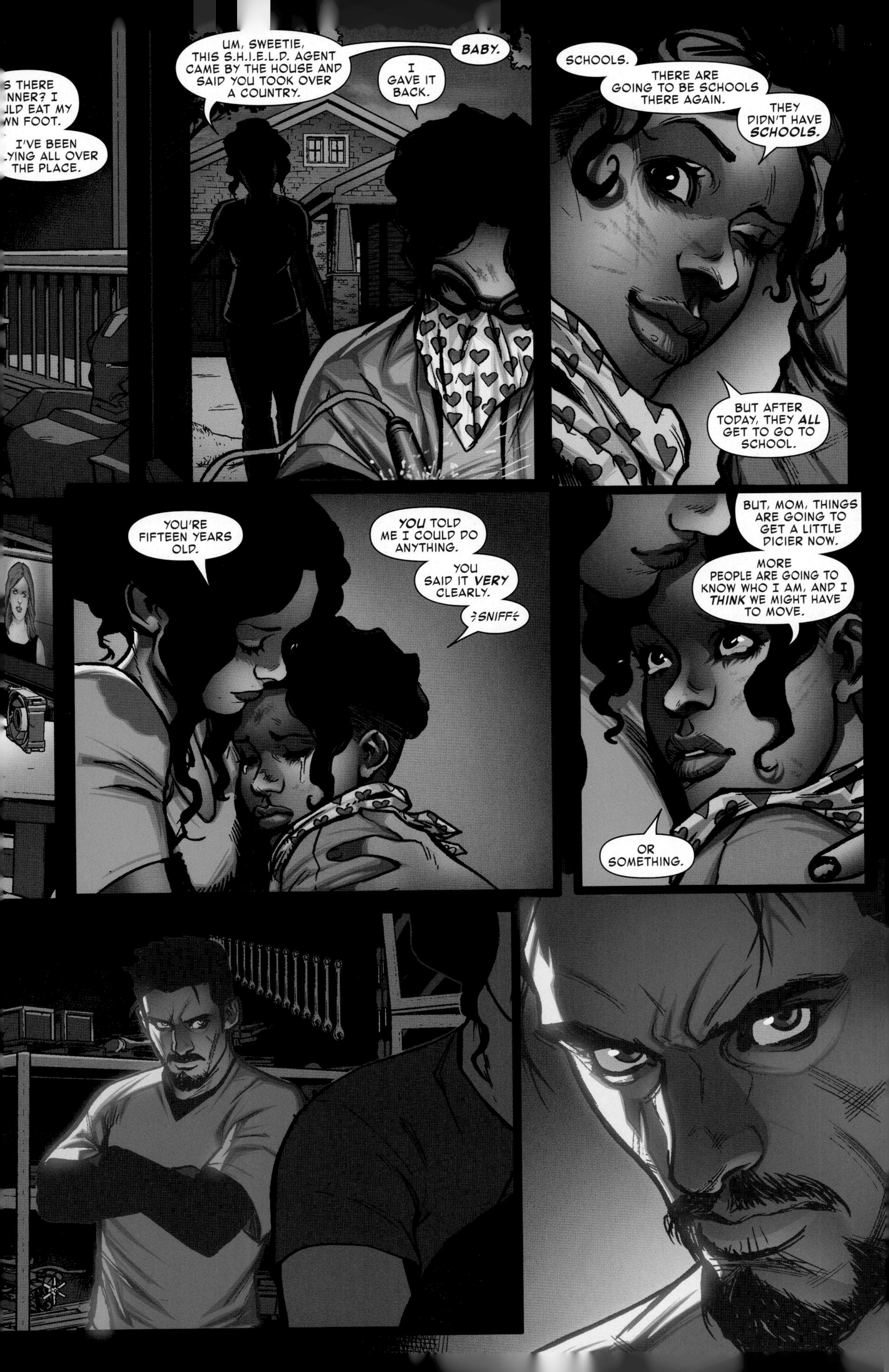

S THERE
NNER? I
LD EAT MY
WN FOOT.
I'VE BEEN
YING ALL OVER
THE PLACE.
UM, SWEETIE, THIS S.H.I.E.L.D. AGENT CAME BY THE HOUSE AND SAID YOU TOOK OVER A COUNTRY.
BABY.
I GAVE IT BACK.
SCHOOLS.
THERE ARE GOING TO BE SCHOOLS THERE AGAIN.
THEY DIDN'T HAVE SCHOOLS.
BUT AFTER TODAY, THEY ALL GET TO GO TO SCHOOL.
YOU'RE FIFTEEN YEARS OLD.
YOU TOLD ME I COULD DO ANYTHING.
YOU SAID IT VERY CLEARLY.
SNIFF
BUT, MOM, THINGS ARE GOING TO GET A LITTLE DICIER NOW.
MORE PEOPLE ARE GOING TO KNOW WHO I AM, AND I THINK WE MIGHT HAVE TO MOVE.
OR SOMETHING.

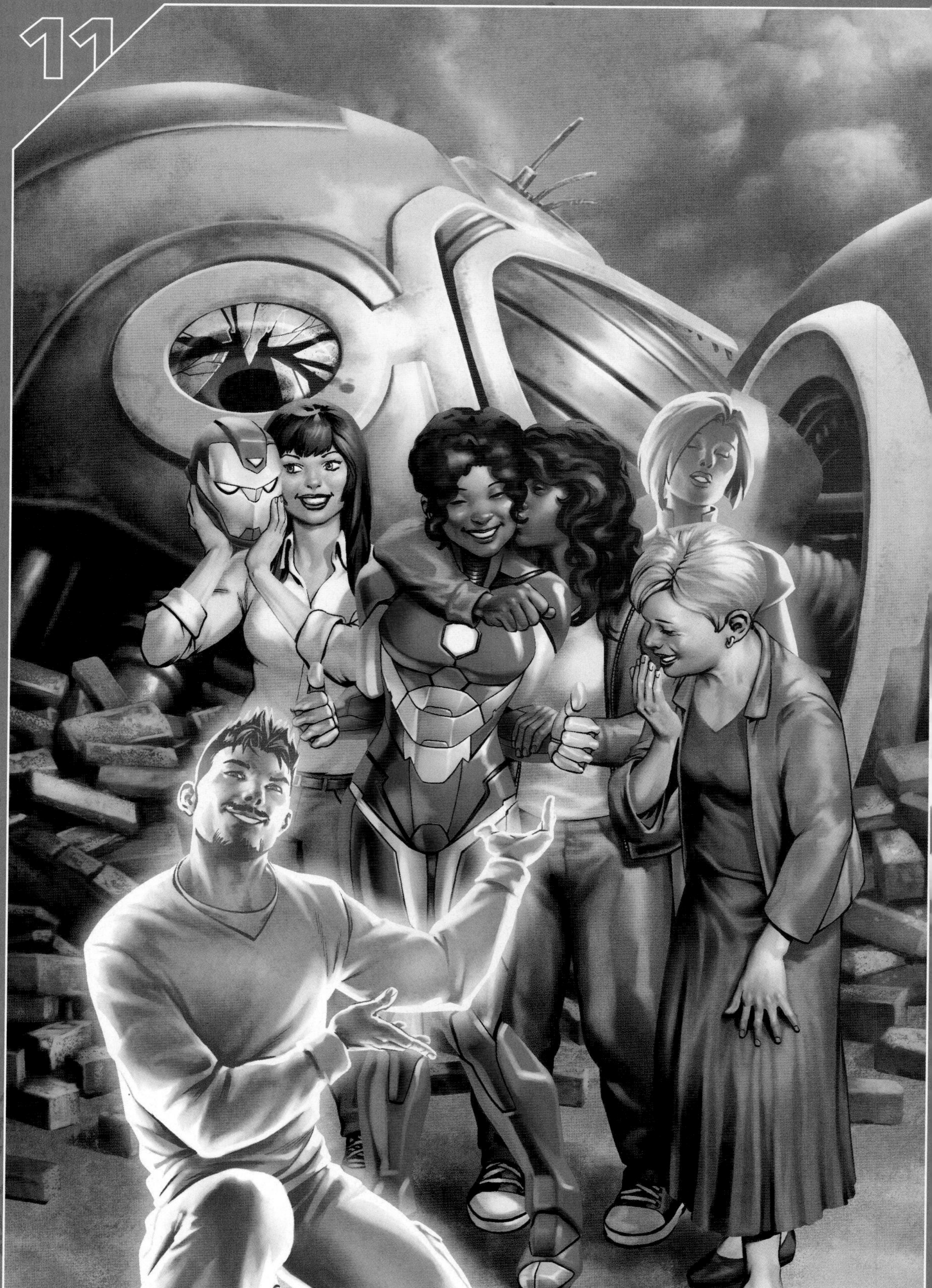
11

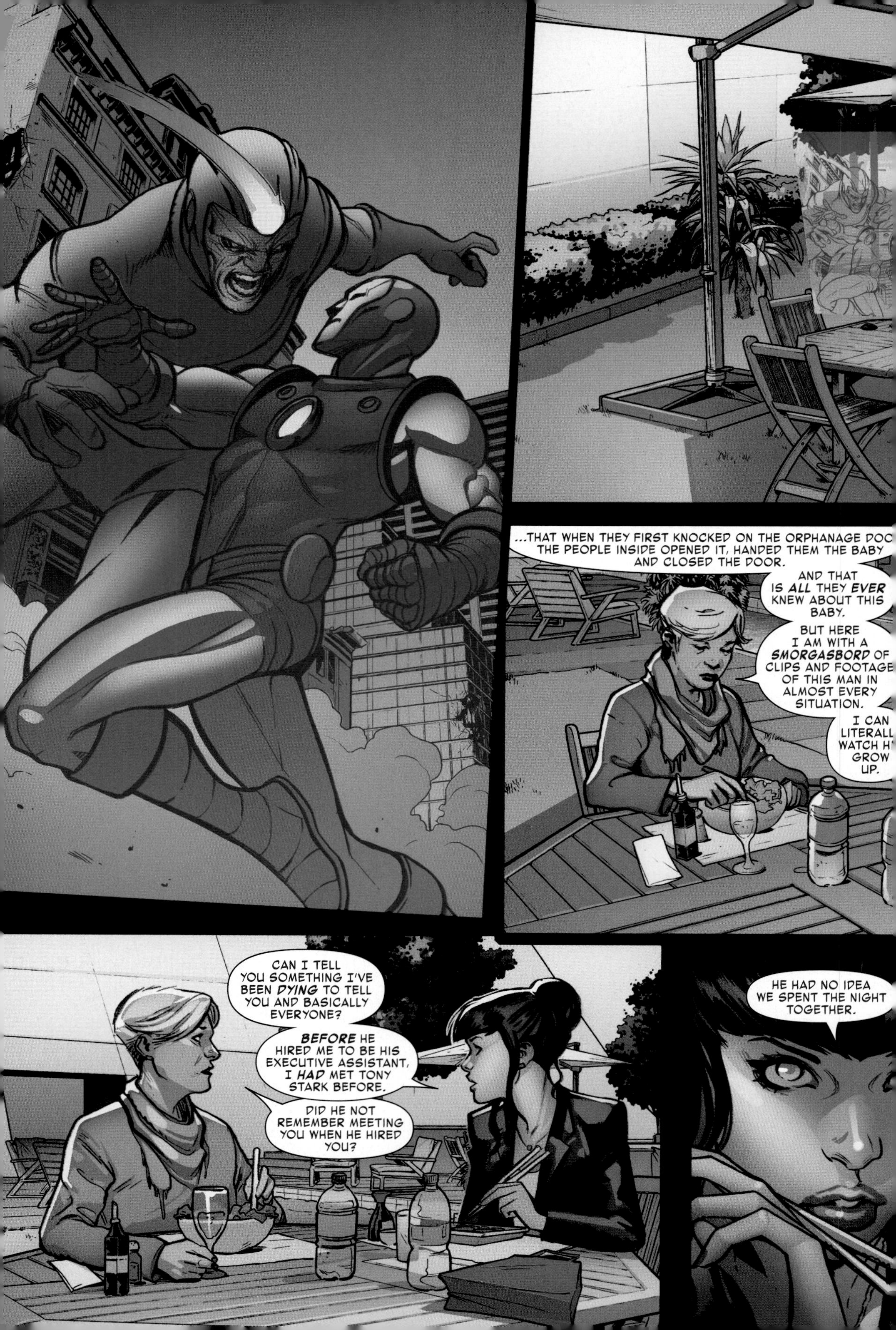

...THAT WHEN THEY FIRST KNOCKED ON THE ORPHANAGE DOO
THE PEOPLE INSIDE OPENED IT, HANDED THEM THE BABY AND CLOSED THE DOOR.
AND THAT IS ALL THEY EVER KNEW ABOUT THIS BABY.
BUT HERE I AM WITH A SMORGASBORD OF CLIPS AND FOOTAGE OF THIS MAN IN ALMOST EVERY SITUATION.
I CAN LITERALL WATCH H GROW UP.
CAN I TELL YOU SOMETHING I'VE BEEN DYING TO TELL YOU AND BASICALLY EVERYONE?
BEFORE HE HIRED ME TO BE HIS EXECUTIVE ASSISTANT, I HAD MET TONY STARK BEFORE.
DID HE NOT REMEMBER MEETING YOU WHEN HE HIRED YOU?
HE HAD NO IDEA WE SPENT THE NIGHT TOGETHER.

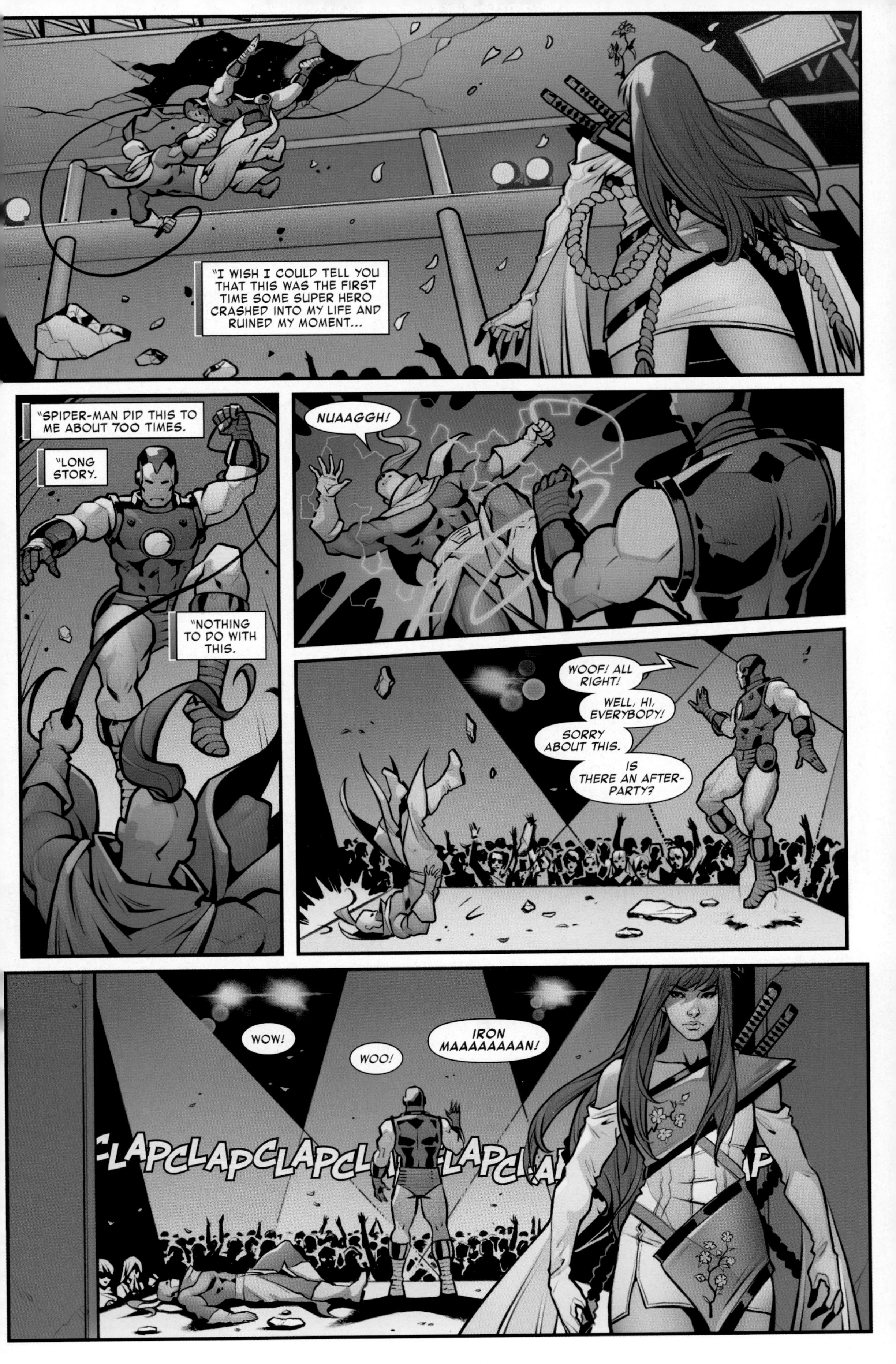
"I WISH I COULD TELL YOU THAT THIS WAS THE FIRST TIME SOME SUPER HERO CRASHED INTO MY LIFE AND RUINED MY MOMENT...
"SPIDER-MAN DID THIS TO ME ABOUT 700 TIMES.
"LONG STORY.
"NOTHING TO DO WITH THIS.
NUAAGGH!
WOOF! ALL RIGHT!
WELL, HI, EVERYBODY!
SORRY ABOUT THIS.
IS THERE AN AFTER-PARTY?
WOW!
WOO!
IRON MAAAAAAAAN!
CLAPCLAPCLAPCLAPCLAPCLAPCLAPCLAP

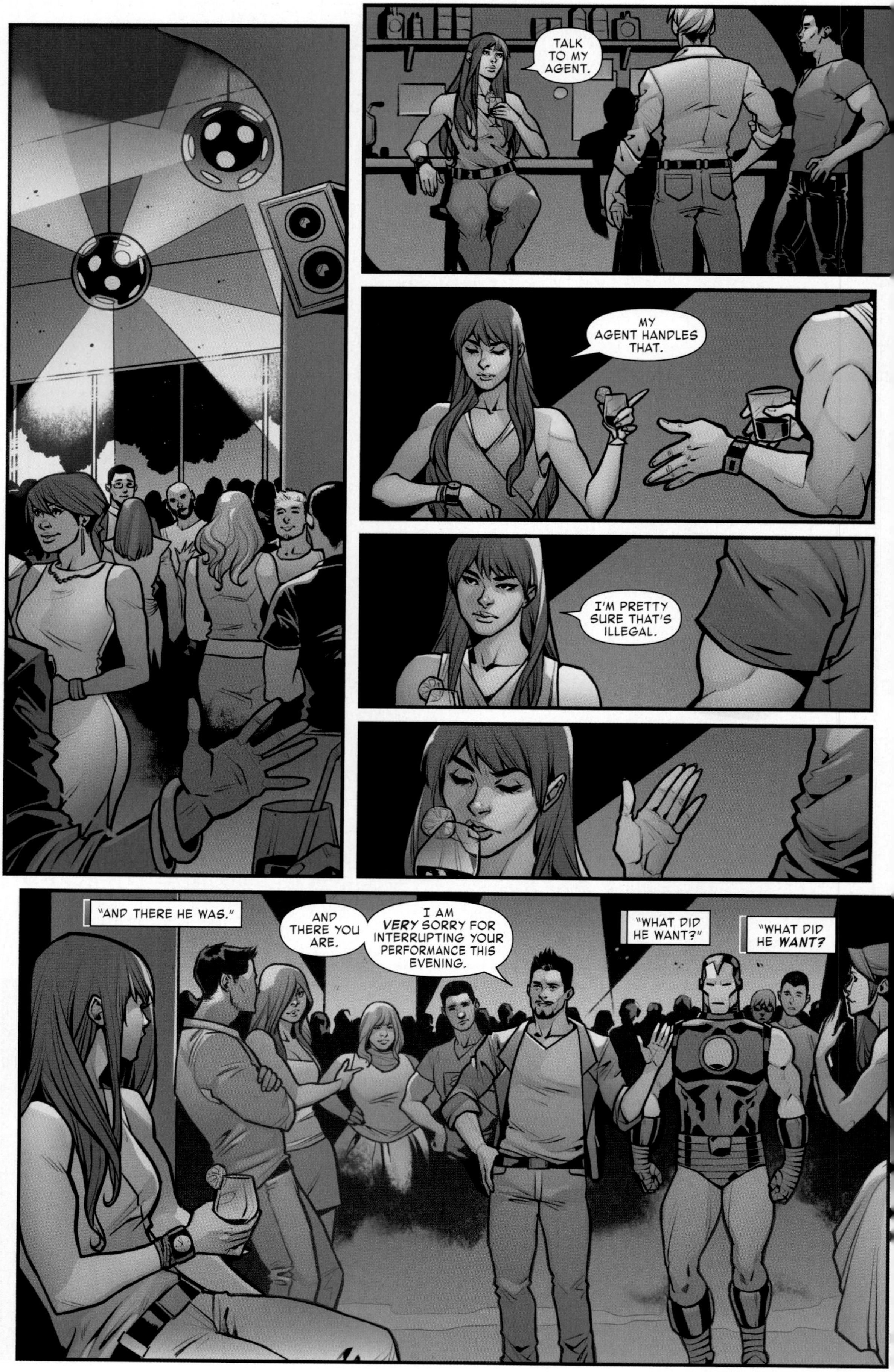

TALK TO MY AGENT.
MY AGENT HANDLES THAT.
I'M PRETTY SURE THAT'S ILLEGAL.
"AND THERE HE WAS."
AND THERE YOU ARE.
I AM *VERY* SORRY FOR INTERRUPTING YOUR PERFORMANCE THIS EVENING.
"WHAT DID HE WANT?"
"WHAT DID HE *WANT?*

DID ANYONE EVER TELL YOU YOU SHOULD BE A MODEL?

I'M TONY STARK.

CUTE.

MARY JANE WATSON.

I KNOW.

WHAT DO YOU KNOW?

I KNOW YOU'RE A QUEENS GIRL MAKING YOUR WAY IN THE BIG, BAD WORLD.

AND *HERE* YOU ARE...IN MILAN. KICKING ASS. MAKING YOUR WAY.

UNTIL SOME STUPID AVENGER BODYGUARD CAME IN AND RUINED IT.

KTANG

"THIS WAS BACK WHEN TONY PRETENDED IRON MAN WAS A DIFFERENT GUY...HIS BODYGUARD.

"REMEMBER THAT?"

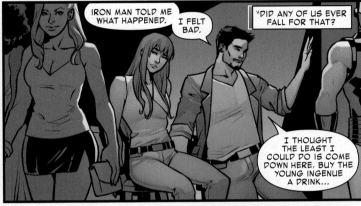

IRON MAN TOLD ME WHAT HAPPENED. I FELT BAD.

"DID ANY OF US EVER FALL FOR THAT?

I THOUGHT THE LEAST I COULD DO IS COME DOWN HERE, BUY THE YOUNG INGENUE A DRINK...

...OR A DINNER...

...OR TAKE HER TO THE CARIBBEAN FOR THE NEXT TWO WEEKS...

UGH!

"UGH"?

DOES THAT KIND OF THING REALLY WORK?

YOU KNOW, IT'S INTERESTING...

...IT *DOES* WORK.

I DON'T ALWAYS TRUST THE STANDARDS OF WOMEN IT WORKS ON...

YET...

...YET I KEEP DOING IT.

WHY DON'T YOU TRY BEING HONEST?

SOME OF US GIRLS *LIKE* HONEST.

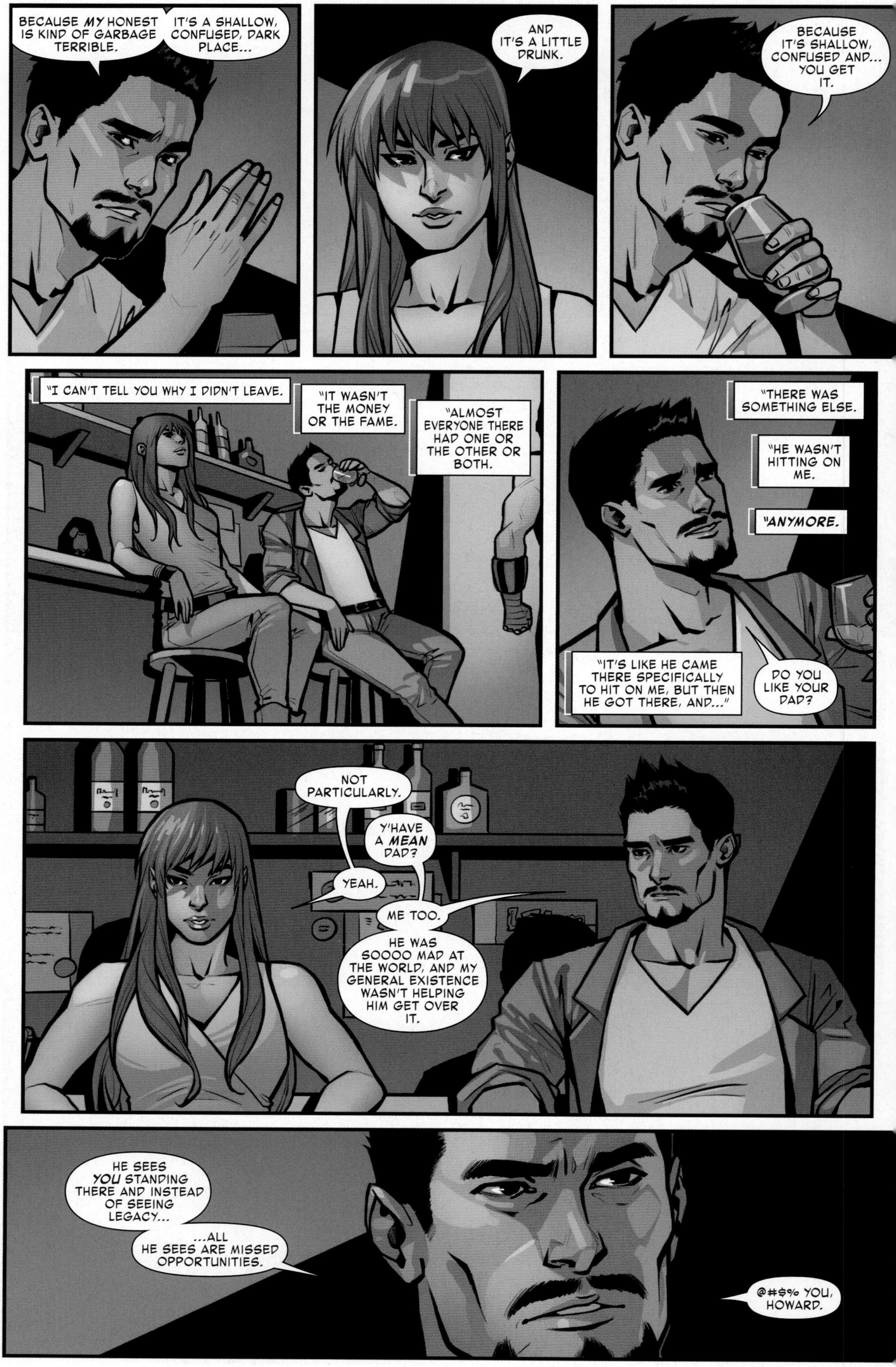
BECAUSE MY HONEST IS KIND OF GARBAGE TERRIBLE.
IT'S A SHALLOW, CONFUSED, DARK PLACE...
AND IT'S A LITTLE DRUNK.
BECAUSE IT'S SHALLOW, CONFUSED AND... YOU GET IT.
"I CAN'T TELL YOU WHY I DIDN'T LEAVE.
"IT WASN'T THE MONEY OR THE FAME.
"ALMOST EVERYONE THERE HAD ONE OR THE OTHER OR BOTH.
"THERE WAS SOMETHING ELSE.
"HE WASN'T HITTING ON ME.
"ANYMORE.
"IT'S LIKE HE CAME THERE SPECIFICALLY TO HIT ON ME, BUT THEN HE GOT THERE, AND..."
DO YOU LIKE YOUR DAD?
NOT PARTICULARLY.
Y'HAVE A MEAN DAD?
YEAH.
ME TOO.
HE WAS SOOOO MAD AT THE WORLD, AND MY GENERAL EXISTENCE WASN'T HELPING HIM GET OVER IT.
HE SEES YOU STANDING THERE AND INSTEAD OF SEEING LEGACY...
...ALL HE SEES ARE MISSED OPPORTUNITIES.
@#$% YOU, HOWARD.

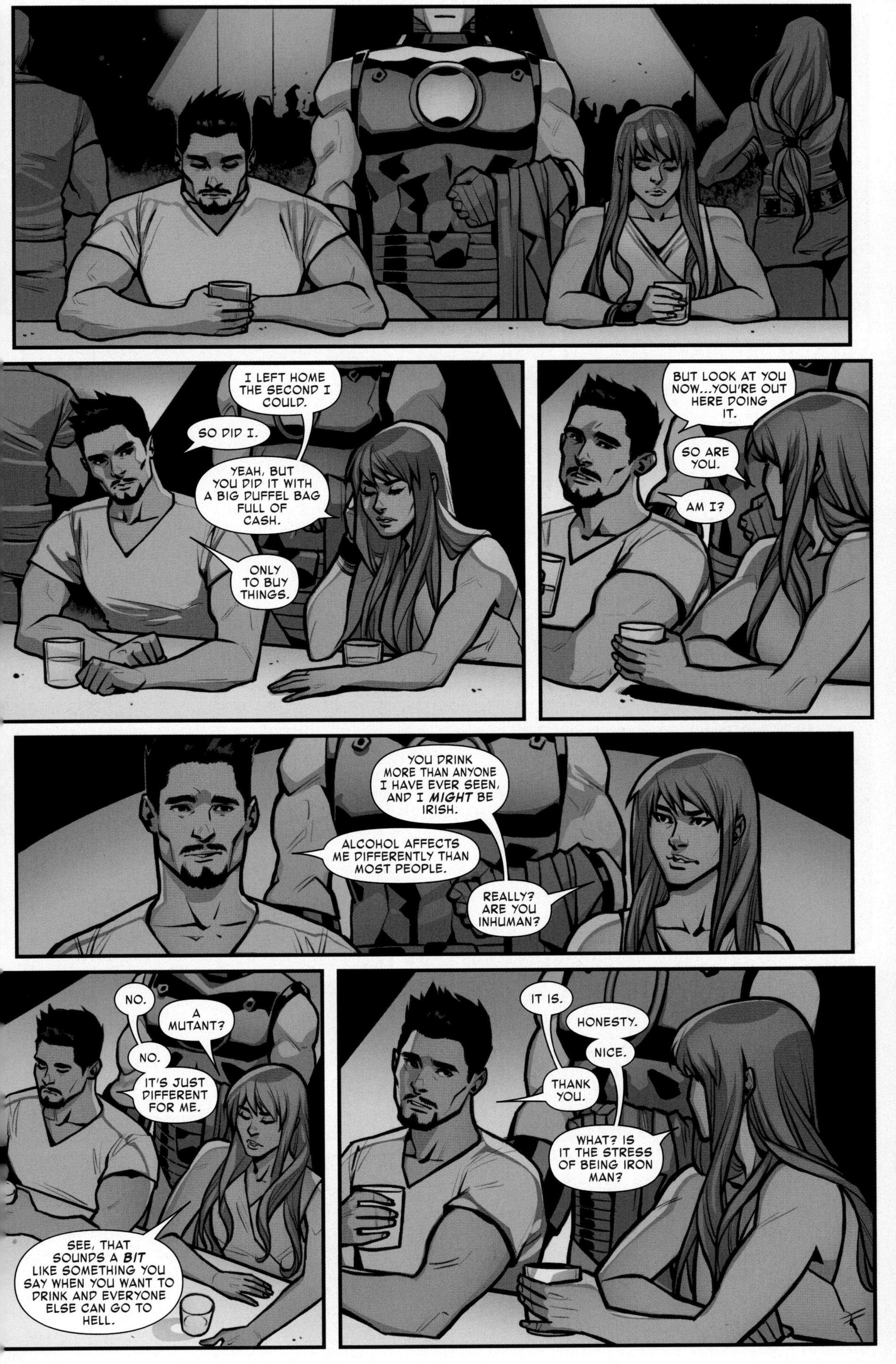
I LEFT HOME THE SECOND I COULD.
SO DID I.
YEAH, BUT YOU DID IT WITH A BIG DUFFEL BAG FULL OF CASH.
ONLY TO BUY THINGS.
BUT LOOK AT YOU NOW...YOU'RE OUT HERE DOING IT.
SO ARE YOU.
AM I?
YOU DRINK MORE THAN ANYONE I HAVE EVER SEEN, AND I *MIGHT* BE IRISH.
ALCOHOL AFFECTS ME DIFFERENTLY THAN MOST PEOPLE.
REALLY? ARE YOU INHUMAN?
NO.
A MUTANT?
NO.
IT'S JUST DIFFERENT FOR ME.
SEE, THAT SOUNDS A *BIT* LIKE SOMETHING YOU SAY WHEN YOU WANT TO DRINK AND EVERYONE ELSE CAN GO TO HELL.
IT IS.
HONESTY.
NICE.
THANK YOU.
WHAT? IS IT THE STRESS OF BEING IRON MAN?

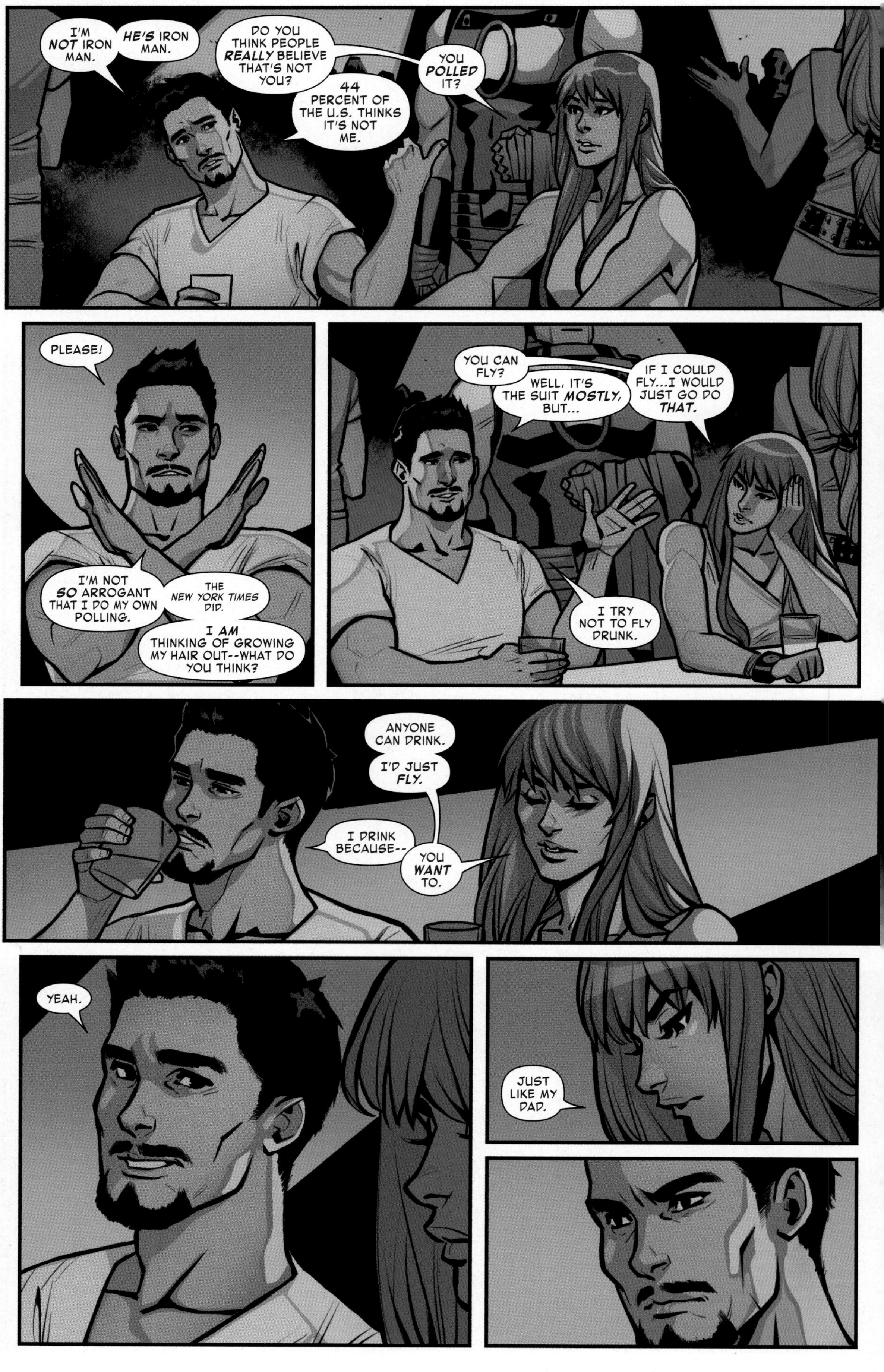

I'M NOT IRON MAN.
HE'S IRON MAN.
DO YOU THINK PEOPLE REALLY BELIEVE THAT'S NOT YOU?
YOU POLLED IT?
44 PERCENT OF THE U.S. THINKS IT'S NOT ME.
PLEASE!
I'M NOT SO ARROGANT THAT I DO MY OWN POLLING.
THE NEW YORK TIMES DID.
I AM THINKING OF GROWING MY HAIR OUT--WHAT DO YOU THINK?
YOU CAN FLY?
WELL, IT'S THE SUIT MOSTLY, BUT...
IF I COULD FLY...I WOULD JUST GO DO THAT.
I TRY NOT TO FLY DRUNK.
ANYONE CAN DRINK.
I'D JUST FLY.
I DRINK BECAUSE--
YOU WANT TO.
YEAH.
JUST LIKE MY DAD.

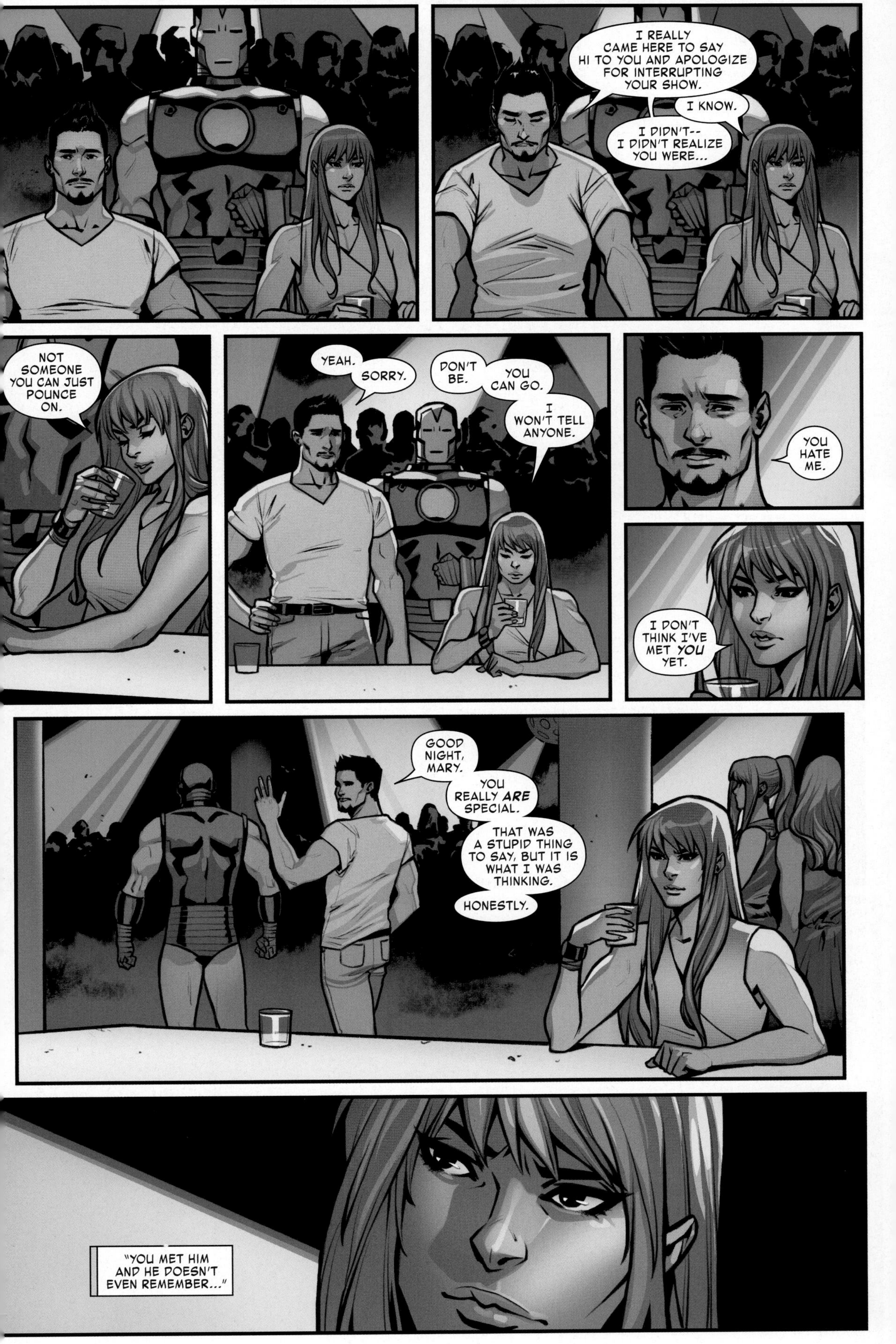
I REALLY CAME HERE TO SAY HI TO YOU AND APOLOGIZE FOR INTERRUPTING YOUR SHOW.
I KNOW.
I DIDN'T-- I DIDN'T REALIZE YOU WERE...
NOT SOMEONE YOU CAN JUST POUNCE ON.
YEAH.
SORRY.
DON'T BE.
YOU CAN GO.
I WON'T TELL ANYONE.
YOU HATE ME.
I DON'T THINK I'VE MET *YOU* YET.
GOOD NIGHT, MARY.
YOU REALLY *ARE* SPECIAL.
THAT WAS A STUPID THING TO SAY, BUT IT IS WHAT I WAS THINKING.
HONESTLY.
"YOU MET HIM AND HE DOESN'T EVEN REMEMBER..."

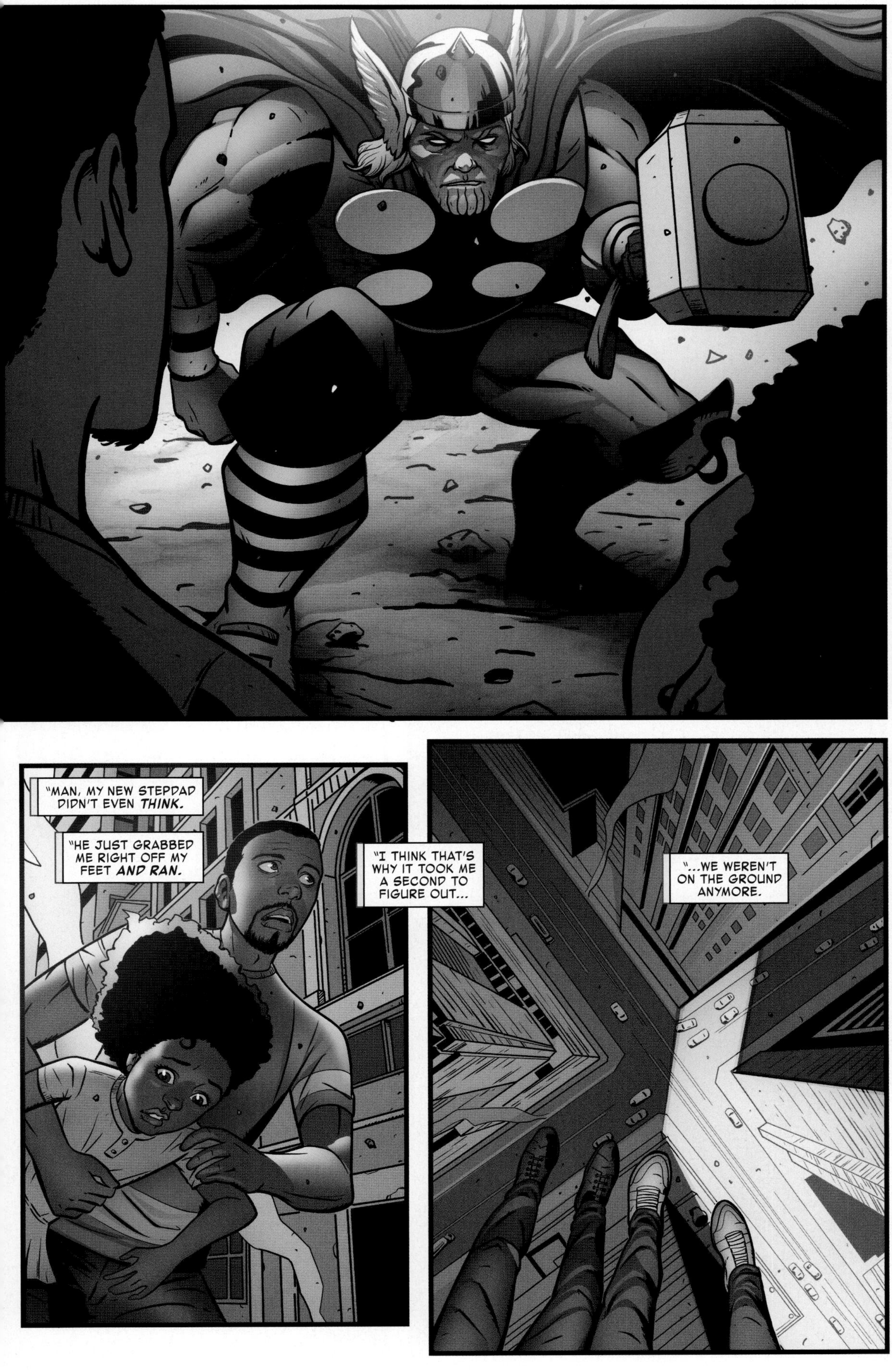
"MAN, MY NEW STEPDAD DIDN'T EVEN *THINK.*
"HE JUST GRABBED ME RIGHT OFF MY FEET *AND RAN.*
"I THINK THAT'S WHY IT TOOK ME A SECOND TO FIGURE OUT...
"...WE WEREN'T ON THE GROUND ANYMORE.

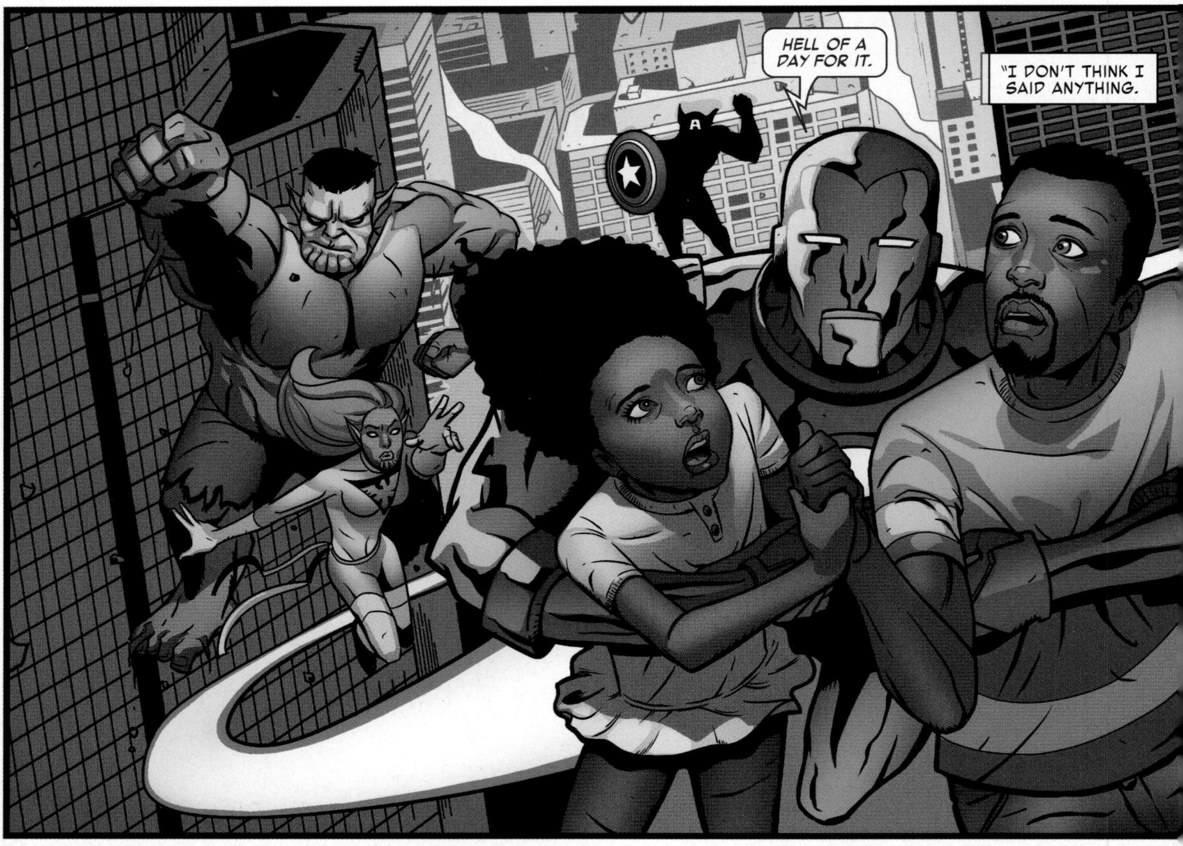
"I DON'T THINK I SAID ANYTHING.
HELL OF A DAY FOR IT.

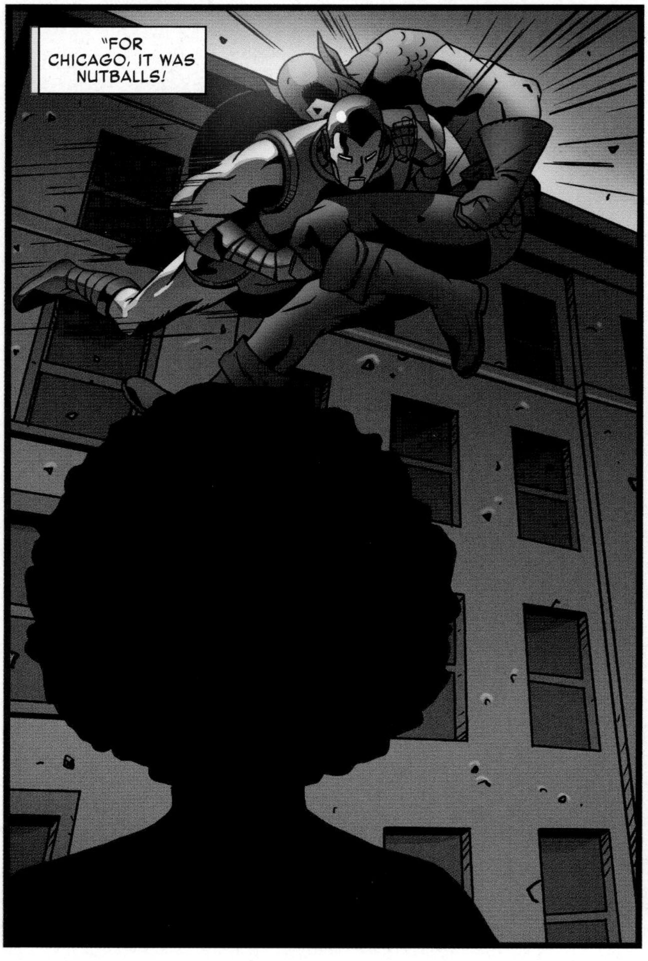
"FOR CHICAGO, IT WAS NUTBALLS!

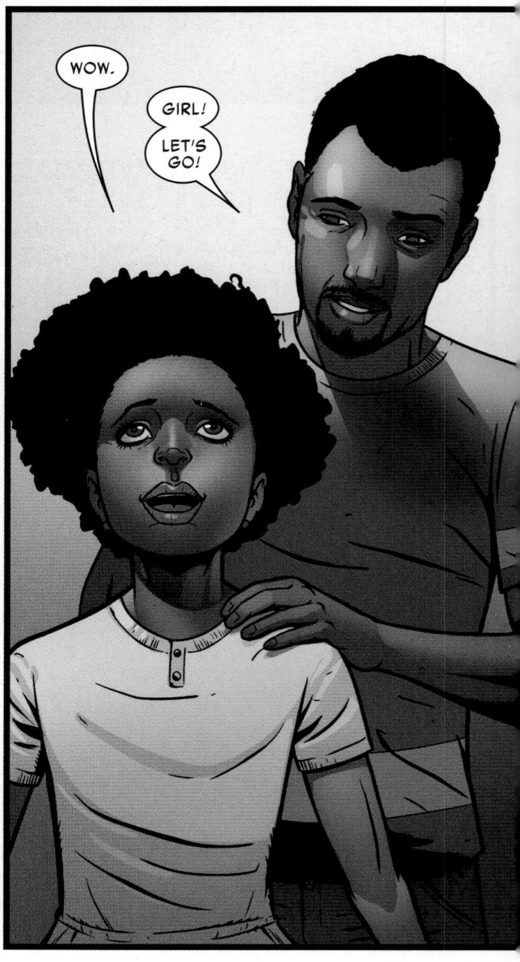
WOW.
GIRL!
LET'S GO!

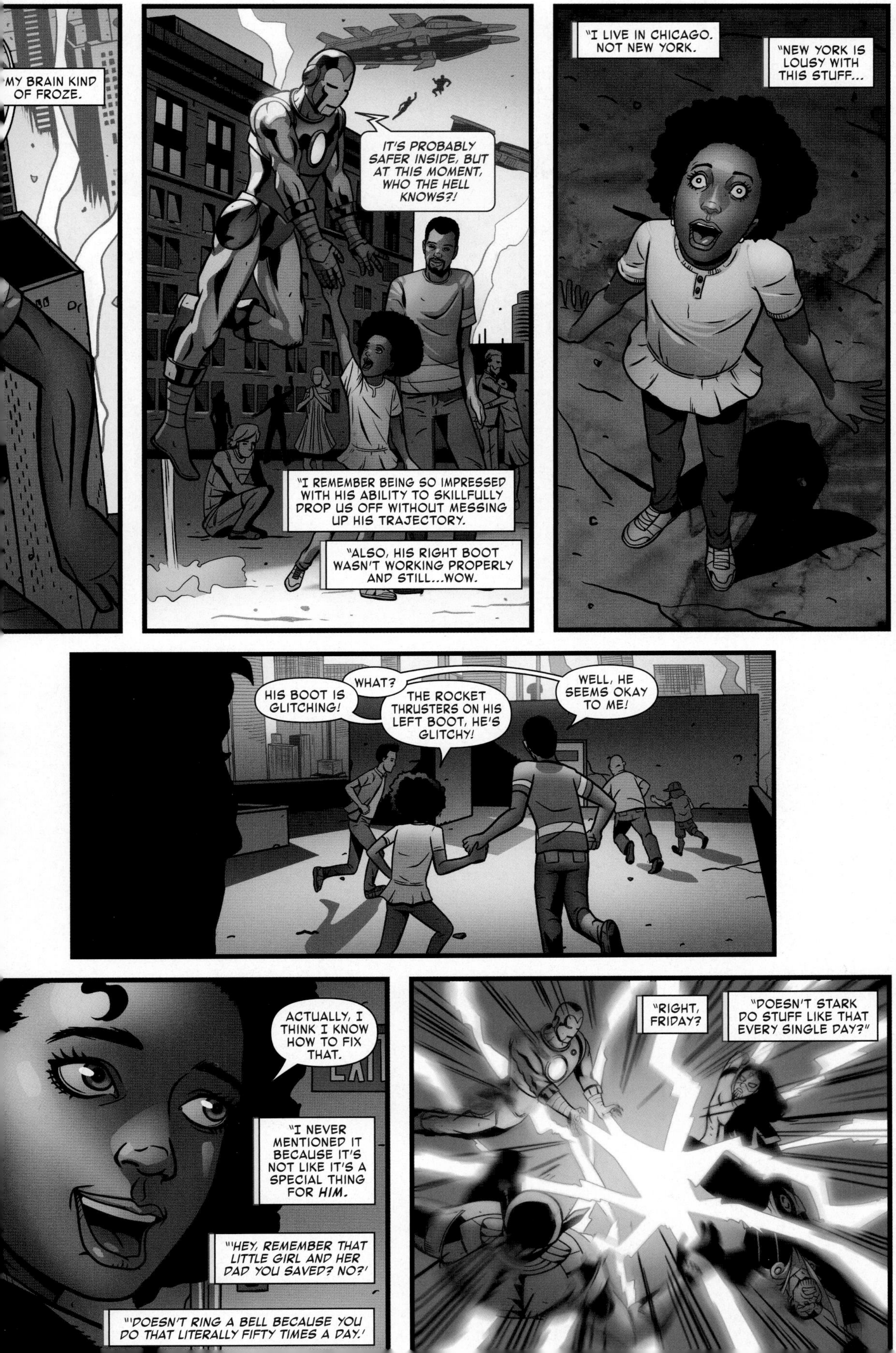

"MY BRAIN KIND OF FROZE.
IT'S PROBABLY SAFER INSIDE, BUT AT THIS MOMENT, WHO THE HELL KNOWS?!
"I REMEMBER BEING SO IMPRESSED WITH HIS ABILITY TO SKILLFULLY DROP US OFF WITHOUT MESSING UP HIS TRAJECTORY.
"ALSO, HIS RIGHT BOOT WASN'T WORKING PROPERLY AND STILL...WOW.
"I LIVE IN CHICAGO. NOT NEW YORK.
"NEW YORK IS LOUSY WITH THIS STUFF...
HIS BOOT IS GLITCHING!
WHAT?
THE ROCKET THRUSTERS ON HIS LEFT BOOT, HE'S GLITCHY!
WELL, HE SEEMS OKAY TO ME!
ACTUALLY, I THINK I KNOW HOW TO FIX THAT.
"I NEVER MENTIONED IT BECAUSE IT'S NOT LIKE IT'S A SPECIAL THING FOR HIM.
"'HEY, REMEMBER THAT LITTLE GIRL AND HER DAD YOU SAVED? NO?'
"'DOESN'T RING A BELL BECAUSE YOU DO THAT LITERALLY FIFTY TIMES A DAY.'
"RIGHT, FRIDAY?
"DOESN'T STARK DO STUFF LIKE THAT EVERY SINGLE DAY?"

NEXT: THE SEARCH FOR TONY STARK!

11 LETTER BY BRIAN MICHAEL BENDIS

Hi. It's Brian. I've been writing IRON MAN for a few years but this is my first letter column. I wanted to take a moment to talk about this issue. We have some VERY special guest artists with us, whom I will get to in a minute, but I wanted to tell you about who this issue is dedicated to and why.

I live in Portland, Oregon. When you move to a new neighborhood, one of the big X factors is your neighbors. Who will they be? Will we like each other? Will we go to war over a shrub? We had just left one of those great old neighborhoods where we became friends and family with almost all of our neighbors. We were worried about missing out on that special feeling.

That's when we met our NEW across-the-street neighbors of the last seven years...the Cheeks. Let me tell you about Dick Cheek. Make the jokes. He's heard them all.

His name is Richard Cheek and I soon found out he's a real super hero.

Dick and his wife, Helen, both in their eighties, and their eight adult children (!) are just amazing people. Great positive energy EVERYWHERE they go. Big on community. BIG on helping out anyone who needs a little help, be it through church, community organizing or just looking out. Almost to an unbelievable degree.

I could literally spend this entire issue listing kindnesses I know of or witnessed them do. It's exhaustive. It's crazy. Who is this nice? For all these years, they did us neighborly kindnesses that we never asked for. Did I say he was in his eighties? Yes. But you couldn't tell. Such a zest for life.

It just so happened, after the first time I had met him, I had to run off to a Marvel retreat. In the cab on the way to the airport, the cab driver looked at Dick's house, turned to me and said: "Oh my God! You live across the street from the Cheeks. He saved my father's life in the war. He's a genuine war hero. I wouldn't be here if not for him. Has he ever told you about that?"

The next time I got a chance to ask him, he blew it off warmly and just chuckled. Then, I heard from his children that he was the real deal.

I will honor his service by not speaking of things he clearly did not want spoken of...but he was a war hero.

As our relationship developed over the years, he told me that his priest happened to be a huge comic book fan and wanted to talk to me about the spirituality of comics over dinner. The Jew in me expected a "hip" younger priest into SPIDER-MAN or GUARDIANS OF THE GALAXY. You know, for the kids! I was surprised to find this big, gray-haired, Brian-Dennehy-with-a-priest-collar shake my hand and say, "I love ALIAS and *Powers.*" To have a man of the cloth tell you how much he loves your basically rated R work was the beginning of a surreal and spiritually exciting dinner. One of the most fun dinners I've ever had. It changed my work. For the better.

So over the last few years, my wife started including the Cheeks at our semi-regular Friday night dinners. A dinner MOSTLY for our Portland comics peer group. So many of my friends, who just happen to be some of your favorite comic creators, have become big fans and friends of the Cheeks as well.

Well, as it goes, this summer both Helen and Dick started to feel their age. I was at their 65th wedding anniversary party, and they showed a slide show of family, mountain hiking, world travel and real adventure that was awe-inspiring to say the least. When the Cheeks started to slow down you could feel it.

Dick's health started to slip and he had been in hospice for most of the summer. We would visit and Helen would be frustrated that she was in the hospital because Dick needed her...and he said the exact same thing about her. Just heartwarming. My wife and I have been happily married for over 20 years and it gave US relationship goals.

During his time in hospice, Dick came over. He could feel everyone's stress about the situation. He came over just to tell me, "Hey, tell everyone that I'm okay. That I've lived a long and fortunate life. My kids are amazing, my wife loves me and I think I left the world a little better than the way I found it. I'm really okay with everything that's happening now. I'm good to go."

And then he said, after attending dozens of dinners at my house with all of your favorite kind of comic creators, "Hey, did I ever tell you that I was friends with Walt Kelly?"

After seven years of knowing each other, I turned to him and said with an incredulous smile, "No, Dick, I did not know you were friends with one of the greatest cartoonists of all time." He then pulled out the correspondence between the two of them, and the original art that Walt Kelly had given him as a present, and some other insane Walt Kelly memorabilia. I was blown away, and I told our mutual friend, and one of the artists of this issue, Taki Soma--and Taki said, "That's my favorite artist of all time." I guess I'm not surprised, but I am surprised, because when I told Dick, he gave Taki and me his Walt Kelly original art, memorabilia and correspondence.

I didn't want to take it. He has kids. They should have it. I told the sons. They made it very clear that Dick wanted us to have it. I said I could donate it to a library cartoonist archive. I was told no. He wanted us to have it. It might even be why we met, so one of his lifelong prize possessions could have a truly appreciative home.

Seven years and this war-hero super hero never told me he was one of us. Secret nerd!

The reason this specific issue is dedicated to him is that a couple weeks ago, his son walked over just to say hi to my wife and me. Stunned to have just learned this himself, he asked us, "Did you know that my father, when he has time, goes to hospitals and just holds the babies?"

We were as stunned as he was. Who does that? Who does that and doesn't tell anybody?

Yeah, the most unbelievable concept in this issue was based on the true Dick Cheek. I was told this as I was thinking, what's the coolest thing Tony Stark could've done that no one knows he's done? I really wrote that question down for this issue and then Dick's son comes over and drops this on me.

So, inspired, I wrote this issue and I went over and I told them. Of course, he was a little embarrassed, but his wife and his kids were thrilled.

Then this issue started to reveal a fragmented structure, and I thought this gave us this great opportunity to spotlight some different artists for this issue. Stefano was going to need a little bit of a break to get to our big Legacy story next issue anyhow, and I thought this was a great opportunity to join Kelly Sue DeConnick's "Visible Women" Twitter campaign and shine a spotlight on some female creators in this book filled with female voices. And now Taki Soma makes her Marvel Comics debut for an issue especially dedicated to a good friend of both of ours. He gave us something special to keep of his and we wanted to give you something of him.

Kate Niemczyk blew me away with her work on MOCKINGBIRD, and I have been dying to do something with her--and Tom Brevoort, in his travels, showed me the world of Kiichi Mizushima. It's like she fell out of the sky to bring the perfect voice to her chapter. I would like to report that, behind the scenes, Stefano and all the artists had an amazing creative experience. They have been emailing all month. The book was made with love from beginning to end, just like the man the book is dedicated to.

The reason I'm telling you all of this is, about two hours ago, he passed away. In my heart, I hoped that I could give him this issue before he passed, but he passed this morning before it went to print.

I don't know when you'll be reading this, but if you're reading it the day it came out, I think you can agree that the world has been a hot mess lately. One of my personal ways of dealing with the stress of it is knowing that there are people in the world like the Cheeks.

I thought you'd like a reminder, too. They are people who do kindnesses because that's what you're supposed to do. In his honor, today, if you find someone that needs a little kindness, maybe stop and do it. Do that.

Be an honest-to-goodness real super hero like Dick Cheek. A kindness is all it takes.

— BENDIS!

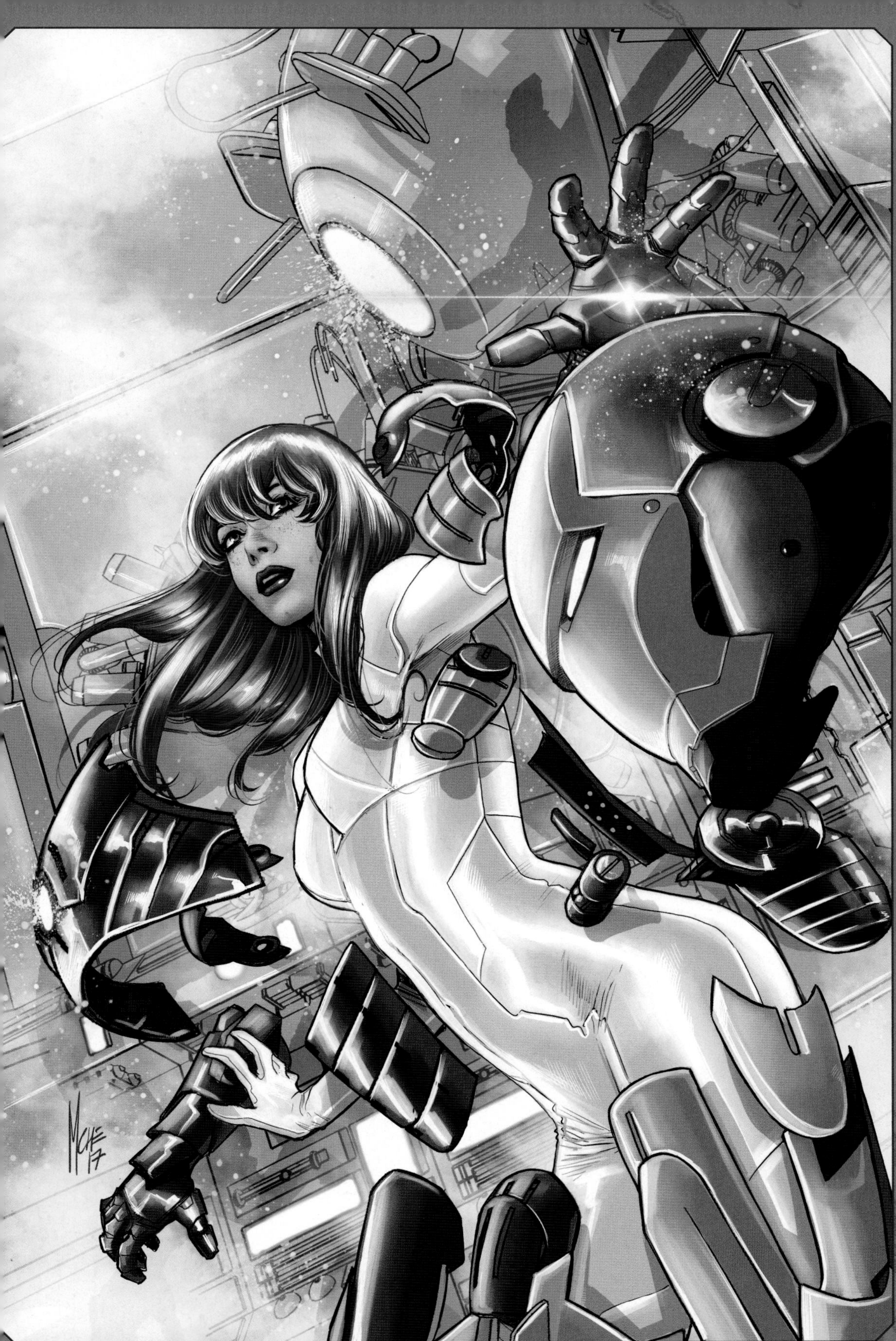
MCHE
17

MARCO CHECCHETTO

9 MARY JANE VARIANT

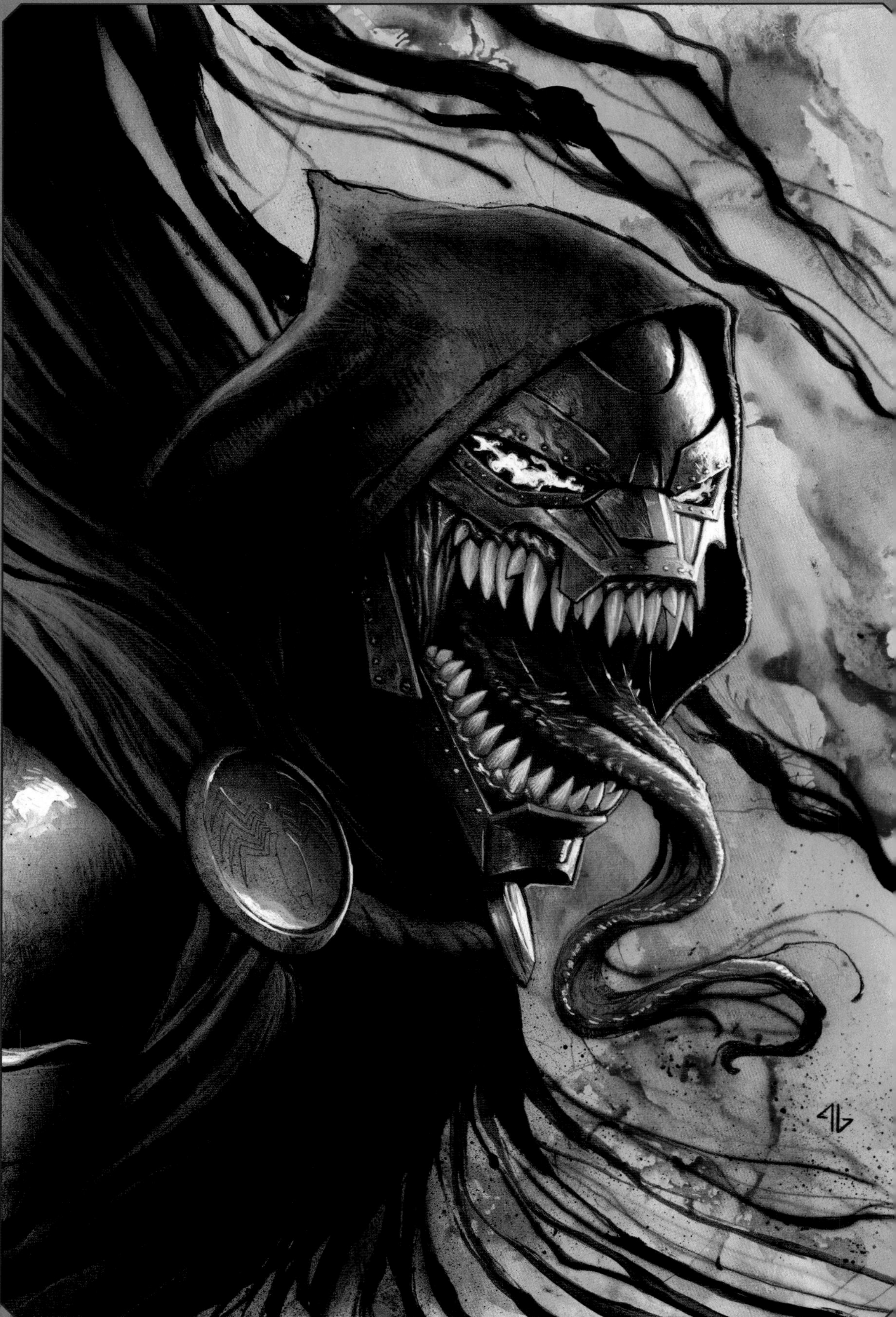

ADI GRANOV

11 VENOMIZED VILLAINS VARIANT

STEFANO CASELLI

ISSUE 8, PAGE 21 ART

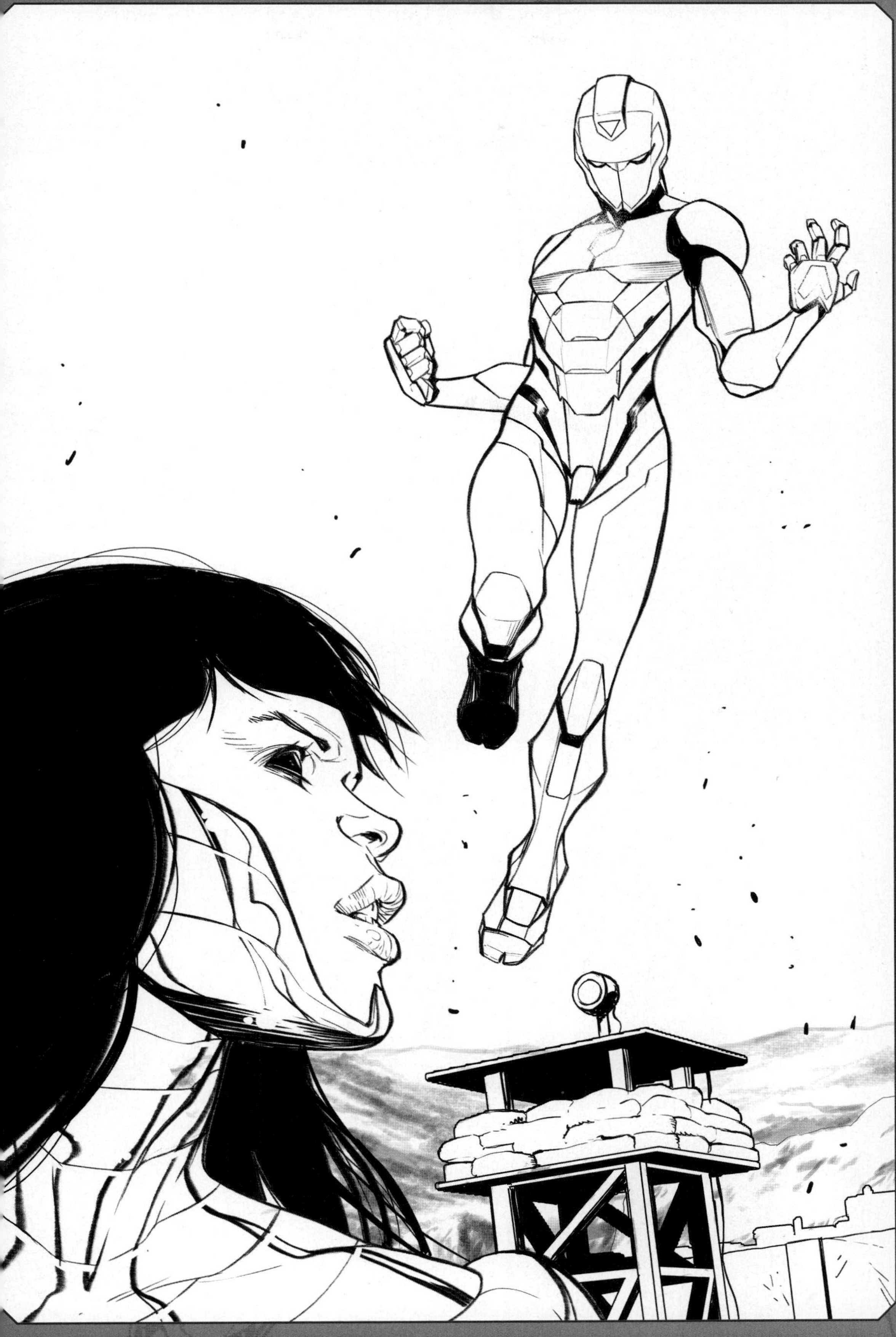

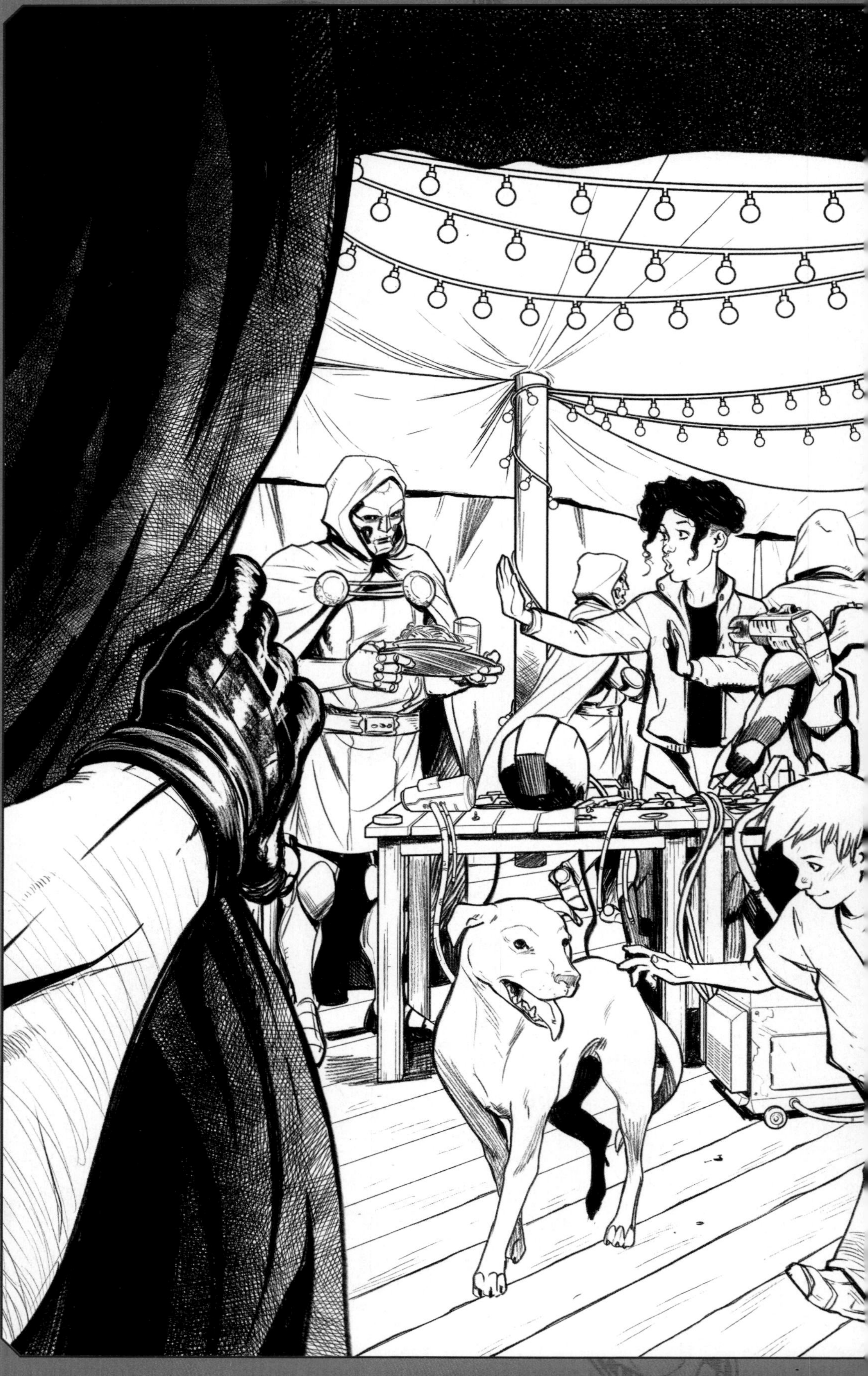

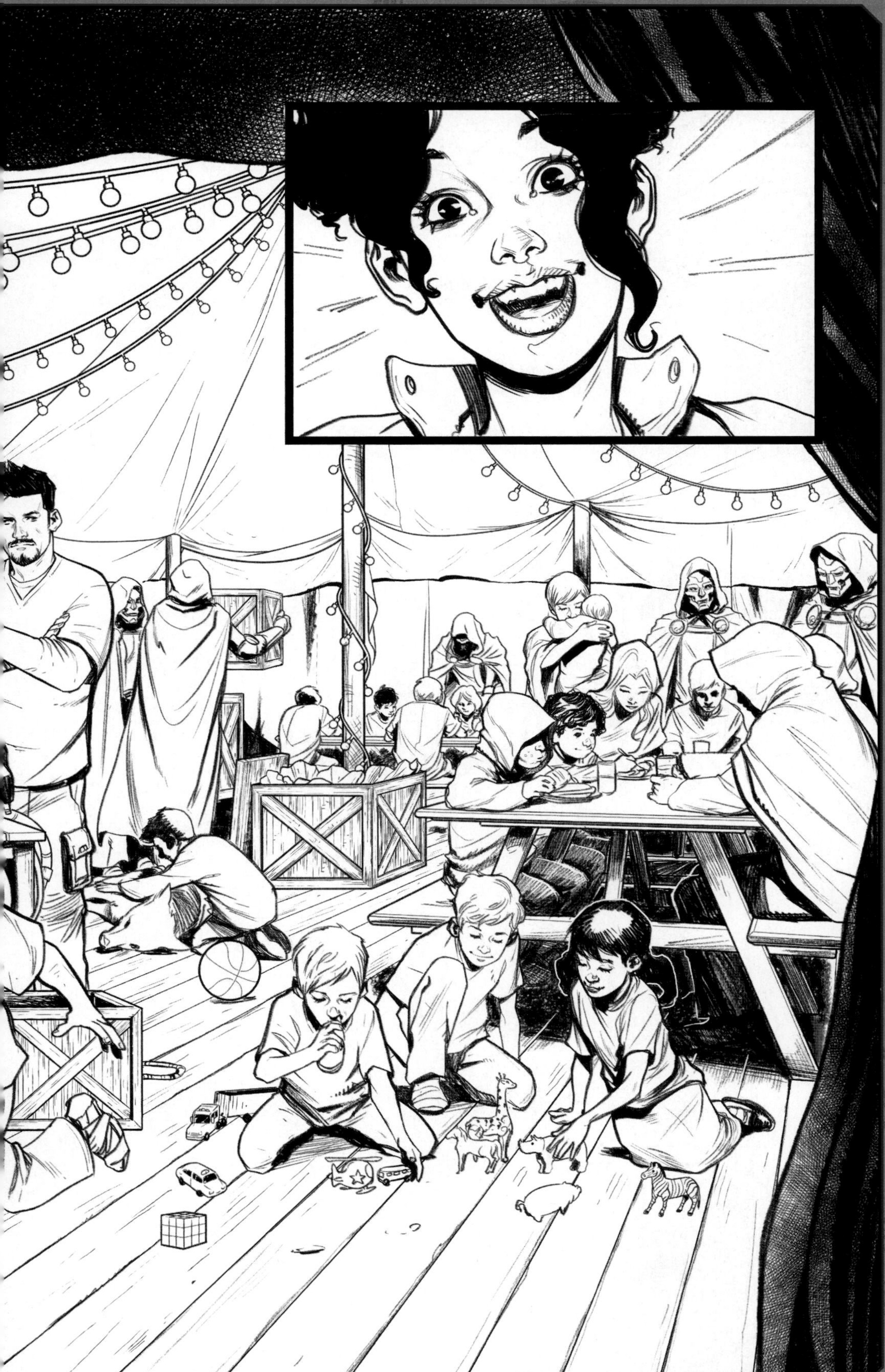

KATE NIEMCZYK

ISSUE 11, PAGE 4 ART

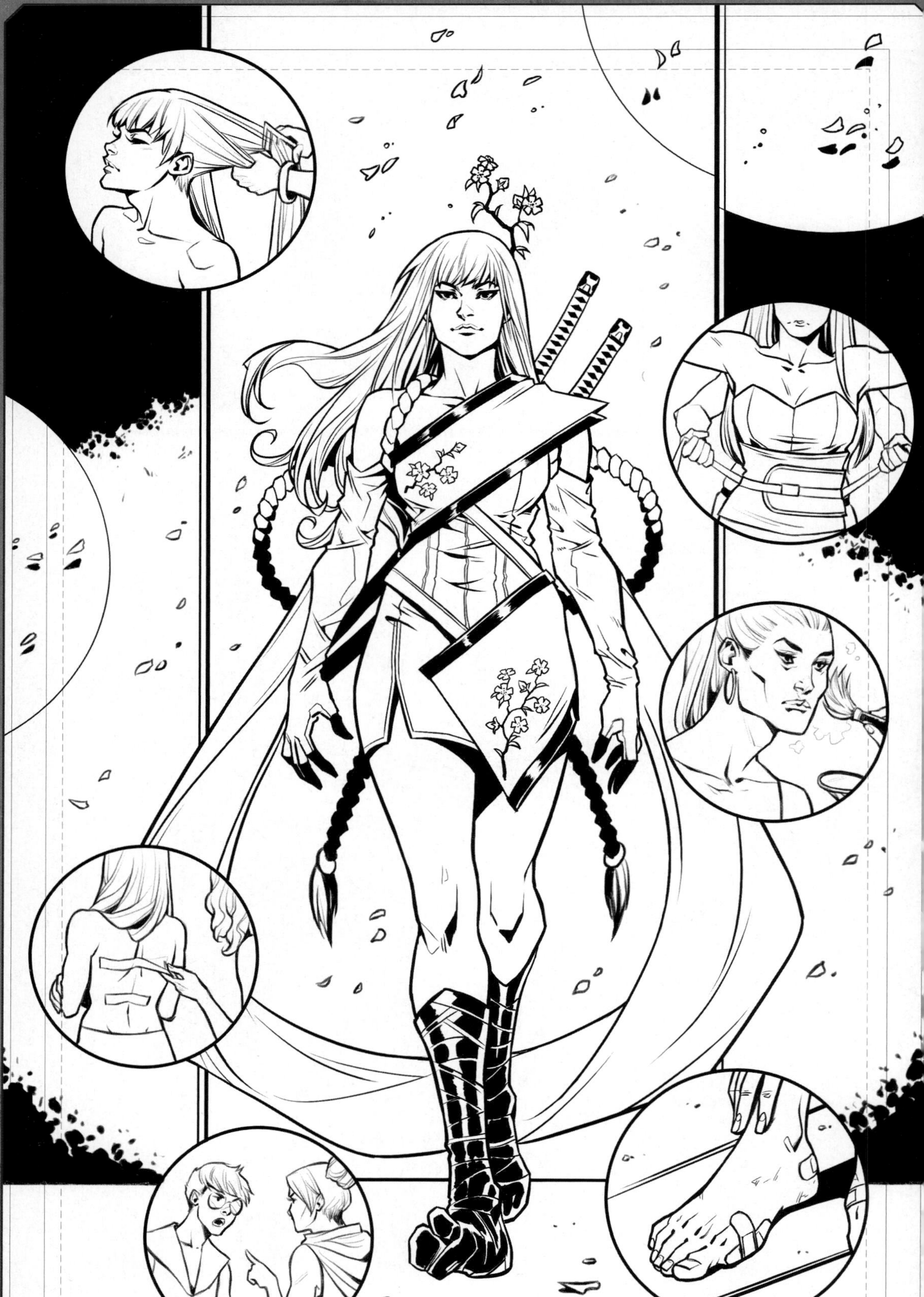